11th Workshop on Multiword Expressions

(MWE 2015)

Held at NAACL HLT 2015

Denver, Colorado, USA
4 June 2015

ISBN: 978-1-5108-0438-8

Printed from e-media with permission by:

Curran Associates, Inc.
57 Morehouse Lane
Red Hook, NY 12571

Some format issues inherent in the e-media version may also appear in this print version.

Printed by Curran Associates, Inc. (2015)

For permission requests, please contact the Association for Computational Linguistics at the address below.

Association for Computational Linguistics
209 N. Eighth Street
Stroudsburg, Pennsylvania 18360

Phone: 1-570-476-8006
Fax: 1-570-476-0860

acl@aclweb.org

Additional copies of this publication are available from:

Curran Associates, Inc.
57 Morehouse Lane
Red Hook, NY 12571 USA
Phone: 845-758-0400
Fax: 845-758-2634
Email: curran@proceedings.com
Web: www.proceedings.com

Introduction

The 11th Workshop on Multiword Expressions (MWE 2015) took place on June 4, 2015 in Denver, Colorado, USA, in conjunction with the 2015 Conference of the North American Chapter of the Association for Computational Linguistics – Human Language Technologies (NAACL HLT 2015) and was endorsed by the Special Interest Group on the Lexicon of the Association for Computational Linguistics (SIGLEX), as well as SIGLEX's Section dedicated to the study and research of Multiword Expressions (SIGLEX-MWE).

The workshop has been held almost every year since 2003 in conjunction with ACL, EACL, NAACL, COLING and LREC. By now, it provides the main venue of the field for interaction, sharing of resources and tools and collaboration efforts for advancing the computational treatment of Multiword Expressions (MWEs), attracting the attention of an ever-growing community from all around the world working on a variety of languages and MWE types.

MWEs include idioms (storm in a teacup, sweep under the rug), fixed phrases (in vitro, by and large), noun compounds (olive oil, laser printer), compound verbs (take a nap, bring about), among others. These, while easily mastered by native speakers, are a key issue and a current weakness for natural language parsing and generation, as well as real-life applications depending on some degree of semantic interpretation, such as machine translation, just to name a prominent one among many. However, thanks to the joint efforts of researchers from several fields working on MWEs, significant progress has been made in recent years, especially concerning the construction of large-scale language resources. For instance, there is a large number of recent papers that focus on acquisition of MWEs from corpora, and others that describe a variety of techniques to find paraphrases for MWEs. Current methods use a plethora of tools such as association measures, machine learning, syntactic patterns, web queries, etc.

In the call for papers we solicited submissions about major challenges in the overall process of MWE treatment, both from the theoretical and the computational viewpoint, focusing on original research related (but not limited) to the following topics:

- Lexicon-grammar interface for MWEs
- Parsing techniques for MWEs
- Hybrid parsing of MWEs
- Annotating MWEs in treebanks
- MWEs in Machine Translation and Translation Technology
- Manually and automatically constructed resources
- Representation of MWEs in dictionaries and ontologies
- MWEs and user interaction
- Multilingual acquisition

- Multilingualism and MWE processing
- Models of first and second language acquisition of MWEs
- Crosslinguistic studies on MWEs
- The role of MWEs in the domain adaptation of parsers
- Integration of MWEs into NLP applications
- Evaluation of MWE treatment techniques
- Lexical, syntactic or semantic aspects of MWEs

Submission modalities included long papers and short papers. From a total of 27 submissions, of which 14 were long papers and 13 were short papers, we accepted 5 long papers for oral presentation and 3 as posters. We further accepted 3 short papers for oral presentation and 3 as posters. The overall acceptance rate is 52%.

The workshop also featured an invited talk by Paul Kay (International Computer Science Institute, UC Berkeley) and Laura A. Michaelis (Department of Linguistics and Institute of Cognitive Science, University of Colorado Boulder) on "How Constructions Mean".

Acknowledgements

We would like to thank the members of the Program Committee for the timely reviews and the authors for their valuable contributions.

Valia Kordoni, Kostadin Cholakov, Markus Egg, Stella Markantonatou, Shuly Wintner
Co-Organizers

Organizers:

Valia Kordoni, Humboldt Universität zu Berlin (Germany)
Kostadin Cholakov, Humboldt Universität zu Berlin (Germany)
Markus Egg, Humboldt Universität zu Berlin (Germany)
Stella Markantonatou, Institute for Language and Speech Processing (ILSP) - Athena Research Center (Greece)
Shuly Wintner, University of Haifa (Israel)

Program Committee:

Dimitra Anastasiou, University of Bremen (Germany)
Eleftherios Avramidis, DFKI GmbH (Germany)
Tim Baldwin, University of Melbourne (Australia)
Núria Bel, Pompeu Fabra University (Spain)
Lars Borin, University of Gothenburg (Sweden)
Jill Burstein, ETS (USA)
Aoife Cahill, ETS (USA)
Helena Caseli, Federal University of Sao Carlos (Brazil)
Ken Church, IBM Research (USA)
Paul Cook, University of New Brunswick (Canada)
Béatrice Daille, Nantes University (France)
Gaël Dias, University of Caen Basse-Normandie (France)
Stefan Evert, Friedrich-Alexander-Universität Erlangen-Nürnberg (Germany)
Roxana Girju, University of Illinois at Urbana-Champaign (USA)
Ed Hovy, Carnegie Mellon University (USA)
Kyo Kageura, University of Tokyo (Japan)
Su Nam Kim, Monash University (Australia)
Dimitrios Kokkinakis, University of Gothenburg (Sweden)
Ioannis Korkontzelos, University of Manchester (UK)
Lori Levin, Carnegie Mellon University (USA)
Patricia Lichtenstein, University of California, Merced (USA)
Marie-Catherine de Marneffe, The Ohio State University (USA)
Takuya Matsuzaki, Nagoya University (Japan)
Yusuke Miyao, National Institute of Informatics (Japan)
Preslav Nakov, Qatar Computing Research Institute - Qatar Foundation (Qatar)
Malvina Nissim, University of Bologna (Italy)
Joakim Nivre, University of Uppsala (Sweden)
Diarmuid Ó Séaghdha, University of Cambridge and VocalIQ (UK)
Jan Odijk, University of Utrecht (The Netherlands)
Yannick Parmentier, Universite d'Orleans (France)
Pavel Pecina, Charles University Prague (Czech Republic)

Scott Piao, Lancaster University (UK)
Barbara Plank, University of Copenhagen (Denmark)
Carlos Ramisch, Aix-Marseille University (France)
Martin Riedl, University of Darmstadt (Germany)
Will Roberts, Humboldt University Berlin (Germany)
Agata Savary, Université François Rabelais Tours (France)
Violeta Seretan, University of Geneva (Switzerland)
Ekaterina Shutova, University of California, Berkeley (USA)
Beata Trawinski, IDS Mannheim (Germany)
Yulia Tsvetkov, Carnegie Mellon University (USA)
Yuancheng Tu, Microsoft (USA)
Aline Villavicencio, Federal University of Rio Grande do Sul (Brazil)
Veronika Vincze, Hungarian Academy of Sciences (Hungary)
Martin Volk, University of Zurich (Switzerland)
Tom Wasow, Stanford University (USA)
Eric Wehrli, University of Geneva (Switzerland)

Invited Speaker:

Laura A. Michaelis

Table of Contents

Conference Program

Thursday, June 4, 2014

Oral Session 1

09:00–09:30 *A Method of Accounting Bigrams in Topic Models*
Michael Nokel and Natalia Loukachevitch

09:30–10:00 *Multiword Expression Identification with Recurring Tree Fragments and Association Measures*
Federico Sangati and Andreas van Cranenburgh

10:00–10:30 *How to Account for Idiomatic German Support Verb Constructions in Statistical Machine Translation*
Fabienne Cap, Manju Nirmal, Marion Weller and Sabine Schulte im Walde

10:30–11:00 ***Coffee Break***

Oral Session 2

11:00–11:20 *A Multiword Expression Data Set: Annotating Non-Compositionality and Conventionalization for English Noun Compounds*
Meghdad Farahmand, Aaron Smith and Joakim Nivre

11:20–11:40 *Modeling the Statistical Idiosyncrasy of Multiword Expressions*
Meghdad Farahmand and Joakim Nivre

11:40–12:00 *Clustering-based Approach to Multiword Expression Extraction and Ranking*
Elena Tutubalina

Thursday, June 4, 2014 (continued)

Invited Talk by Laura A. Michaelis

12:00–13:00 *How Constructions Mean*
Paul Kay and Laura A. Michaelis

13:00–14:00 ***Lunch***

14:00–14:30 ***Poster Booster Session (5 minutes per poster)***

Never-Ending Multiword Expressions Learning
Alexandre Rondon, Helena Caseli and Carlos Ramisch

The Impact of Multiword Expression Compositionality on Machine Translation Evaluation
Bahar Salehi, Nitika Mathur, Paul Cook and Timothy Baldwin

The Bare Necessities: Increasing Lexical Coverage for Multi-Word Domain Terms with Less Lexical Data
Branimir Boguraev, Esme Manandise and Benjamin Segal

Phrase translation using a bilingual dictionary and n-gram data: A case study from Vietnamese to English
Khang Nhut Lam, Feras Al Tarouti and Jugal Kalita

Annotation and Extraction of Multiword Expressions in Turkish Treebanks
Gülşen Eryiğit, Kübra ADALI, Dilara Torunoğlu-Selamet, Umut Sulubacak and Tuğba Pamay

Event Categorization beyond Verb Senses
Aron Marvel and Jean-Pierre Koenig

14:30–15:30 ***Poster Session***

15:30–16:00 ***Coffee Break***

Thursday, June 4, 2014 (continued)

Oral Session 3

16:00–16:30 *Muddying The Multiword Expression Waters: How Cognitive Demand Affects Multiword Expression Production*
Adam Goodkind and Andrew Rosenberg

16:30–17:00 *Building a Lexicon of Formulaic Language for Language Learners*
Julian Brooke, Adam Hammond, David Jacob, Vivian Tsang, Graeme Hirst and Fraser Shein

A Method of Accounting Bigrams in Topic Models

Michael Nokel
Yandex,
Moscow, Russian Federation
mnokel@yandex-team.ru

Natalia Loukachevitch
Lomonosov Moscow State Univeristy,
Moscow, Russian Federation
louk_nat@mail.ru

Abstract

The paper describes the results of an empirical study of integrating bigram collocations and similarities between them and unigrams into topic models. First of all, we propose a novel algorithm PLSA-SIM that is a modification of the original algorithm PLSA. It incorporates bigrams and maintains relationships between unigrams and bigrams based on their component structure. Then we analyze a variety of word association measures in order to integrate top-ranked bigrams into topic models. All experiments were conducted on four text collections of different domains and languages. The experiments distinguish a subgroup of tested measures that produce top-ranked bigrams, which demonstrate significant improvement of topic models quality for all collections, when integrated into PLSA-SIM algorithm.

1 Introduction

Topic modeling is one of the latest applications of machine learning techniques to natural language processing. Topic models identify which topics relate to each document and which words form each topic. Each topic is defined as a multinomial distribution over terms and each document is defined as multinomial distribution over topics (Blei et al., 2003). Topic models have achieved noticeable success in various areas such as information retrieval (Wei and Croft, 2006), including such applications as multi-document summarization (Wang et al., 2009), text clustering and categorization (Zhou et al., 2009), and other natural language processing tasks such as word sense disambiguation (Boyd-Graber et al., 2007), machine translation (Eidelman et al., 2012). Among most well-known models are Latent Dirichlet Allocation (LDA) (Blei et al., 2003), which is based on Dirichlet prior distribution, and Probabilistic Latent Semantic Analysis (PLSA) (Hofmann, 1999), which is not connected with any parametric prior distribution.

One of the main drawbacks of the topic models is that they utilize "bag-of-words" model that discards word order and is based on the word independence assumption. There are numerous studies, where the integration of collocations, n-grams, idioms and multi-word terms into topic models is investigated. However, it often leads to a decrease in the model quality due to increasing size of a vocabulary or to a complication of the model, which require time-intensive computation (Wallach, 2006; Griffiths et al., 2007; Wang et al., 2007).

The paper proposes a novel approach taking into account bigram collocations and relationship between them and unigrams in topic models (such as *citizen – citizen of country – citizen of union – European citizen – state citizen*; *categorization – document categorization – term categorization – text categorization*). This allows us to create a novel method of integrating bigram collocations into topic models that does not consider bigrams being as "black boxes", but maintains the relationship between unigrams and bigrams based on their component structure. The proposed algorithm leads to significant improvement of topic models quality measured in perplexity and topic coherence (Newman et al., 2010)

Proceedings of NAACL-HLT 2015, pages 1–9,
Denver, Colorado, May 31 – June 5, 2015.

without complications of the model.

All experiments were carried out using PLSA algorithm and its modifications on four corpora of different domains and languages: the English part of Europarl parallel corpus, the English part of JRC-Acquis parallel corpus, ACL Anthology Reference corpus, and Russian banking magazines.

The rest of the paper is organized as follows. In the section 2 we focus on related work. Section 4 describes the datasets used in experiments, all preprocessing steps and metrics used to evaluate the quality. Section 3 proposes a novel algorithm PLSA-SIM that incorporates bigrams and similarities between them and unigrams into topic models. In the section 5 we perform an extensive analysis of a variety of measures for integrating top-ranked bigrams into topic models. And in the last section we draw conclusions.

2 Related Work

The idea of using collocations in topic models is not a novel one. Nowadays there are two kinds of methods proposed to deal with this problem: creation of a unified probabilistic model and preliminary extraction of collocations and n-grams with further integration into topic models.

Most studies belong to the first kind of methods. So, the first movement beyond "bag-of-words" assumption has been made by Wallach (2006), where the Bigram Topic Model was presented. In this model word probabilities are conditioned on the immediately preceding word. The LDA Collocation Model (Griffiths et al., 2007) extends the Bigram Topic Model by introducing a new set of variables and thereby giving a flexibility to generate both unigrams and bigrams. Wang et al. (2007) proposed the Topical N-Gram Model that adds a layer of complexity to allow the formation of bigrams to be determined by the context. Hu et al. (2008) proposed the Topical Word-Character Model challenging the assumption that the topic of an n-gram is determined by the topics of composite words within the collocation. This model is mainly suitable for Chinese language. Johnson (2010) established connection between LDA and Probabilistic Context-Free Grammars and proposed two probabilistic models combining insights from LDA and Adaptor Grammars to integrate collocations and proper names into the topic model.

While all these models have a theoretically elegant background, they are very complex and hard to compute on real datasets. For example, Bigram Topic Model has W^2T parameters, compared to WT for LDA and $WT + DT$ for PLSA, where W is the size of vocabulary, D is the number of documents, and T is the number of topics. Therefore such models are mostly of theoretical interest.

The algorithm proposed in (Lau et al., 2013) belongs to the second type of methods that use collocations in topic models. The authors extract bigram collocations via t-test and replace separate units by top-ranked bigrams at the preprocessing step. They use two metrics of topic quality: perplexity and topic coherence (Newman et al., 2010) and conclude that incorporating bigram collocations into topics results in worsening perplexity and improving topic coherence.

Our current work also belongs to the second type of methods and distinguishes from previous papers such as (Lau et al., 2013) in that our approach does not consider bigrams as "black boxes", but maintains information about the inner structure of bigrams and relationships between bigrams and component unigrams, which leads to improvement in both metrics: perplexity and topic coherence.

The idea to utilize prior natural language knowledge in topic models is not a novel one. So, Andrzejewski et al. (2009) incorporated domain-specific knowledge by Must-Link and Cannot-Link primitives represented by a novel Dirichlet Forest prior. These primitives control that two words tend to be generated by the same or separate topics. However, this method can result in an exponential growth in the encoding of Cannot-Link primitives and thus has difficulty in processing a large number of constraints (Liu, 2012). Another method of incorporating such knowledge is presented in (Zhai, 2010) where a semi-supervised EM-algorithm was proposed to group expressions into some user-specified categories. To provide a better initialization for EM-algorithm the method employs prior knowledge that expressions sharing words and synonyms are likely to belong to the same group. Our current work distinguishes from these ones in that we incorporate similarity links between unigrams and bigrams into the topic model in a very natural way counting their co-occurrences in documents. The proposed approach does not increase the complexity of the original PLSA algorithm.

3 PLSA-SIM algorithm

As mentioned above, original topic models utilize the “bag-of-words” assumption that assumes word independence. And bigrams are usually added to topic models as “black boxes” without any ties with other words. So, bigrams are added to the vocabulary as single tokens and in each document containing any of added bigrams the frequencies of unigram components are decreased by the frequencies of bigrams (Lau et al., 2013). Thus “bag-of-words” assumption holds.

However, there are many similar unigrams and bigrams that share the same lemmas (i.e, *correction – correction of word – error correction – spelling correction*; *rail – rail infrastructure – rail transport – use of rail*) and others in documents. We should note such bigrams do not only have identical words, but many of them maintain semantic and thematic similarity. At the same time other bigrams with the same words (i.e., idioms) can have significant semantic differences. To take into account these different situations, we hypothesized that similar bigrams sharing the same unigram components should often belong to the same topics, if they often co-occur within the same texts.

To verify this hypothesis we precompute sets of similar unigrams and bigrams sharing the same lemmas and propose novel PLSA-SIM algorithm that is the modification of the original PLSA algorithm. We will rely on the description found in (Vorontsov and Potapenko, 2014) and use the following notations (further in the paper we will use notation “term” when speaking about both unigrams and bigrams):

- D – the collection of documents;
- T – the set of inferred topics;
- W – the vocabulary (the set of unique terms found in the collection D);
- $\Phi = \{\phi_{wt} = p(w|t)\}$ – the distribution of terms w over topics t;
- $\Theta = \{\theta_{td} = p(t|d)\}$ – the distribution of topics t over documents d;
- $S = \{S_w\}$ – the sets of similar terms (S_w is the set of terms similar to w, that is $S_w = \{w \bigcup_v wv \bigcup_v vw\}$, where w is the lemmatized unigram, while wv and vw are lemmatized bigrams);
- n_{dw}, n_{ds} – the number of occurrences of the terms w, s in the document d;
- $\hat{n}_{wt}$ – the estimate of frequency of the term w in the topic t;
- $\hat{n}_{td}$ – the estimate of frequency of the topic t in the document d;
- $\hat{n}_t$ – the estimate of frequency of the topic t in the text collection D;
- n_d – the number of words in the document d.

The pseudocode of PLSA-SIM algorithm is presented in the Algorithm 1. The only modifications of the original algorithm concern line 7, where we take into account pre-computed sets of similar terms. Thus, the weight of such terms is increased within each document.

Algorithm 1: PLSA-SIM algorithm: PLSA with similar terms

Input: collection of documents D, number of topics $|T|$, initial distributions Θ and Φ, sets of similar terms S

Output: distributions Θ and Φ

1 **while** *not meet the stop criterion* **do**
2   **for** $d \in D,\ w \in W,\ t \in T$ **do**
3     $\hat{n}_{wt} = 0,\ \hat{n}_{td} = 0,\ \hat{n}_t = 0$
4   **for** $d \in D,\ w \in W$ **do**
5   **for** $t \in T$ **do**
6       $P(t|d,w) = \frac{\phi_{wt}\theta_{td}}{\sum_{s \in T} \phi_{ws}\theta_{sd}}$
7       $\hat{n}_{wt}, \hat{n}_{td}, \hat{n}_t += (n_{dw} + \sum_{s \in S_w} n_{ds}) P(t|d,w)$
8   **for** $d \in D,\ w \in W$ **do**
9     $\phi_{wt} = \frac{\hat{n}_{wt}}{\hat{n}_t}$
10   **for** $d \in D,\ t \in T$ **do**
11     $\theta_{td} = \frac{\hat{n}_{td}}{n_d}$

So, if similar unigrams and bigrams co-occur within the same document, we try to carry them to the same topics. We consider such terms having semantic and thematic similarities. However, if unigrams and bigrams from the same set S_w do not co-occur within the same document, we do no modifications to the original algorithm PLSA. We consider such terms having semantic differences.

4 Datasets and Evaluation

4.1 Datasets and Preprocessing

In our experiments we used English and Russian text collections obtained from different sources:

- For the English part of our study we took three different collections:
  - Europarl multilingual parallel corpus. It was extracted from the proceedings of the European Parliament (`http://www.statmt.org/europarl`). The English part includes almost 54 million words and 9672 documents.
  - JRC-Acquis multilingual parallel corpus. It represents selected texts of the EU legislation written between the 1950s and 2005 (`http://ipsc.jrc.ec.europa.eu/index.php?id=198`). The English part contains almost 45 million words and 23545 documents.
  - ACL Anthology Reference Corpus. It contains scholarly publications about Computational Linguistics (`http://acl-arc.comp.nus.edu.sg/`). The corpus includes almost 42 million words and 10921 documents.
- For the Russian part of our study we took 10422 Russian articles from several economics-oriented magazines such as Auditor, RBC, Banking Magazine, etc. These documents contain almost 18.5 million words.

At the preprocessing step documents were processed by morphological analyzers. For the English corpus we used Stanford CoreNLP tools (`http://nlp.stanford.edu/software/corenlp.shtml`), while for the Russian corpus we used our own morphological analyzer. All words were lemmatized. We consider only Adjectives, Nouns, Verbs and Adverbs since function words do not play significant role in forming topics. Besides, we excluded words occurring less than five times per the whole text collection.

In addition, we extracted all bigrams in forms of *Noun + Noun*, *Adjective + Noun* and *Noun + of + Noun* for all English collections, and *Noun + Noun in Genitive* and *Adjective + Noun* for the Russian collection. We should note that we consider trigrams in forms *Noun + of + Noun* as bigrams since they consist of two content words. We take into account only such bigrams since topics are mainly identified by nouns and noun groups.

4.2 Evaluation Framework

As for the inferred topics quality, we consider four different intrinsic measures. The first measure is **Perplexity** since it is the standard criterion of topic models quality (Daud et al., 2010):

$$Perplexity(D) = \exp\left(-\frac{1}{n}\sum_{d\in D}\sum_{w\in d} n_{dw}\ln p(w|d)\right), \quad (1)$$

where n is the number of all considered words in the collection, D is the set of documents in the collection, n_{dw} is the number of occurrences of the word w in the document d, $p(w|d)$ is the probability of appearing the word w in the document d.

The less the value of perplexity is the better the model predicts words w in documents D. Although there were numerous studies arguing that perplexity is not suited to topic model evaluation (Chang et al., 2009; Newman et al., 2010), it is still commonly used for comparing different topic models. Since it is well-known that perplexity computed on the same training collection is susceptible to overfitting and can give optimistically low values (Blei et al., 2003) we use the standard method of computing hold-out perplexity described in (Asuncion et al., 2009). In our experiments we split the collections randomly into the training sets D, on which models are trained, and the validation sets D', on which hold-out perplexity is computed (in the proportion $|D| : |D'| = 9 : 1$).

Another method of evaluating topic model quality is using **expert opinions**. We provided annotators with inferred topics from the same text collections and instructed them to decide whether the topic was to some extent coherent, meaningful and interpretable. The indicator of topic usefulness is the ease by which one could think of a short label to describe a topic (Newman et al., 2010). In the Table 1 we present incoherent topic that cannot be given any label and coherent one with label given by experts.

Top words from topic	Label
have, also, commission, state, more, however	–
vessel, fishing, fishery, community, catch, board	*fishing*

Table 1: Examples of incoherent and coherent topics

Since involving experts is time-consuming and expensive, there were several attempts to propose a method for automatic evaluation of topic models quality that would go beyond perplexity and would be correlated with expert opinions. The formulation of such a problem is very complicated since experts can quite strongly disagree with each other. However, it was recently shown that it is possible to evaluate topic coherence automatically using word semantics with precision, almost coinciding with experts (Newman et al., 2010; Mimno et al., 2011). The proposed metric measures interpretability of topics based on human judgement (Newman et al., 2010). As topics are usually presented to users via their top-N topic terms, the *topic coherence* evaluates whether these top terms correspond to the topic or not. Newman et al. (2010) proposed an automated variation of the coherence score based on pointwise mutual information (**TC-PMI**):

$$TC\text{-}PMI(t) = \sum_{j=2}^{10} \sum_{i=1}^{j-1} \log \frac{P(w_j, w_i)}{P(w_j)P(w_i)}, \quad (2)$$

where $(w_1, w_2, \ldots, w_{10})$ are the top-10 terms in a topic, $P(w_i)$ and $P(w_j)$ are probabilities of unigrams w_i and w_j respectively, while $P(w_j, w_i)$ is the probability of bigram (w_j, w_i). The final measure of topic coherence is calculated by averaging $TC\text{-}PMI(t)$ measure by all topics t.

This score is proven to demonstrate high correlation with human judgement (Newman et al., 2010). The proposed metric considers only top-10 words in each topic since they usually provide enough information to form the subject of the topic and distinguishing features from other topics. Topic coherence is becoming more widely used to evaluate topic model quality along with perplexity. For example, Stevens et al. (2012) showed that this metric is strongly correlated with expert estimates. Also Andrzejewski et al. (2011) simply used it for evaluating topic model quality.

Following the approach proposed by (Mimno et al., 2011) we compute probabilities by dividing the number of documents where the unigram or bigram occurred by the number of documents in the collection. To avoid optimistically high values we use external corpus for this purpose – namely, Russian and English Wikipedia. We should note that we do not consider another variation of topic coherence based on log conditional probability (*TC-LCP*) proposed by (Mimno et al., 2011) since it was shown in (Lau et al., 2013) that it works significantly worse than *TC-PMI*.

We should note that while incorporating the knowledge of similar unigrams and bigrams into topic models in the proposed algorithm, we encourage such terms to be in the top-10 terms in inferred topics. Therefore, we increase TC-PMI metric unintentionally since such terms are likely to co-occur within the same documents. So we decided to use also modification of this metric to consider the first 10 terms, no two of which are from the same set of similar unigrams and bigrams (this metric will be further called as **TC-PMI-nSIM**).

5 Integrating bigrams into topic models

To compare proposed algorithm with the original one we extracted all bigrams found in each document of collections. For ranking bigrams we utilized *Term Frequency (TF)* or one of the following 16 word association measures:

1. *Mutual Information (MI)* (Church and Hanks, 1990);
2. *Augmented MI* (Zhang, 2008);
3. *Normalized MI* (Bouma, 2009);
4. *True MI* (Deane, 2005);
5. *Cubic MI* (Daille, 1995);
6. *Symmetric Conditional Probability* (Lopes and Silva, 1999);
7. *Dice Coefficient (DC)* (Smadja et al., 1996);
8. *Modified DC* (Kitamura and Matsumoto, 1996);
9. *Gravity Count* (Daudaravičius and Marcinkevičienė, 2003);
10. *Simple Matching Coefficient* (Daille, 1995);

11. *Kulczinsky Coefficient* (Daille, 1995);
12. *Yule Coefficient* (Daille, 1995);
13. *Jaccard Coefficient* (Jaccard, 1901);
14. *T-Score*;
15. *Chi Square*;
16. *Loglikelihood Ratio* (Dunning, 1993).

According to the results of (Lau et al., 2013) we decided to integrate top-1000 bigrams into all topic models under consideration. We should note that in all experiments described in the paper we fixed the number of topics and the number of iterations of algorithms to 100.

We conducted experiments with all **17** aforementioned measures on all four text collections in order to compare the quality of the original algorithm PLSA, PLSA with top-1000 bigrams added as "black boxes", and PLSA-SIM algorithm with the same top-1000 bigrams.

According to the results of experiments we have revealed two groups of measures.

The first group contains **11** measures: *MI*, *Augmented MI*, *Normalized MI*, *DC*, *Symmetrical Conditional Probability*, *Simple Matching Coefficient*, *Kulczinsky Coefficient*, *Yule Coefficient*, *Jaccard Coefficient*, *Chi-Square*, and *Loglikelihood Ratio*. We got nearly the same levels of perplexity and topic coherence when top bigrams ranked by these measures were integrated into all tested topic models. This is explained by the fact that these measures rank up very special, non-typical and low frequency bigrams. In the Table 2 we present results of integrating top-1000 bigrams ranked by *MI* for all four text collections.

The second group includes **6** measures: *TF*, *Cubic MI*, *True MI*, *Modified DC*, *T-Score*, and *Gravity Count*. We got worsened perplexity and improved topic coherence, when top bigrams ranked by these measures were integrated into PLSA algorithm as "black boxes". But when they were used in PLSA-SIM topic models, it led to significant improvement of all metrics under consideration. This is explained by the fact that these measures rank up high frequent, typical bigrams. In the Table 3 we present results of integrating top-1000 bigrams ranked by *TF* for all four text collections.

So, we succeed to achieve better quality for both languages using the proposed modification of the original PLSA algorithm and the second group of measures.

Corpus	Model	Perplexity	TC-PMI	TC-PMI-nSIM
Banking	*PLSA*	1724.2	86.1	86.1
	PLSA + bigrams	1714.1	84.2	84.2
	PLSA-SIM + bigrams	1715.4	84.1	84.1
Europarl	*PLSA*	1594.3	53.2	53.2
	PLSA + bigrams	1584.6	55	55
	PLSA-SIM + bigrams	1591.3	55.2	55.2
JRC	*PLSA*	812.1	67	67
	PLSA + bigrams	815.4	66.3	66.3
	PLSA-SIM + bigrams	815.6	66.4	66.4
ACL	*PLSA*	2134.7	74.8	74.8
	PLSA + bigrams	2138.1	75.5	75.5
	PLSA-SIM + bigrams	2144.8	75.8	75.8

Table 2: Results of integrating top-1000 bigrams ranked by MI into topic models

Corpus	Model	Perplexity	TC-PMI	TC-PMI-nSIM
Banking	*PLSA*	1724.2	86.1	86.1
	PLSA + bigrams	2251.8	98.8	98.8
	PLSA-SIM + bigrams	**1450.6**	**156.5**	**102.6**
Europarl	*PLSA*	1594.3	53.2	53.2
	PLSA + bigrams	1993.5	57.3	57.3
	PLSA-SIM + bigrams	**1431.6**	**127.7**	**84.7**
JRC	*PLSA*	812.1	67	67
	PLSA + bigrams	1038.9	72	72
	PLSA-SIM + bigrams	**743.7**	**108.4**	**76.9**
ACL	*PLSA*	2134.7	74.8	74.8
	PLSA + bigrams	2619.3	73.7	73.7
	PLSA-SIM + bigrams	**1806.4**	**152.7**	**87.8**

Table 3: Results of integrating top-1000 bigrams ranked by TF into topic models

For the expert evaluation of topic model quality we invited two linguistic experts and gave them topics inferred by the original PLSA algorithm and by the proposed PLSA-SIM algorithm with top-1000 bigrams ranked by TF (term frequency). The task was to classify given topics into 2 classes: whether they can be given a subject name (we will further mark such topics as '+') or not (we will further mark such topics as '–'). In the Table 4 we present results for all text collections except ACL Anthology Reference Corpus because for the correct markup advance knowledge in computational linguistics is required.

Corpus	Model	Expert 1		Expert 2	
		+	–	+	–
Banking	*PLSA*	93	7	92	8
	PLSA + bigrams	92	8	95	5
	PLSA-SIM + bigrams	**95**	**5**	**97**	**3**
JRC	*PLSA*	98	2	90	10
	PLSA + bigrams	96	4	97	3
	PLSA-SIM + bigrams	**100**	**0**	**100**	**0**
Europarl	*PLSA*	91	9	99	1
	PLSA + bigrams	94	6	99	1
	PLSA-SIM + bigrams	**99**	**1**	**100**	**0**

Table 4: Results of expert markup of topics

As we can see, in the case of PLSA-SIM algorithm with top-1000 bigrams ranked by TF the amount of inferred topics, for which labels can be given, is increased for all text collections. It is also worth noting that adding bigrams as "black boxes" does not increase the amount of such inferred topics. This result also confirms that the proposed algorithm improves the quality of topic models.

In the Table 5 we present top-5 words from one random topic for each corpus for original PLSA and PLSA-SIM algorithms with top-1000 bigrams ranked by TF. Within each text collection we present topics discussing the same subject.

We should note that we used only intrinsic measures of topic model quality in the paper. In the future we would like to test improved topic models in such applications of information retrieval as text clustering and categorization.

Banking		Europarl	
PLSA	PLSA-SIM	PLSA	PLSA-SIM
Banking	*Financial system*	*Financial*	*Economic crisis*
Bank	*Financial market*	*Crisis*	*Financial crisis*
Sector	*Financial sector*	*Have*	*European economy*
Financial	*Financial*	*European*	*Time of crisis*
System	*Financial institute*	*Market*	*Crisis*
JRC-Acquis		**ACL**	
PLSA	PLSA-SIM	PLSA	PLSA-SIM
Transport	*Transport*	*Tag*	*Tag*
Road	*Transport service*	*Word*	*Tag set*
Nuclear	*Road transport*	*Corpus*	*Tag sequence*
Vehicle	*Transport sector*	*Tagger*	*Unknown word*
Material	*Air transport*	*Tagging*	*Speech tag*

Table 5: Top-5 words from topics inferred by PLSA and PLSA-SIM algorithms

6 Conclusion

The paper presents experiments on integrating bigrams and similarities between them and unigrams into topic models. At first, we propose the novel algorithm PLSA-SIM that incorporates similar unigrams and bigrams into topic models and maintains relationships between bigrams and unigram components. The experiments were conducted on the English parts of Europarl and JRC-Acquis parallel corpora, ACL Anthology Reference corpus and Russian banking articles distinguished two groups of measures ranking bigrams. The first group produces top bigrams, which, if added to topic models either as "black boxes" or not, results in nearly the same quality of inferred topics. However, the second group produces top bigrams, which, if added to the proposed PLSA-SIM algorithm, results in significant improvement in all metrics under consideration.

Acknowledgements

This work is partially supported by RFBR grant N14-07-00383.

References

David Andrzejewski, Xiaojin Zhu, and Mark Craven. 2009. *Incorporating Domain Knowledge into Topic Modeling via Dirichlet Forest Priors*. Proceedings of the 26th Annual International Conference on Machine Learning: 25–32.

David Andrzejewski and David Buttler. 2011. *Latent Topic Feedback for Information Retrieval*. Proceedings of the 17th ACM SIGKDD International Conference on Knowledge Discovery and Data Mining: 600–608.

Arthur Asuncion, Max Welling, Padhraic Smyth, Yee Whye Teh. 2009. *On Smoothing and Inference for Topic Models*. Proceedings of the 25th International Conference on Uncertainty in Artificial Intelligence: 27–34.

David M. Blei, Andrew Y. Ng, and Michael I. Jordan. 2003. *Latent Dirichlet Allocation*. Journal of Machine Learning Research, volume 3: 993–1022.

Gerlof Bouma. 2009. *Normalized (Pointwise) Mutual Information*. Proceedings of the Biennial GSCL Conference: 31–40.

Jordan Boyd-Graber, David M. Blei, and Xiaojin Zhu. 2007. *A Topic Model for Word Sense Disambiguation*. Proceedings of the 2007 Joint Conference on Empirical Methods in Natural Language Processing and Computational Natural Language Learning: 1024–1033.

Jonathan Chang, Jordan Boyd-Graber, Sean Gerrish, Chong Wang, David M. Blei. 2009. *Reading Tea Leaves: How Human Interpret Topic Models*. Proceedings of the 24th Annual Conference on Neural Information Processing Systems: 288–296.

Kenneth Ward Church, and Patrick Hanks. 1990. *Word Association Norms, Mutual Information, and Lexicography*. Computational Linguistics, volume 16: 22–29.

Beatrice Daille. 1995. *Combined Approach for Terminology Extraction: Lexical Statistics and Linguistic Filtering* PhD Dissertation. University of Paris, Paris.

Ali Daud, Juanzi Li, Lizhu Zhou, Faqir Muhammad. 2010. *Knowledge discovery through directed probabilistic topic models: a survey*. Frontiers of Computer Science in China, 4(2): 280–301.

Vidas Daudaravičius and Rūta Marcinkevičienė. 2003. *Gravity Counts for the Boundaries of Collocations*. International Journal of Corpus Linguistics, 9(2): 321–348.

Paul Deane. 2005. *A Nonparametric Method for Extraction of Candidate Phrasal Terms*. Proceedings of the 43rd Annual Meeting of the ACL: 605–613.

Ted Dunning. 1993. *Accurate Methods for the Statistics of Surprise and Coincidence*. International Journal of Computational Linguistics, 19(1): 61–74.

Vladimir Eidelman, Jordan Boyd-Graber, and Philip Resnik. 2012. *Topic Models for Dynamic Translation Model Adaptation*. Proceedings of the 50th Annual Meeting of the Association of Computational Linguistics, volume 2: 115–119.

Thomas L. Griffiths, Mark Steyvers, and Joshua B. Tenenbaum. 2007. *Topics in Semantic Representation*. Psychological Review, 114(2): 211–244.

Thomas Hofmann. 1999. *Probabilistic Latent Semantic Indexing*. Proceedings of the 22nd Annual International SIGIR Conference on Research and Development in Information Retrieval: 50–57.

Wei Hu, Nobuyuki Shimizu, Hiroshi Nakagawa, and Huanye Shenq. 2008. *Modeling Chinese Documents with Topical Word-Character Models*. Proceedings of the 22nd International Conference on Computational Linguistics: 345–352.

Paul Jaccard. 1901. *Distribution de la flore alpine dans le Bassin des Dranses et dans quelques regions voisines*. Bull. Soc. Vaudoise sci. Natur. V. 37. Bd. 140: 241–272.

Mark Johnson M. 2010. *PCFGs, Topic Models, Adaptor Grammars and Learning Topical Collocations and the Structure of Proper Names*. Proceedings of the 48th Annual Meeting of the ACL: 1148–1157.

Mihoko Kitamura, and Yuji Matsumoto. 1996. *Automatic Extraction of Word Sequence Correspondences in Parallel Corpora*. Proceedings of the 4th Annual Workshop on Very Large Corpora: 79–87.

Jey Han Lau, Timothy Baldwin, and David Newman. 2013. *On Collocations and Topic Models*. ACM Transactions on Speech and Language Processing, 10(3): 1–14.

Bing Liu. 2012. *Sentiment Analysis and Opinion Mining*. Synthesis Lectures on Human Language Technologies, Morgan & Claypool Publishers.

Jose Gabriel Pereira Lopes, and Joaquim Ferreira da Silva. 1999. *A Local Maxima Method and a Fair Dispersion Normalization for Extracting Multiword Units*. Proceedings of the 6th Meeting on the Mathematics of Language: 369–381.

David Mimno, Hanna M. Wallach, Edmund Talley, Miriam Leenders, Andrew McCallum. 2011. *Optimizing Semantic Coherence in Topic Models*. Proceedings of EMNLP'11: 262–272.

David Newman, Jey Han Lau, Karl Grieser, and Timothy Baldwin. 2010. *Automatic Evaluation of Topic Coherence*. Proceedings of Human Language Technologies: The 11th Annual Conference of the North American Chapter of the Association for Computational Linguistics: 100–108.

Frank Smadja, Kathleen R. McKeown, and Vasileios Hatzivassiloglou. 1996. *Translating Collocations for*

Bilingual Lexicons: A Statistical Approach. Computational Linguistics, 22(1): 1–38.

Keith Stevens, Philip Kegelmeyer, David Adnrzejewski, and David Buttler. 2012. *Exploring Topic Coherence over Many Models and Many Topics*. Proceedings of EMNLP-CoNLL'12: 952–961.

Konstantin V. Vorontsov, and Anna A. Potapenko. 2014. *Tutorial on Probabilistic Topic Modeling: Additive Regularization for Stochastic Matrix Factorization*. Proceedings of AIST'2014. LNCS, Springer Verlag-Germany, volume CCIS 439: 28–45.

Hanna M. Wallach. 2006. *Topic Modeling: Beyond Bag-of-Words*. Proceedings of the 23rd International Conference on Machine Learning: 977–984.

Xuerui Wang, Andrew McCallum, and Xing Wei. 2007. *Topical N-grams: Phrase and Topic Discovery, with an Application to Information Retrieval*. Proceedings of the 2007 Seventh IEEE International Conference on Data Mining: 697–702.

Dingding Wang, Shenghuo Zhu, Tao Li, and Yihong Gong. 2009. Multi-Document Summarization using Sentence-based Topic Models. Proceedings of the ACL-IJCNLP 2009 Conference Short Papers: 297–300.

Xing Wei and W. Bruce Croft. 2006. *LDA-Based Document Models for Ad-hoc Retrieval*. Proceedings of the 29th International Conference on Research and Development in Information Retrieval: 178–185.

Zhongwu Zhai, Bing Liu, Hua Xu, and Peifa Jia. 2010. *Grouping Product Features Using Semi-Supervised Learning with Soft-Constraints*. Proceedings of the 23rd International Conference on Computational Linguistics: 1272–1280.

Wen Zhang, Taketoshi Yoshida, Tu Bao Ho, and Xijin Tang. 2008. *Augmented Mutual Information for Multi-Word Term Extraction*. International Journal of Innovative Computing, Information and Control, 8(2): 543–554.

Shibin Zhou, Kan Li, and Yushu Liu. 2009. *Text Categorization Based on Topic Model*. International Journal of Computational Intelligence Systems, volume 2, No. 4: 398–409.

Multiword Expression Identification with Recurring Tree Fragments and Association Measures

Federico Sangati
Fondazione Bruno Kessler (FBK)
Trento, Italy
sangati@fbk.eu

Andreas van Cranenburgh
Huygens ING, Royal Netherlands Academy of Arts & Sciences; ILLC, Univ. of Amsterdam.
andreas.van.cranenburgh@huygens.knaw.nl

Abstract

We present a novel approach for the identification of multiword expressions (MWEs). The methodology extracts a large set of recurring syntactic fragments from a given treebank using a Tree-Kernel method. Differently from previous studies, the expressions underlying these fragments are arbitrarily long and can include intervening gaps. In the initial study we use these fragments to identify MWEs as a parsing task (in a supervised manner) as proposed by Green et al. (2011). Here we obtain a small improvement over previous results. In the second part, we compare various association measures in reranking the expressions underlying these fragments in an unsupervised fashion. We show how a newly defined measure (Log Inside Ratio) based on statistical parsing techniques is able to outperform classical association measures in the French data.

1 Introduction

According to many current linguistic theories, language users produce and understand sentences without necessarily fully decomposing them into 'words' and 'rules'; rather, multiword units may function as the elementary building blocks (Goldberg, 1995; Kay and Fillmore, 1997; Stefanowitsch and Gries, 2003). A growing literature is emerging which focuses on "idiosyncratic interpretations that cross word boundaries (or spaces)" (Sag et al., 2002) also referred to as multiword expressions (MWEs) . These expressions, such as "to beat around the bush", can be arbitrarily long. An important question for computational linguistics is how to identify such building blocks using statistical regularities in large corpora (Zuidema, 2006; Ramisch et al., 2012).

Most of the work on the identification of MWEs has focused on very short expressions, typically bigrams (Evert, 2005) or trigrams (Lyse and Andersen, 2012) using unsupervised techniques based on word association measures. Recent work (Green et al., 2011, 2013) has incorporated full phrase-structure trees in the process of multiword expression identification, obtaining a 36.4% F1 absolute improvement in MWE identification using a Tree-Substitution Grammar over an *n*-gram surface statistics baseline (Ramisch et al., 2010). However, one needs to note that the French Treebank (Abeillé et al., 2003) used in this study, contains explicitly tagged MWEs (as a special phrasal category), and therefore the comparison between supervised and unsupervised identification is not entirely fair.

In the current work, we present a hybrid method using both phrase-structure representation of MWEs, and association measures for ranking them in an unsupervised fashion (see table 1 for a quick comparison between the current work and previous approaches). We make use of a Tree-Kernel method (Collins and Duffy, 2002) for extracting a large set of recurring syntactic fragments from a given treebank.

The rest of the paper is organized as follows: in section 2 we present the idea of adopting recurring tree fragments extracted from a treebank using a Tree Kernel. In section 3 we introduce the treebanks from which tree fragments are extracted. Next we perform two types of experiments: in section 4 we employ the extracted fragments for supervised identification of multiword expressions as a supervised parsing task; in section 5, we compare how well different association measures rerank the expressions underlying the extracted fragments in an unsupervised fashion.

Proceedings of NAACL-HLT 2015, pages 10–18,
Denver, Colorado, May 31 – June 5, 2015.

	Ramisch et al. (2010)	Green et al. (2013)	This work
Unsupervised	Yes	No	Yes
Association measures	Yes	No	Yes
Syntax	POS tags	flat rules	hierarchical
Gaps	No	No	Yes
Representation	⟨ JJ_mountain, NN_bike ⟩	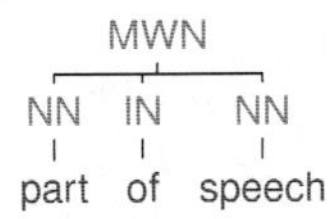	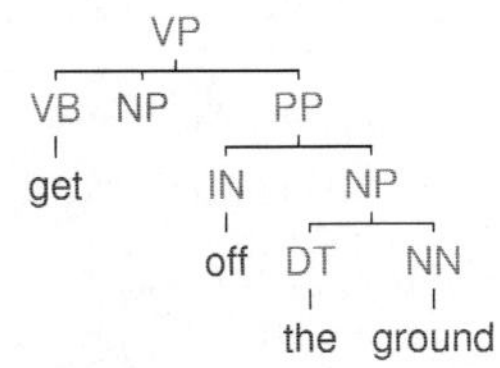

Table 1: Comparison of the current work with previous approaches.

2 Recurring Fragments

In our work, we investigate ways of automatically detecting MWEs in large treebanks by searching for recurring patterns. The patterns consist of tree fragments that occur two or more times in the treebank. This is an ideal constraint if we want to assume that a necessary condition for a fragment to yield a MWE is to *recur multiple times in a representative corpus*.

This is also one of the original motivations behind the Data-Oriented Parsing (DOP) framework in which "idiomaticity is the rule rather than the exception" (Scha, 1990). For instance, if we have seen the MWE "pain in the neck" several times before, we should store the whole fragment for later use.

Data-Oriented Parsing has been most successfully implemented (Bod, 1992; Bod et al., 2003) with Tree Substitution Grammars (TSGs), A Tree-Substitution Grammar consists of a bag of elementary trees. In DOP, these are arbitrarily large fragments extracted from a treebank corresponding to syntactic constructions. They can include any number of lexical units, with possible intervening gaps, and are therefore very suited to represent MWEs ranging from fixed idiomatic cases such as "kick the bucket" to more flexible expressions such as "break *X* up" and "as far as *X* is concerned" to even longer constructions such as "everything you always wanted to know about *X* but were afraid to ask."

Since extracting all possible fragments from a large treebank is impossible (the number of possible fragments grows exponentially with the size of a tree) it is necessary to work with a restricted set of fragments. Several sampling methods have been proposed (Bod, 2001; Zuidema, 2007; Cohn et al., 2010), but all include some limitations (e.g., use of random sampling methods, restriction in the size of the fragments, number of lexical items).

An alternative is to use a Tree Kernel which quantifies the similarity of trees (Collins and Duffy, 2002). Sangati et al. (2010) introduces `FragmentSeeker`, an algorithm based on a Tree Kernel that makes the similarities between trees explicit by extracting recurring tree fragments. `FragmentSeeker` is based on a dynamic programming algorithm which compares every pair of trees of a given treebank and extracts a list of maximal overlapping fragments in all the pairs.

In a recent effort, van Cranenburgh (2014) developed an improved algorithm[1] for fragment extraction which runs in linear average time in the size of the treebank (it is 30 times faster than the original implementation on the Penn treebank). This substantial speedup is due to the incorporation of the Fast Tree Kernel (Moschitti, 2006), and opens up the possibility of handling much larger treebanks.

Figure 1 shows an example of a pair of trees sharing a common fragment (with lexical items depicted in blue and non-lexical terminals in green).

The fragments extracted with these tools have proven to be successful for several NLP tasks such as statistical parsing, as in DOP (Sangati and Zuidema, 2011; van Cranenburgh and Bod, 2013), authorship attribution (van Cranenburgh, 2012), and native language detection (Swanson and Charniak, 2012, 2013).

[1]The tool is publicly available at `https://github.com/andreasvc/disco-dop`

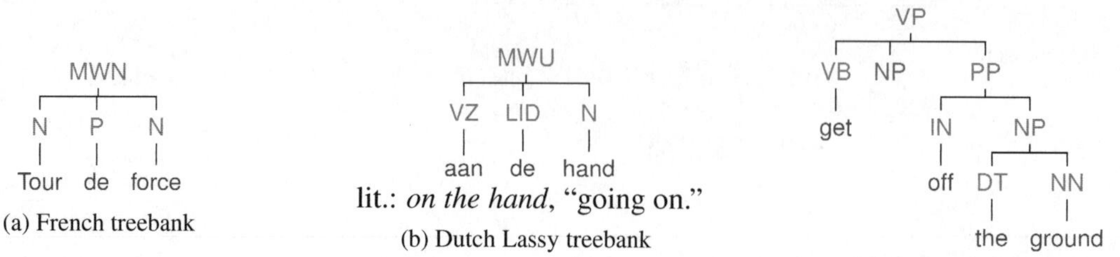

(a) French treebank

(b) Dutch Lassy treebank

(c) Annotated English Gigaword

Figure 2: A comparison of treebanks and their MWE annotation. (a) French treebank; flat MWE annotation. (c) Dutch Lassy treebank; flat MWE annotation. (b) Annotated English Gigaword; no MWE annotation.

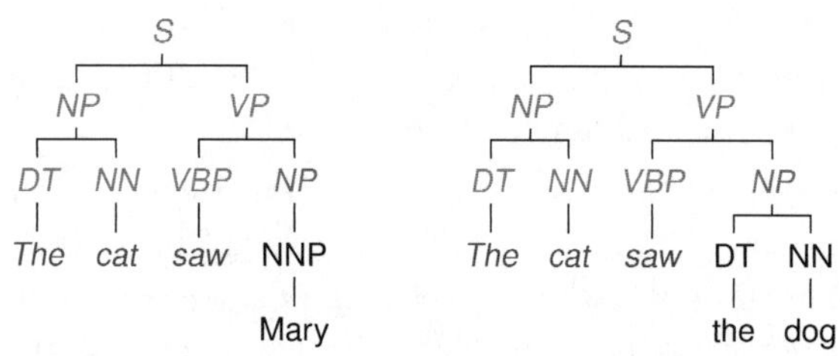

Figure 1: An example of two syntactic trees sharing a common fragment (highlighted).

3 Treebanks

We are using three different treebanks for extracting MWEs across three languages: French, Dutch and English. See table 2 for statistics on treebank sizes and number of fragments, and figure 2 for a comparison of the MWE annotations in the treebanks.

Treebank	Trees	Total Frags	Selected Frags
French	13K	274K	86K
Dutch	52K	536K	193K
English	500K	4.3M	2.8M

Table 2: Treebank size and number of fragments extracted and employed in the experiments. The last column reports the number of fragments after filtering out all those which do not contain at least a content word and a non-punctuation word.

3.1 French Treebank

We adopt the version of the French Treebank (Abeillé et al., 2003) from June 2010 used in Green et al. (2011). In this treebank MWEs are annotated with a flat bracketing (see figure 2a), that is, all words are grouped non-hierarchically, immediately under a single phrase which has a specific label per each phrasal category (e.g., MWV for verbal expression, MWN for nominal expressions, etc). We use this corpus for both supervised (parsing) and unsupervised (association measures) identification of MWEs .

3.2 Dutch Treebank

For Dutch, we employ the LASSY Small treebank (Noord, 2009) which is a syntactically annotated and manually verified corpus of 1 million words. As shown in figure 2b, the MWE annotation is flat as in the French Treebank, but a single category (MWU) is used to label them. We use this treebank for both supervised and unsupervised identification of MWEs.

3.3 Annotated English Gigaword

For English, we use the Annotated English Gigaword treebank[2] which contains more than 180 million automatically parsed sentences.

The size of this treebank is still prohibitively large even for the fast version of `FragmentSeeker`. We therefore decided to use only a sample of the treebank by selecting one out of every 150 sentences. This leaves us with a treebank of 500K structures, still 10 times larger than the Dutch treebank. However, since we want to extract MWEs, we are only interested in fragments with at least two lexical items. This restriction enables us to apply a further optimization to the algorithm which substantially boosts the extraction speed: after indexing sentences by the words they contain, we compare every tree structure only to other structures sharing at least two words.

[2] http://catalog.ldc.upenn.edu/LDC2012T21

The annotation of the English Gigaword treebank follows the Penn Treebank scheme (Marcus et al., 1994) which does not include any special category for MWEs. As we have no gold standard for MWE annotation, we can only employ this treebank for unsupervised experiments and qualitative analysis. However, as shown in figure 2c, this annotation preserves the full hierarchical structure of MWEs and allows us to employ the full potential of Tree Kernels for extracting arbitrarily large MWEs with possible intervening gaps.

4 Finding MWEs by parsing

Green et al. (2011) introduce the idea of using a parsing model to identify MWEs. This is a supervised methodology as it requires a training treebank with gold MWE labels. The experiments of this section will therefore be performed on the French and Dutch treebanks.

4.1 Parsing Methodology

As parsing model we use the Double-DOP (2DOP) model (Sangati and Zuidema, 2011), as implemented in the `disco-dop` parser (van Cranenburgh and Bod, 2013). The resulting TSG grammar is constituted by the recurring fragments extracted from the training portion of the treebank (as explained in section 2) and additionally the Context-Free Grammar (CFG) rules occurring once (in order to ensure better coverage over the test sentences). In a TSG, fragments are combined by means of the substitution operation to derive the tree structures of novel sentences (see figure 4 for an example of fragments combination). We redirect the reader to Bod et al. (2003) for more details about TSG parsing.

In our models we use simple relative frequencies as fragment probabilities. As preprocessing we apply a set of manual state splits, heuristics for head-outward binarization, and an unknown word model for assigning POS tags to out-of-vocabulary words. For Dutch, we use the same preprocessing as described in van Cranenburgh and Bod (2013). For French, we apply similar preprocessing as Green et al. (2013)[3].

[3]For the binarization we apply the markovization setting $h = 1, v = 1$, i.e., no additional parent annotation, and every child constituent is conditioned on the previous two siblings.Note that Green et al. (2013) uses $h = \infty, v = 1$ markovization (Green, personal communication).

4.2 Results

In table 3 we present the comparison of the overall parsing results on the French and Dutch treebanks together with the MWE detection score. The overall parsing results (F1 score, exact match) are not specific to MWEs, but describe the general quality of the parsing model. The MWE-F1 score is an F1 score of correctly parsed MWE constituents.

For French we compare our model (2DOP) against two systems reported in Green et al. (2013), i.e., the factored Stanford parser and a TSG-DP parser in which tree fragments are drawn from a Dirichlet process (DP) prior (Cohn et al., 2010). Our system performs better than the other systems, both in terms of overall parsing results and MWE identification specifically.

For Dutch, since this is the first attempt to extract MWEs via parsing, we compare our result with a simple PCFG baseline. Our 2DOP model performs well above the baseline both in terms of parsing and MWE identification.

Finally, table 4 presents the detailed results for the identification of the MWEs for each category in the French treebank. Our system performs better in 4 out of 8 categories compared with the Stanford parser and the DP-TSG model. The Dutch results consist of a single category, so we do not report a further breakdown.

Parser	F1	EX	MWE-F1
FRENCH			
Green et al. (2013): DP-TSG	76.9	16.0	71.3
Green et al. (2013): Stanford	79.0	17.6	70.5
disco-dop, 2DOP	**79.3**	**19.9**	**71.9**
DUTCH			
disco-dop, PCFG baseline	63.9	21.8	50.4
disco-dop, 2DOP	**77.0**	**35.2**	**75.3**

Table 3: Performance of the parsing models on the French and Dutch treebanks, with respect to parsing results (F1 score and exact match) and the MWE-F1 score, for sentences ≤ 40 words.

5 Identifying MWEs with Tree Fragments and Association Measures

In this section we focus on the unsupervised detection of MWEs. We start with the same Tree Kernel

	#gold	DP-TSG	Stanford	This work
MWN	457	65.7	64.8	**68.9**
MWADV	220	**77.2**	75.0	70.0
MWP	162	79.5	81.2	**81.9**
MWC	47	85.8	**86.3**	80.7
MWV	26	56.2	**57.1**	55.9
MWPRO	17	75.3	72.2	**78.1**
MWD	15	65.1	**68.4**	66.7
MWA	8	36.0	26.1	**37.5**
Total	955	71.3	70.5	**71.9**

Table 4: French MWE identification, F1 score per category, for sentences ≤ 40 words.

methodology illustrated in section 2 for extracting the set of recurring fragments from the various treebanks. Next, we apply various association measures (AMs) for ranking these fragments and compare how they perform in distinguishing those fragments underlying MWEs from the others.

In section 5.3 we conduct a case study on the English treebank for which we have no MWE annotations, whereas in section 5.4 we apply a quantitative analysis to assess how the AMs perform in the French and the Dutch treebank (for which we have gold MWE annotations).

5.1 Signatures

Differently from most existing works on MWEs discovery, our methodology does not focus on MWEs of a specific type or size. However, the association measures that are commonly employed are strongly influenced by the length of the expressions, i.e., shorter expressions tend to have higher association scores. Moreover, since we also take into account fragments with possible gaps, we need to be careful in distinguishing fully lexicalized expressions from those containing intervening phrasal categories.

We therefore devise a way to partition the set of extracted fragments into a number of bins. All fragments belonging to the same bin share the same signature and are therefore mutually comparable (in terms of their association scores). The signature of a fragment is a sequence $\{L, X\}^+$ of symbols obtained by mapping each frontier node of the fragment to L if it is a lexical node, or X if it is a non-lexical node. Figure 3 shows an example of a fragment and its corresponding signature.

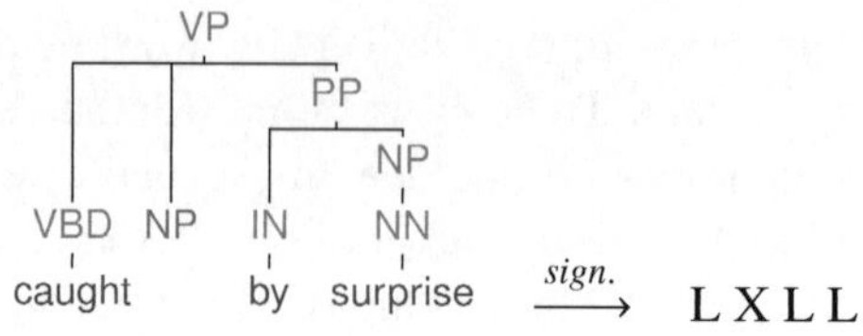

Figure 3: Example of a fragment (of length 4 with a gap in the second position) with its signature.

5.2 Association Measures

A number of Association Measures (AM) have been defined in the literature to assess the cohesiveness of a potential MWE. In this work we take into consideration two standard association measures, the Pointwise Mutual Information (PMI) and the Log-Likelihood Ratio (LLR). Both AMs are generalized to arbitrarily long expressions, and are defined over the sequence of symbols $S_1, S_2, \ldots, S_n$, where S_i is the pair $\langle \text{pos}_i, \text{word}_i \rangle$, with pos_i and word_i being the pre-terminal label and lexical item of the i-th frontier node, respectively; $\text{word}_i = \emptyset$ if the i-th frontier node is a non-lexical item. In addition, we define a novel association measure, namely the Log Inside Ratio (LIR), based on probabilities of a probabilistic TSG underlying the extracted fragments.

PMI The Multivariate Generalization of Pointwise Mutual Information, also referred to as Total Correlation (Watanabe, 1960) and Multi-Information (Studený and Vejnarová, 1998; Van de Cruys, 2011), is defined as follows:

$$\text{PMI}(S_1, S_2, \ldots, S_n) = \log \frac{p(S_1, S_2, \ldots, S_n)}{\prod_{i=1}^{n} p(S_i)}$$

where $p(S_1, S_2, \ldots, S_n)$ is the relative frequency with which the signature $S_1, S_2, \ldots, S_n$ has been seen within the set of fragments sharing the same signature, and $p(S_i)$ is the relative frequency of seeing the symbol S_i in the i-th position of the signature within the same set of fragments.

LLR The Log-Likelihood Ratio generalized for a sequence with an arbitrary number of symbols (Su, 1991) is defined as follows:

$$\text{LLR}(S_1, \ldots, S_n) = \log \frac{p(S_1, \ldots, S_n)}{\sum_{\sigma \in \text{CSP}(S_1, \ldots, S_n)} \prod_{s \in \sigma} p(s)}$$

where the numerator is as in PMI, while the denominator represents the probability of the sequence to be derived from contiguous spans. More precisely, CSP($S_1, \ldots, S_n$) returns the ways (σ) of partitioning the sequence $S_1, \ldots, S_n$ in contigous spans (s).[4]

LIR The Log Inside Ratio is a newly derived association measure which specifies the probability that a Probabilistic TSG (PTSG) grammar generates a given fragment in a single step with respect to the total probability of generating it in any possible way, i.e., by combining smaller fragments together. Figure 4 shows an example of how a TSG can generate the same fragment in multiple ways. The LIR is computed as follows:

$$\text{LIR}(\text{frag}) = \log \frac{p(\text{frag})}{\mathit{inside}(\text{frag})}$$

where the numerator is the probability of the fragment according to the PTSG extracted from the treebank,[5] while the denominator is the total probability with which the grammar generates the given fragment starting from its root category (in any possible way).

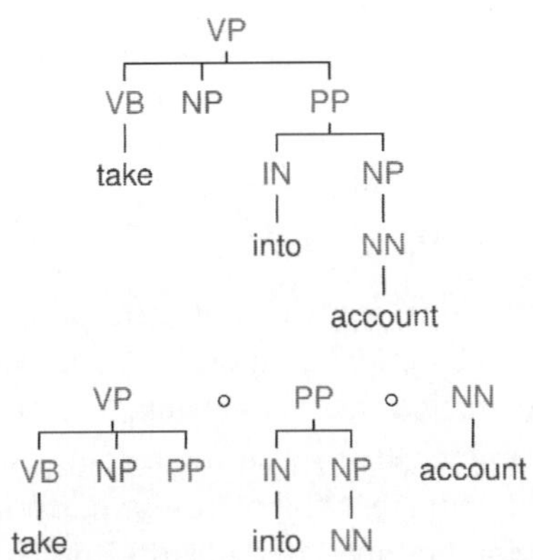

Figure 4: Example of how a TSG can generate the same fragment in two different ways, i.e., in a single step (above), and in 3 subsequent steps (below).

5.3 Case Study on English Treebank

We have conducted a case study on the English treebank, for which no MWE gold labels are available. In this initial study we limited the qualitative analysis to the PMI association measure.

The histogram in figure 5 reports the distribution of the extracted fragments in the most common signature bins. This includes fragments with up to 7 terminals at the frontier nodes, with at most 3 non-lexical nodes (X in the signatures). Tables 5 and 6 present a list of fragments starting with the verb *take* with and without a gap in the second position, sorted by the PMI measure. In both cases there is a contrast between MWEs at the top of the list (e.g., take into account) and more compositional expressions at the bottom (e.g., take QP years to, take the money).

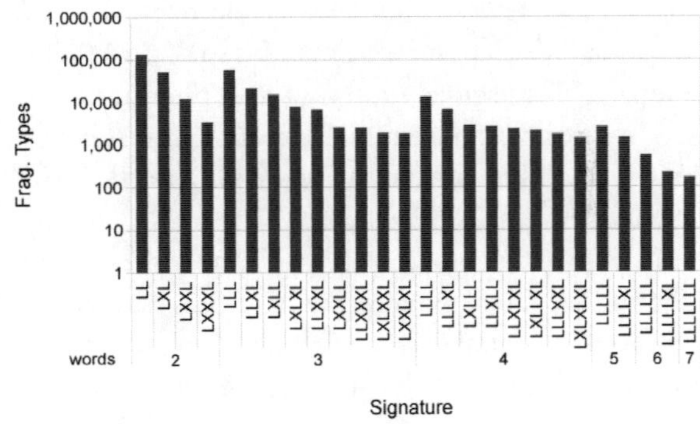

Figure 5: Distribution of the 2.8M recurring fragments extracted from the English treebank into the various signature bins. Only bins with at least 100 fragment types are reported.

5.4 Quantitative Results on French and Dutch

Quantitative evaluation of MWE identification is a non-trivial task. Typically, association measures are tuned so that only expressions above a specific threshold are considered MWEs. Alternatively, precision and recall measures on a full reference data or on n-best lists are used (Evert and Krenn, 2001). In our case the task is more challenging as we would need to fix a different threshold value for each set of fragments sharing the same signature. We therefore decided to resort to a novel evaluation metric which would enable us to compare how the various AMs rerank the full list of expressions sharing the same signature in a more neutral and informative way.

We do so by calculating, for each signature bin, the percentage of MWEs present in subsequently smaller portions of the reranked list, limiting the evaluation

[4] *CSP* stands for *Contiguous Sequence Partition*. As an example, CSP(S_1, S_2, S_3) = $\{[[S_1, S_2], [S_3]]; [[S_1], [S_2, S_3]]; [[S_1], [S_2], [S_3]]\}$

[5] Here we use the same PTSG as in the parsing experiments of the previous section.

PMI	Freq.	Sequence Pattern
18.0	6	VB_take NP IN_into NN_account
14.6	6	VB_take NP IN_for VBN_granted
13.6	7	VB_take DT NN_look IN_at
12.9	6	VB_take NP TO_to NN_court
12.5	6	VB_take NN RB_away IN_from
12.4	17	VB_take NP RB_away IN_from
12.0	6	VB_take JJ NN_action TO_to
11.2	5	VB_take NP RB_away IN_from
10.5	6	VB_take QP NNS_years TO_to
8.3	10	VB_take DT NN_time TO_to

Table 5: List of English fragments conforming to the sequence pattern VB_take X L L, sorted by PMI.

PMI	Freq.	Sequence Pattern
15.3	13	VB_take IN_into NN_account
9.8	5	VB_take NN_responsibility IN_for
9.7	8	VB_take NN_credit IN_for
9.3	12	VB_take DT_a NN_look
8.4	88	VB_take NN_advantage IN_of
8.4	7	VB_take NN_place IN_on
8.3	6	VB_take NN_effect IN_in
8.1	14	VB_take NNS_steps TO_to
...	...	...
4.6	6	VB_take DT_the NN_money

Table 6: A sample of English fragments conforming to the sequence pattern VB_take L L, sorted by PMI.

to fewer and fewer candidates at the beginning of the list (as association measures tend to place MWEs on top). This metric is similar to the "precision at k" used in Information Retrieval, except that instead of using a fixed integer k, we use varying portions of the list (i.e., $1, 1/2, 1/3, \ldots, 1/10$).

Figure 6 shows the resulting graphs for the three AMs and the most common signatures in the French and Dutch treebanks. All curves are usually monotonically increasing, indicating that for all measures the concentration of MWEs increases at the top of the reranked list. PMI and LLR often overlap (they are mathematically identical for expressions of length 2), with LLR being slightly better for French and PMI for Dutch. Finally LIR is consistently better than the other 2 AMs for French while being worse or on a par with the others for Dutch. We are currently investigating the reason for this discrepancy. Our current hypotheses are: (i) the French treebank makes use of several MWE categories while the Dutch treebank has a single MWE category, and (ii) Dutch MWEs tend to be less rigid than the French ones.

Table 7 shows a single-figure F1 evaluation of the three AMs, obtained by aggregating the top $1/5$ candidates of each bin. For this evaluation, recall and precision are computed, with the gold set consisting of all the extracted lexicalized fragments with MWE gold tags.[6] According to these results the Log Inside Ratio (LIR) performs best for both French and Dutch. This evaluation is not ideal, as our method aims to go beyond the small, contiguous MWE strings annotated in the treebanks. In addition, manual inspection of the selected candidates reveals that many of them are MWEs, while not part of the gold standard. This should be addressed in future work with a manual evaluation.

Treebank	PMI	LLR	LIR
French	33.0	32.3	45.8
Dutch	49.4	46.6	50.5

Table 7: F1 scores for the top $1/5$ candidates of each bin as ranked by the three AMs evaluated against MWEs in extracted recurring fragments.

[6]Only fully lexicalized fragments are selected, since the treebanks do not annotate any MWEs with open slots.

6 Conclusion

We have presented a novel approach for the identification of MWEs based on recurring fragments automatically extracted from a treebank. We have shown that a probabilistic tree-substitution grammar (PTSG) constructed with these fragments outperforms previous results for the supervised identification of MWEs. Finally we have conducted a study to asses how various association measures (AMs) can rerank the extracted fragments for the unsupervised identification of MWE. Here we proposed a new measure based on PTSG, the Log Inside Ratio, which shows competitive results when compared against other classical association measures.

Acknowledgments

We kindly acknowledge the three anonymous reviewers and Katja Abramova for very useful feedback as well as the PARSEME European Cost Action (IC1207) for promoting this collaboration.

FRENCH

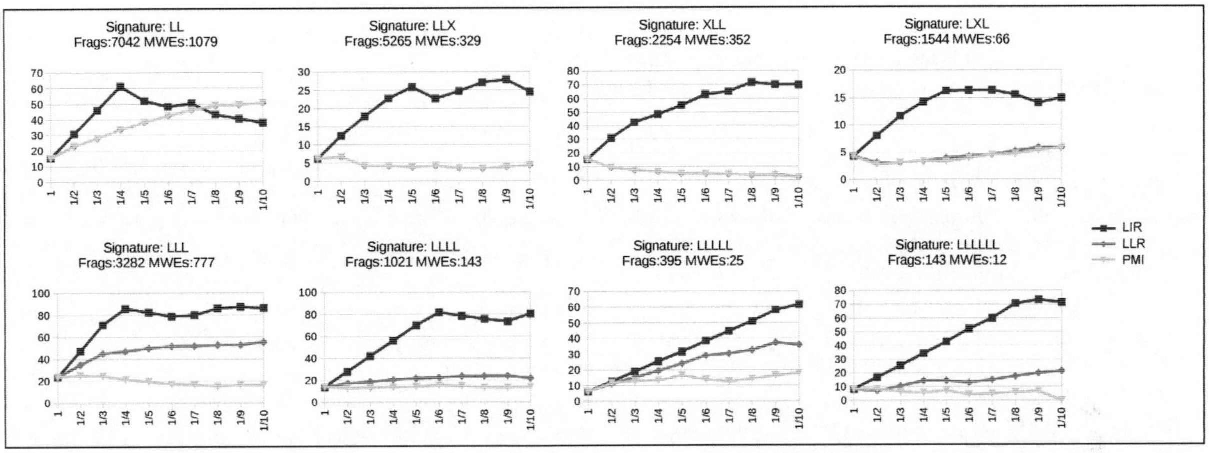

DUTCH

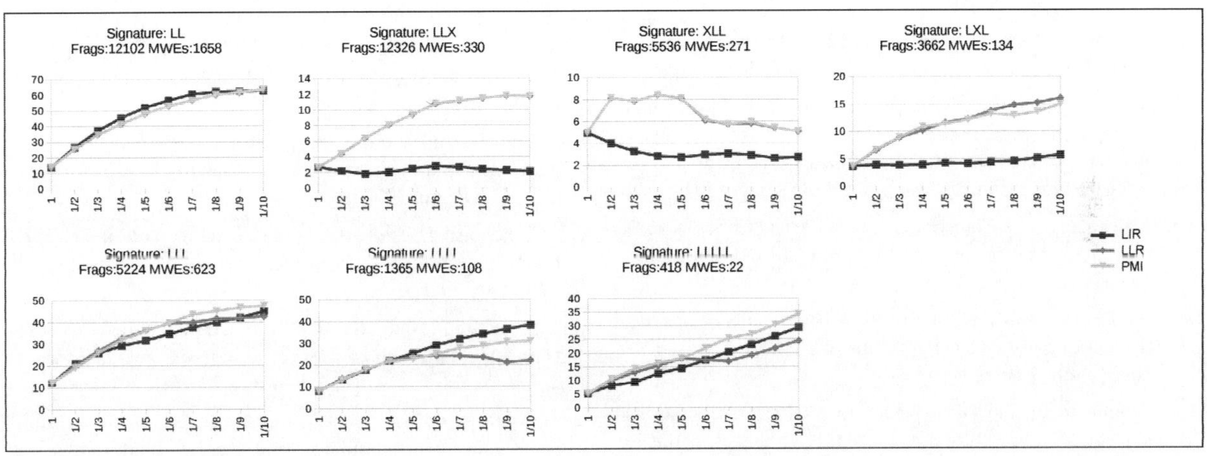

Figure 6: Results for the French and Dutch treebanks when ranking of the MWEs for various signatures according to several association measures. Each line reports how the percentage of MWEs (y-axis) changes when restricting the list to fewer and fewer top candidates. More specifically, we compute the percentage of MWE in the full list of fragments (1), in the first half (1/2), the first third (1/3), and so on until the first tenth (1/10).

References

Abeillé, Anne, Lionel Clément, and François Toussenel (2003). *Building a Treebank for French*, volume 20 of *Text, Speech and Language Technology*, pp. 165–188. Springer.

Bod, Rens (1992). A Computational Model of Language Performance: Data Oriented Parsing. In *Proc. of COLING*, pp. 855–859.

Bod, Rens (2001). What is the minimal set of fragments that achieves maximal parse accuracy? In *Proc. of ACL*, pp. 69-76.

Bod, Rens, Khalil Sima'an, and Remko Scha (2003). *Data-Oriented Parsing*. University of Chicago Press.

Cohn, Trevor, Phil Blunsom, and Sharon Goldwater (2010). Inducing Tree-Substitution Grammars. *Journal of Machine Learning Research*, 11:3053–3096.

Collins, Michael and Nigel Duffy (2002). New Ranking Algorithms for Parsing and Tagging: Kernels over Discrete Structures, and the Voted Perceptron. In *Proceedings of ACL*, pp. 263–270.

Evert, Stefan (2005). *The Statistics of Word Co-Occurrences: Word Pairs and Collocations*. PhD thesis, University of Stuttgart, Stuttgart, Germany.

Evert, Stefan and Brigitte Krenn (2001). Methods for the qualitative evaluation of lexical association measures. In *Proceedings of ACL*, pp. 188–195.

Goldberg, A.E. (1995). *Constructions: A Construction Grammar Approach to Argument Structure*. Univ. Of Chicago Press.

Green, Spence, Marie-Catherine de Marneffe, John Bauer, and Christopher D. Manning (2011). Multiword Expression Identification with Tree Substitution Grammars: A Parsing tour de force with French. In *Proceedings of EMNLP*, pp. 725–735.

Green, Spence, Marie-Catherine de Marneffe, and Christopher D. Manning (2013). Parsing models for identifying multiword expressions. *Comput. Linguist.*, 39(1):195–227.

Kay, Paul and Charles J. Fillmore (1997). Grammatical Constructions and Linguistic Generalizations: the What's X Doing Y? Construction. *Language*, 75:1–33.

Lyse, Gunn Inger and Gisle Andersen (2012). Collocations and statistical analysis of n-grams: Multiword expressions in newspaper text. In *Exploring Newspaper Language*. John Benjamins Publishing Company.

Marcus, Mitchell, Grace Kim, Mary Ann Marcinkiewicz, Robert MacIntyre, Ann Bies, Mark Ferguson, Karen Katz, and Britta Schasberger (1994). The Penn Treebank: annotating predicate argument structure. In *Proc. of HLT*, pp. 114–119.

Moschitti, Alessandro (2006). Making Tree Kernels Practical for Natural Language Learning. In *Proceedings of EACL*.

Noord, Gertjan Van (2009). Huge parsed corpora in lassy. In *Proceedings of TLT7*, Groningen, Netherlands.

Ramisch, Carlos, Vitor De Araujo, and Aline Villavicencio (2012). A broad evaluation of techniques for automatic acquisition of multiword expressions. In *Proc. of ACL SRW 2012*, pp. 1–6.

Ramisch, Carlos, Aline Villavicencio, and Christian Boitet (2010). mwetoolkit: a framework for multiword expression identification. In *Proceedings of LREC*, pp. 662–669.

Sag, Ivan A., Timothy Baldwin, Francis Bond, Ann Copestake, and Dan Flickinger (2002). Multiword Expressions: A Pain in the Neck for NLP. In Gelbukh, Alexander, ed., *Computational Linguistics and Intelligent Text Processing, LCNS* vol. 2276, pp. 1–15. Springer Berlin Heidelberg.

Sangati, Federico and Willem Zuidema (2011). Accurate Parsing with Compact Tree-Substitution Grammars: Double-DOP. In *Proceedings of EMNLP*, pp. 84–95.

Sangati, Federico, Willem Zuidema, and Rens Bod (2010). Efficiently Extract Recurring Tree Fragments from Large Treebanks. In *Proceedings of LREC*, pp. 219–226.

Scha, Remko (1990). Taaltheorie en taaltechnologie: competence en performance. In de Kort, Q. A. M. and G. L. J. Leerdam, eds., *Computertoepassingen in de Neerlandistiek*, LVVN-jaarboek, pp. 7–22. Landelijke Vereniging van Neerlandici, Almere. [Language theory and language technology: Competence and Performance] in Dutch.

Stefanowitsch, Anatol and Stephan Th. Gries (2003). Collostructions: Investigating the interaction of words and constructions. *International Journal of Corpus Linguistics*, 8:209–243.

Studený, Milan and Jirina Vejnarová (1998). The multiinformation function as a tool for measuring stochastic dependence. In *Learning in graphical models*, pp. 261–297. Springer.

Swanson, Ben and Eugene Charniak (2013). Extracting the native language signal for second language acquisition. In *Proceedings of NAACL*, pp. 85–94.

Swanson, Benjamin and Eugene Charniak (2012). Native language detection with tree substitution grammars. In *Proceedings of ACL*, pp. 193–197.

van Cranenburgh, Andreas (2012). Literary authorship attribution with phrase-structure fragments. In *Proceedings of CLFL*, pp. 59–63.

van Cranenburgh, Andreas (2014). Extraction of phrase-structure fragments with a linear average time tree kernel. *Computational Linguistics in the Netherlands Journal*, 4:3–16.

van Cranenburgh, Andreas and Rens Bod (2013). Discontinuous parsing with an efficient and accurate DOP model. In *Proceedings of IWPT*, pp. 7–16.

Van de Cruys, Tim (2011). Two multivariate generalizations of pointwise mutual information. In *Proceedings of the Workshop on Distributional Semantics and Compositionality*, pp. 16–20.

Watanabe, Satosi (1960). Information theoretical analysis of multivariate correlation. *IBM Journal of research and development*, 4(1):66–82.

Zuidema, Willem (2006). What are the productive units of natural language grammar? In *Proc. of CoNLL*, pp. 29–36.

Zuidema, Willem (2007). Parsimonious Data-Oriented Parsing. In *Proceedings of EMNLP-CoNLL*, pp. 551–560.

How to Account for Idiomatic German Support Verb Constructions in Statistical Machine Translation

Fabienne Cap[1], **Manju Nirmal**[2], **Marion Weller**[1,2], **Sabine Schulte im Walde**[2]

[1] CIS, Ludwig-Maximilian University of Munich – cap@cis.uni-muenchen.de
[2] IMS, University of Stuttgart – (nirmalmu|wellermn|schulte)@ims.uni-stuttgart.de

Abstract

Support-verb constructions (i.e., multiword expressions combining a semantically light verb with a predicative noun) are problematic for standard statistical machine translation systems, because SMT systems cannot distinguish between literal and idiomatic uses of the verb. We work on the German to English translation direction, for which the identification of support-verb constructions is challenging due to the relatively free word order of German. We show that we achieve improved translation quality for verb-object support-verb constructions by marking the verbs when occuring in such constructions. Additional evaluations revealed that our systems produce more correct verb translations than a contrastive baseline system without verb markup.

1 Introduction

It is widely acknowledged in the NLP community that multiword expressions (MWEs) are a challenge for many NLP applications (Sag et al., 2002), due to their idiosyncratic behaviour at different levels of linguistic description. In this paper we address German support verb constructions (SVCs) in statistical machine translation.[1]

Support-verb constructions, also known as *light-verb constructions*,[2] are multiword expressions combining a verb and a predicative noun. The verb neither contributes its full meaning to the construction, nor is the meaning completely void (Butt, 2003; Langer, 2009). For example, the verb *take* does not contribute its full meaning to the SVC *take a bath*, but nevertheless its semantic contribution is different to the verb *make* in the SVC *make a bath* (Butt, 2003). Often, an SVC is close in meaning to a corresponding full verb, e.g., the SVC *make a contribution* is synonymous to the verb *contribute*. Table 1 presents examples for English and for German SVCs and synonymous full verbs, where the predicative nouns are embedded in a noun phrase (V+NP) or a prepositional phrase (V+PP).

	English	
V+NP	make a contribution	contribute
V+PP	take into account	consider
	German	
V+NP	einen Beitrag leisten lit. *a contribution achieve*	beitragen *to contribute*
V+PP	in Frage stellen lit. *in question put*	hinterfragen *to question*

Table 1: Examples of English and German SVCs.

Support-verb constructions are problematic for phrase-based statistical machine translation (SMT) systems, as these systems consider texts to consist of word sequences, without distinguishing between the literal meanings of the verbs vs. their idiomatic meaning within an SVC. In this paper, we will show that we can achieve improved translation quality by marking the verbs that occur within **V+NP** SVCs. The marking distinguishes the SVC verbs from independent occurrences of the verb and thus enables the SMT system to learn different translations for the different kinds of occurrences. We focus on German SVCs, which are particularly challenging due to the morphological richness and the relatively free word

[1]The work presented in this paper is part of the Master's Thesis of Manju Nirmal, cf. (Nirmal, 2015).

[2]in German: *Funktionsverbgefüge*

Proceedings of NAACL-HLT 2015, pages 19–28,
Denver, Colorado, May 31 – June 5, 2015.

order in German. While Carpuat and Diab (2010) included some English SVCs into their pilot study on evaluating MWEs through SMT, to our knowledge there is no other previous work on SVCs in the context of SMT.

2 SVCs in Statistical Machine Translation

Default translation: In SMT, translations are "learned" from parallel data. Out of a set of possible translations derived from that data, the SMT decoder selects the most probable one. Today, most SMT systems translate whole phrases instead of single words, which allows to take some context of the word into account. Moreover, a language model and an reodering model are consulted in order to promote fluent translations. Nevertheless it is often the most frequent translation of a word which is chosed by the decoder. For example, the German verb *"vertreten"* is most often translated as "represent" in the training data. A standard phrase-based SMT system thus considers "represent" as a suitable translation for *"vertreten"*. However, when occurring in the context of an SVC like *"die Auffassung* ***vertreten****"*, a translation into "**represent** the view" is clearly wrong. Instead, *"vertreten"* should in this case be translated into "take" in order to yield the correct translation into "**take** the view". However, this is only one translation scenario. Sometimes, the German SVC is not translated into an English SVC but a different construction. For example, *"Auffassung vertreten"* is often translated as "being of the opinion that". In other cases, the SVC is identical in both languages: e.g. *"Rolle spielen"* - "play a role".

Dazu **leistet** die Effizienz des Vermittlungsverfahrens einen substanziellen **Beitrag**. *To that* **make** *the effectiveness of the codecision procedure a substantial* **contribution**.
The effectiveness of the codecision procedure has **made** a substantial **contribution** in this case .

Table 2: Example for a non-adjacent SVC.

Non-adjacent SVCs: If the verb and its object are directly adjacent, a phrase-based system with sufficient coverage of the SVC in question is likely to correctly translate the SVC as one phrase. However, if the verb appears isolated, which is not uncommon in German, it is much more difficult for the SMT system to recognize that the verb should not be translated by its "default", but by the SVC-specific translation. The example in Table 2 illustrates that several words may occur between the components of the SVC *"Beitrag leisten"*.

Note that some SVCs allow for more intervening words than others. In Table 3, the comparison of the average distance between the verb and the noun within the two SVCs *"Beitrag leisten"* and *"Rechnung tragen"* shows considerable differences.

SVC		distance
Beitrag leisten	*to make a contribution*	5.44
Rechnung tragen	*to account for*	2.62

Table 3: Average distance of SVC components.

The mean distances are derived from 3,549 occurrences of the SVC *"Beitrag leisten"* and 1,868 occurrences of the SVC *"Rechnung tragen"* within the Europarl corpus (Koehn, 2005). They were calculated by substracting the lower position in the sentence from the higher position for either the noun or the verb. Whenever the verb and the noun occurred directly adjacent, the score yields "1".

Methodology: In order to enable the SMT system to distinguish occurrences of a verb within an SVC from independent occurrences, we add a special markup to the verbs occurring in an SVC. By introducing this markup, the translations for independent verbs with a literal meaning are separated from those of verbs occurring in an SVC context. Thus, the SMT system can learn the SVC-translation of a verb not only when it occurs directly adjacent to the noun, but also for SVCs with many intervening words between the components. In such cases, the SVC is chopped and stored in different phrases of the SMT system. For a standard SMT system without markup it is almost impossible to learn the correct translation of the verb.

3 Related Work

MWEs in general: Multiword expressions have been a recurrent focus of attention within theoretical, cognitive, and in the last decade also within computational linguistics: The workshops on multiword expressions attached to major CL conferences[3] celebrated their 10th anniversary in 2014, and the SIGLEX-MWE has initiated three special issues in NLP journals.

After initial approaches mainly focused on characterising the computationally challenging properties of multiword expressions (such as Sag et al. (2002) and Villavicencio et al. (2005)) and automatically identifying various types of multiword expressions in corpora (such as Baldwin and Villavicencio (2002), Villavicencio (2003) and Bannard (2007) who extracted English particle verbs), the focus of interest moved towards deeper semantic models of specific types of multiword expressions and towards integrating multiword expressions into applications.

Compositionality of MWEs: A wide range of semantic approaches has been concerned with distinguishing degrees of compositionality within multiword expressions, addressing

- noun compounds (Zinsmeister and Heid (2004), Reddy et al. (2011), Schulte im Walde et al. (2013)),
- particle verbs (McCarthy et al. (2003), Bannard (2005), Cook and Stevenson (2006), Ramisch et al. (2008)),
- light-/support-verb constructions (Bannard (2007), Fazly et al. (2007), Fazly et al. (2009)),
- various MWE types (Lin (1999), Katz and Giesbrecht (2006), Fazly and Stevenson (2008), Evert (2009))

The most prominent approach exploring measures of association strength within multiword expressions, in order to distinguish literal from collocational interpretations, is probably (Evert, 2005).

Addressing the compositionality of multiword expressions is a crucial ingredient for lexicography and NLP applications, to know whether the expression should be treated as a whole, or through its parts, and what the expression means. Examples of applications that have profited from integrating the semantics of multiword expressions are Part-of-Speech Tagging (Constant and Sigogne, 2011), Parsing (Wehrli, 2014), Information Retrieval (Acosta et al., 2011), and SMT (Carpuat and Diab, 2010; Weller et al., 2014), see below for details.

[3] `http://multiword.sourceforge.net`

MWEs in SMT: Previous work regarding multiword expressions in SMTcan be divided into *static* approaches, where the training data is modified in order to facilitate a standard SMT system to learn suitable MWE translations and *dynamic* approaches where the modification takes place in the phrase table of the SMT system.

Static approaches include (Lambert and Banchs, 2005), who first extract bilingual – English and Spanish – MWEs based on parsed data and then merge them into "super-tokens", which later is treated as a unit by the SMT system. Similarly, Carpuat and Diab (2010) merge parts of English MWEs extracted from lexica into larger units in order to improve English to Arabic SMT. In addition, they increase the maximal phrase size from 5 in conventional systems to 10 words per phrase. More recently, Cholakov and Kordoni (2014) described a static approach to handle English phrasal verbs – extracted from lexical ressources – for translation into Bulgarian, where the particles are usually not separated from the verbs.

While static approaches have shown to improve translation quality, they do not allow for context-dependent decisions on how to translate MWEs. Instead of modifying MWEs in the training data, *dynamic* approaches handle MWEs directly in the phrase table of the SMT system. Ren et al. (2009) present an approach to handle bilingual Chinese - English MWEs. These are extracted from domain-specific parallel text and then added as separate phrases to the training data. In a subsequent step, the resulting phrase table is then annotated with a boolean variable indicating the presence or absence of an MWE. This approach was then taken one step further by Carpuat and Diab (2010), who worked with longer phrases and indicated not only the presence, but also the number of MWEs in each phrase. Finally, Cholakov and Kordoni (2014) further improved the dynamic approach in that they, in addition to the number of MWEs in a phrase, also encoded linguistic features of the phrasal verbs they investigated, like transitivity or separability.

In terms of translation quality, both static and dynamic approaches performed more or less equally well, except for (Cholakov and Kordoni, 2014), who found considerable improvements for the dynamic approach incorporating linguistic features.

DE	*"Sie wollen herausfinden, welche **Rolle** der Riesenplanet bei der Entwicklung des Sonnensystems **gespielt** hat."* *they wanted to find out, what **role** the giant-planet for the development of-the solar-system **played** has.*
EN	"They want to find our what **role** the giant planet has **played** in the development of the solar system ."

Table 4: German word order allows for many intervening words between a verb and its object, here: *"Rolle gespielt"*.

Relation to the presented work In this paper, we pursue a static approach, i.e. we modify the training data of the SMT system, but leave the system itself as it is. We extract MWEs directly from the parallel training data (like Lambert and Banchs (2005) and Ren et al. (2009)) using parsed data (to account for the flexible word order of German) and word association measures (similarly to Ren et al. (2009)). In contrast to previous static approaches, where the MWEs were joined together to form a single unit, we only mark the verb of a support verb construction. We have shown with the example of *"Beitrag leisten"* above that German word order allows for many intervening words between the two components. Joining German MWEs together may thus lead to highly influent sentences.

4 Extraction and Markup of SVC verbs

This section provides more details on our methodology. The general procedure is done in five steps, with steps 1–4 explained in the following subsections, and step 5 described in Section 5:

1. extract verb-object pairs (on lemma-level) from the parsed training data
2. identify SVCs (on lemma-level) in this set using standard word association measures
3. create several SVC sets with different degrees of idiomaticity
4. re-visit the training data and mark the verbs of SVCs (on token-level) accordingly
5. run SMT systems trained on data with verb markup based on the different SVC sets (cf. Section 5)

4.1 Verb-Object Pair Extraction To obtain a set of SVCs, we first extract verb-object pairs from dependency-parsed data. In a second step, all of these potential SVCs are scored and ranked by association measures. The SVC candidates with the highest association scores constitute the set of SVCs to be marked in both the parallel training data as well as in the data to be translated.

For extracting the SVC candidates, we follow the extraction method outlined in Scheible et al. (2013) who describe a set of guidelines to induce the complete set of argument and adjunct phrases from dependency-parses (Bohnet, 2010). While in this study we focus on *verb-object* pairs, our extraction method allows for an easy extension to also cover other types of SVCs, such as *preposition+noun+verb* triples.

The example given in Table 4 illustrates the need for parsed data when working with German: due to the flexible word order already illustrated in Section 2, verb and object are often not adjacent, but allow for the insertion of several phrases (*[the giant planet]$_{SUBJ}$ [for the development [of the solar system]$_{PP}$]$_{PP}$*) or sub-ordinate clauses between them. Furthermore, parsed data allows for an extraction of verb-object pairs on lemma-basis in order to generalise over the morphological variants of verbs and nouns. From the example in Table 4, we would extract the verb–object lemma pair *"Rolle spielen"*.

4.2 Identification of SVCs The resulting list of SVC verb-object candidate pairs does not only contain idiomatic SVCs, but also literal verb–object combinations. In order to identify the subset of SVCs, we measure the association strength between the verb and the object. For this, we opted for the often-used *log-likelihood* measure implemented in the UCS-toolkit (Evert, 2005). Assuming that verb-object pairs with a high association score are likely to be idiomatic, we rank the SVC candidate pairs according to their association scores.

4.3 Datasets Based on the ranked list of verb–object pairs by a word association measure, we decided to investigate different thresholds to the log-likelihood scores in order to identify idiomatic SVCs among the set of verb-object pairs and thus approximate different degrees of idiomaticity. We set these thresholds at log-likelihood scores of 1,000, 500,

	training		testing	
	types	token	types	token
all	30,6572	1,102,166	794	881
freq≥5	25,610	713,734	461	537
LL ≥ 1000	338	181,818	58	94
LL ≥ 500	693	240,369	95	139
LL ≥ 350	1,024	271,908	120	168
LL ≥ 250	1,473	304,148	142	191

Table 5: Number of SVCs in the training data and test set when applying different log-likelihood (LL) thresholds.

350 and 250. Note that the degree of idiomaticity decreases with the loglikelihood score, while the amount of noise in form of literal verb-object pairs being erroneosly taken for SVCs increases. Nevertheless, we performed no manual cleaning of these lists. According to the various thresholds, we obtained different sets of presumably idiomatic verb–object pairs to be marked for the SMT system, and all pairs occurring in the sets are considered SVCs.

Table 5 shows the number of all extracted verb-object pairs from the German part of the parallel data, and the number of pairs with a freqency ≥ 5. Note that we discarded verb-object pairs with a frequency < 5 as we consider these to be too sparse to be translated adequately by an SMT system. Table 5 also shows the sizes of the resulting sets of SVCs, both for the training data and the test data.

4.4 Verb Markup For each of the SVC sets given in Table 5, the training data is re-visited and all verbs occurring within SVCs receive a special markup. Generally speaking, we follow here the same procedure as for the extraction. If a verb-object pair occurs in the list of SVCs, the verb is marked by adding the string "_SVC" to the verb. It is important to note that, while the list of SVCs is lemmatized, we keep the inflected verb form in the training data. By introducing this markup, independent verbs with a literal sense are distinct from verbs occurring in SVCs. The SMT system can thus distinguish these two types of verbs and learn different translations for them. The example given in Table 6 illustrates a marked occurrence of *"geleistet"* (in the context of *"Beitrag leisten"* (= "make a contribution") as opposed to an independent occurrence, where *"geleistet"* should be translated literally into "achieved".
In addition to annotating the source-side part of the DE–EN training data, we also need to annotate the

SVC	Das hat einen wichtigen **Beitrag geleistet_SVC**.
	This has an important **contribution made**.
	This has **made** an important **contribution**.
other	Ich glaube , dass sie sehr viel Gutes **geleistet** hat .
	I believe, that it very much good **achieved** *has.*
	I believe that it has **achieved** a great deal of good .

Table 6: Illustration of SVC markup on verbs.

source-side part of the data to be translated, i.e. the data set for parameter tuning and the test set on which we evaluate our systems.

5 SMT Experiments

In order to assess the impact of our SVC verb markup, we trained one baseline SMT system without markup and 4 different systems with our markup (one for each idiomaticity threshold, cf. Table 5). Each of our SMT experiments consists of the following steps:

1. add SVC verb markup to the parallel training data (as described in Section 4)
2. train the SMT system, including word alignment, construction of a phrase-table and a reordering table
3. tune translation parameters using minimun error rate training
4. translate the test set and evaluate the output against one human reference translation

In the following we give details on the data sets we used and some further technical details on our SMT systems. Apart from differing SVC verb markup, all systems are trained identically.

5.1 SMT training data

We trained our systems on data from the annual shared task for statistical machine translation, all of which are accessible for free download.[4] For training, we take the training data from the shared task of 2009, which consists of roughly 1.5 million sentences composed of mainly Europarl (Koehn, 2005) and some news data. The English language model is trained on the monolingual training data of the 2009 shared task, which roughly consists of 22 million sentences. For parameter tuning, we used the test set of the shared task 2013 and for testing the most recent test set of 2014 (~3,000 sentences each).

[4] www.statmt.org

Experiments	BLEU tuning1	BLEU tuning2
Baseline	20.43	20.49
Exp1000	21.04	21.01
Exp500	21.08	21.01
Exp350	20.86	20.89
Exp250	20.85	20.84

Table 7: BLEU scores on the 2014 testset.

System	# sentences with at least one full verb
Reference	2,712
Baseline	2,378
Exp1000	2,412
Exp500	2,413
Exp350	2,412
Exp250	2,411

Table 8: Number of sentences produced by the systems, which contain at least one full verb.

5.2 System Details

We used the Moses toolkit (Koehn et al., 2007) to train standard phrase-based systems with default configurations. We trained an English 5-gram language model using KenLM (Heafield, 2011). For tuning the feature weights, we applied batch-mira with -safe-hope (Cherry and Foster, 2012). In order to ensure stable tuning, we performed two subsequent tuning procedures with identical starting conditions and report on results for both of them.

6 Evaluation

In order to evaluate the translation quality of our systems in comparison to each other and also to a baseline without any markup, we performed a standard MT evaluation using the BLEU metric. In addition, we also performed a semi-automatic evaluation with a focus on verb translations.

6.1 Automatic MT Evaluation

It is common practise to evaluate the performance of an SMT system by comparing its output to one (or more) human reference translations. We follow this line and calculate BLEU scores (Papineni et al., 2001) for each of our systems. Our testset is taken from the 2014 shared task on statistical machine translation ($\sim$ 3,000 words). We tested all BLEU scores for statistical significance using pairwise bootstrap resampling with sample size 1,000 and a p-value of 0.05[5]. Results are givenin Table 7. Compared to the baseline, we found that all of our systems containing verb markup for SVC verbs lead to a significant improvement in terms of BLEU.

The fact that all investigated sets of automatically identified SVCs improve the translation quality in the same magnitude shows that no manual filtering of the SVC sets is required to improve translation quality. Even though the sets certainly contain literal verb-object pairs, their markup does not seem to decrease translation quality. In future experiemnts, we will investigate the effect of manual filtering the SVC lists on translation quality.

6.2 Improved Verb Translations

In addition to the standard evaluation using BLEU scores, we investigated the effect of the SVC verb markup on verb translations in general. In the past, we often observed that verbs are missing in the SMT output. Due to their primary role in the understanding of a sentence, each missing verb translation has a severe effect on the perception of translation quality of humans. In Table 8, we give the number of sentences in which at least one full verb has occurred (note that auxiliary verbs were discarded in this evaluation). From these absolute numbers, it can be seen that each of our systems produces more verbs when compared to the baseline.

In a subsequent evaluation, we compared verb translations separately for each sentence, taking the reference translation the baseline translation and the output of one of our systems (Exp250) into account. The results of this evaluation are given in Table 9. It can be seen that, compared to the baseline, our system yields more verbs that match the reference translation on lemma level (3,648 vs. 3,505).

system	lemma matches the reference		
Baseline	X		X
Exp250		X	X
#verbs	3,505	3,648	2,436

Table 9: Overview of verb counts. 'X' indicates a verb matching the reference verb on lemma-level.

[5]Code to be obtained from `www.ark.cs.smu.edu/MT`

(a) baseline: no verb translation, Exp250: correct translation of the SVC verb.

input	Sie wollen herausfinden, welche **Rolle** der Riesenplanet bei der Entwicklung des Sonnensystems **gespielt** hat. *They wanted to find out, what* **role** *the giant-planet for the development of-the solar-system* **played** *has.*
reference	They want to find out what **role** the giant planet has **played** in the development of the solar system.
baseline	You want to find out what **role** the *Riesenplanet* in the development of the solar system.
Exp250	They want to find out what **role** the *Riesenplanet* **played** in the development of the solar system.

(b) baseline: default translation of the verb, Exp250: SVC translation of the verb.

input	"Ich **vertrete** die **Auffassung**, dass eine hinreichende Grundlage fr eine formelle Ermittlung besteht, sagte er. *I* ***take*** *the* ***view*** *that a sufficient basis for a formal investigation exists, said he.*
reference	"I **am** of the **opinion** that a sufficient basis exits" for a formal investigation, he said.
baseline	I **represent** the **view** that a sufficient basis for a formal investigation is, he said.
Exp250	I **take** the **view** that a sufficient basis for a formal investigation is, he said.

(c) baseline & Exp250: same verb translation, but Exp250 with better noun translation.

input	UBS gab diese Woche bekannt , dass sie **Schritte** gegen einige ihrer Mitarbeiter **unternommen** habe *UBS announced this week, that they* **action** *against some of their employees* **taken** *have*
reference	UBS said this week it had **taken action** against some of its employees.
baseline	UBS was announced this week that they **take steps** against some of their staff have done.
Exp250	UBS was announced this week that they **take action** against some of their staff, after.

Table 10: Comparison of translation outputs from the baseline and Exp250.

Recall that this verb evaluation happened with respect to the verbs occurring in the reference set. We already have seen from the improved BLEU scores that our systems are more similar to the reference translation than the Baseline system. While BLEU scores are calculated on exact matches, the verb evaluation in Table 9 has shown that we produce also more verbs matching the reference on lemma level (thus abstracting over morphological variants). But even this number can only be seen as an approximation of the translation quality. Ideally, a later evaluation would include the German source sentence in the evaluation and reflect whether or not the present verb is a correct translation of the German verb or not (independent of which lexeme the human reference translator chose).

Finally, in Table 10, we give some interesting examples of SVC translations in the context of the whole sentence in which they occurred. In Table 10(a), our system was able to produce the SVC verb that was missing in the baseline translation. In contrast, the baseline produced a verb in Table 10(b), but instead of the SVC verb, a default translation of the verb was produced. This example is particularly interesting as the correct translation of the SVC by our system has no positive effect on the BLEU score, as the human reference translator chose a different construction to translate the SVC. Finally in Table 10(c) we give an example where all systems produced the correct verb (though in a different tense form than the reference), but in addition, our system also yielded an improved translation of the SVC noun. The examples in Table 10 cannot considered to be more than random samples, not strong enough to draw further conclusions from them. However, they show that a more detailed manual evaluation of the translation quality may reveal even more significant improvements of our systems.

6.3 Translation Probabilities

In this section, we study the effects of the verb markup on the resulting translation probabilities. By marking whether a verb appears in an SVC context or not, we expect to see a difference in the respective translation options and probabilities. Table 11 shows entries for translations and the respective probabilities for the verb *treffen* which often occurs in SVCs such as *Entscheidung treffen* (*to make/take a decision*), *Wahl treffen* (*to make a choice*) or *Vorkehrungen treffen* (*to take precautions*).

In the baseline, the predominant translation options are related to *meet*, with a second literal meaning represented by *hit*. Options for translating SVCs (e.g. *make/take*) are listed as well, but their trans-

Baseline		Exp1000			
treffen		*treffen*		*treffen_SVC*	
prob	transl.	prob	transl.	prob	transl.
0.295	meeting	0.315	meeting	0.237	take
0.105	meetings	0.112	meetings	0.176	make
0.086	take	0.074	take	0.032	will
0.059	make	0.048	make	0.022	decide
0.036	meet	0.039	meet	0.019	taken
0.013	be	0.012	be	0.012	reach
0.011	hit	0.012	hit	0.009	will take
0.010	affect	0.011	adopt	0.009	will make
0.010	adopt	0.011	affect	0.009	to take
0.007	taken	0.007	taken	0.009	to make

Table 11: Top-ranked translation possibilities (with probabilities) for the verb *treffen* in the baseline, and its unmarked and marked variants in Exp1000. Valid translations are highlighted.

lation probabilities are considerably smaller. The top-ranked translation possibilities for *treffen* in the Exp1000 system do not differ much from those in the baseline, but the probabilities for the literal translations (highlighted) are higher than those in the baseline, whereas the probabilities for translations in an SVC context are slightly lower compared to the baseline. We assume that the entries *make/take* for the literal translations of *treffen* were derived from usages in SVCs not listed in the set of SVCs on which the annotation for this system was based – keep in mind that 1000 was the highest of the thresholds used and thus resulted in a list of SVCs with a high level of idiomaticity.

When looking at the translation options for *treffen* in an SVC context, we find that there is a considerable change in comparison to the baseline and non-markup entries: translation options for the literal meaning (*meet/hit*) are no longer top-ranked, but instead there are verbs with a light meaning allowing for the respective English SVCs to be realized. While there are a number of variations of the same lemma (*take, taken, will take, to take*), there is also some lexical variation (*take/make/reach [a decision]*) and also one full verb (*decide*) equivalent to one of the SVCs in question.

The comparison of the translation options for the different uses of *treffen* in table 11 illustrates how the verb markup applied to verbs within an SVC separates between the literal translation(s) and those appropriate for an SVC context.

On a sidenote, the selectional preferences of the different usages of *treffen* also reflect its respective meaning: when used with the default meaning of *to meet*[6], the typical object is likely to be a person whereas in the usage as part of an SVC, the object is an abstract concept like *decision* or *choice*.

7 Conclusion and Future Work

We presented an approach to handle SVCs in an German–English SMT system. By marking verbs that occur within an SVC on the source-side, literal translation options are separated from those appropriate in an SVC context. We investigated different degrees of idiomaticity which all lead to significant improvements in BLEU. An additional evaluation of verbs confirmed that the systems with SVC-markup produced more verbs than the baseline and that also an increased amount of verbs matched with the reference translation.

We assume that our strategy of marking the (limited) set of light verbs is not running risk of introducing data sparsity, but the question of how to decide on an optimal set of SVCs remains to be studied more thoroughly in future work. Moreover, we may want to further distinguish the verb markup: while the current markup separates literal translations from SVC-appropriate translations, we could in the future explicitly distinguish translations of *different* SVCs that share the same verb in the source language, but might need different translations as for example in *Massnahme ergreifen* (lit: "to grasp measures", "to take measures") and *Flucht ergreifen* (lit: "to grasp escape", "to esacpe").

An extension to different language pairs would also be interesting – the presented approach can easily be extended to other languages as long as enough data is available as a basis to extract a set of SVCs.

Acknowledgements

This project has received funding from the European Unions Horizon 2020 research and innovation programme under grant agreement No 644402. Moreover, it was funded by the DFG grants *Distributional Approaches to Semantic Relatedness* and *Models of Morphosyntax for Statistical Machine Translation*, and the DFG Heisenberg Fellowship SCHU-2580/1.

[6]The same applies to the second literal meaning *to hit*.

References

Otavio Acosta, Aline Villavicencio, and Viviane Moreira. 2011. Identification and treatment of multiword expressions applied to information retrieval. In *Proceedings of the Workshop on Multiword Expressions: From Parsing and Generation to the Real World*, pages 101–109, Portland, Oregon, USA.

Timothy Baldwin and Aline Villavicencio. 2002. Extracting the unextractable: A case study on verb particles. In *Proceedings of the Sixth Conference on Computational Natural Language Learning*, pages 98–104, Taipei, Taiwan.

Collin Bannard. 2005. Learning about the meaning of verb–particle constructions from corpora. *Computer Speech and Language*, 19:467–478.

Colin Bannard. 2007. A Measure of Syntactic Flexibility for Automatically Identifying Multiword Expressions in Corpora. In *Proceedings of the ACL Workshop on A Broader Perspective on Multiword Expressions*, pages 1–8, Prague, Czech Republic.

Bernd Bohnet. 2010. Top accuracy and fast dependency parsing is not a contradiction. In *Proceedings of the 23rd International Conference on Computational Linguistics*, pages 89–97, Beijing, China.

Miriam Butt. 2003. The Light Verb Jungle. Working Papers in Linguistics 9, Harvard University.

Marine Carpuat and Mona Diab. 2010. Task-based evaluation of multiword expressions: A pilot study in statistical machine translation. In *Proceedings of the Annual Conference of the North American Chapter of the Association for Computational Linguistics*, pages 242–245.

Colin Cherry and George Foster. 2012. Batch Tuning Strategies for Statistical Machine Translation. In *Proceedings of the Human Language Technology Conference of the North American Chapter of the Association for Computational Linguistics*, volume 12, pages 34–35.

Kostadin Cholakov and Valia Kordoni. 2014. Better statistical machine translation through linguistic treatment of phrasal verbs. In *Proceedings of the 2014 Conference on Empirical Methods in Natural Language Processing*.

Matthieu Constant and Anthony Sigogne. 2011. MWU-aware part-of-speech tagging with a CRF model and lexical resources. In *Proceedings of the Workshop on Multiword Expressions: From Parsing and Generation to the Real World*, pages 49–56, Portland, Oregon, USA.

Paul Cook and Suzanne Stevenson. 2006. Classifying particle semantics in English verb-particle constructions. In *Proceedings of the ACL/COLING Workshop on Multiword Expressions: Identifying and Exploiting Underlying Properties*, pages 45–53, Sydney, Australia.

Stefan Evert. 2005. *The statistics of word cooccurrences: Word pairs and collocations*. Ph.D. thesis, University of Stuttgart, Germany.

Stefan Evert. 2009. Corpora and Collocations. In Anke Lüdeling and Merja Kytö, editors, *Corpus Linguistics. An International Handbook.*, volume 2 of *Handbooks of Linguistics and Communication Science*, chapter 58, pages 1212–1248. Mouton de Gruyter, Berlin.

Afsaneh Fazly and Suzanne Stevenson. 2008. A distributional account of the semantics of multiword expressions. *Italian Journal of Linguistics. Alessandro Lenci (guest editor): "From Context to Meaning: Distributional Models of the Lexicon in Linguistics and Cognitive Science"*, 20(1).

Afsaneh Fazly, Suzanne Stevenson, and Ryan North. 2007. Automatically learning semantic knowledge about multiword predicates. *Language Resources and Evaluation*, 41:61–89.

Afsaneh Fazly, Paul Cook, and Suzanne Stevenson. 2009. Unsupervised type and token identification of idiomatic expressions. *Computational Linguistics*, 35(1):61–103.

Kenneth Heafield. 2011. KenLM: Faster and smaller language model queries. In *Proceedings of the EMNLP Workshop on Statistical Machine Translation*, pages 187–197.

Graham Katz and Eugenie Giesbrecht. 2006. Automatic identification of non-compositional multi-word expressions using Latent Semantic Analysis. In *Proceedings of the ACL/COLING Workshop on Multiword Expressions: Identifying and Exploiting Underlying Properties*, pages 12–19, Sydney, Australia.

Philipp Koehn, Hieu Hoang, Alexandra Birch, Chris Callison-Burch, Marcello Federico, Nicola Bertoldi, Brooke Cowan, Wade Shen, Christine Moran, Richard Zens, Chris Dyer, Ondrej Bojar, Alexandra Constantin, and Evan Herbst. 2007. Moses: Open source toolkit for Statistical Machine Translation. In *Proceedings of the 45th Annual Meeting of the Association for Computational Linguistics, Demonstration Session*, pages 177–180.

Philipp Koehn. 2005. Europarl: A parallel corpus for Statistical Machine Translation. In *Proceedings of the 10th Machine Translation Summit*, pages 79–86.

Patrik Lambert and Rafael Banchs. 2005. Data-inferred multi-word expressions for statistical machine translation. In *Proceedings of Machine Translation Summit X*, pages 396–403.

Stefan Langer. 2009. Funktionsverbgefüge und automatische Sprachverarbeitung. Habilitationsschrift, Universität München.

Dekang Lin. 1999. Automatic identification of non-compositional phrases. In *Proceedings of the 37th Annual Meeting of the Association for Computational Linguistics*, pages 317–324, Maryland, MD.

Diana McCarthy, Bill Keller, and John Carroll. 2003. Detecting a continuum of compositionality in phrasal verbs. In *Proceedings of the ACL Workshop on Multiword Expressions: Analysis, Acquisition and Treatment*, pages 73–80, Sapporo, Japan.

Manju Nirmal. 2015. Studying the effect of annotating idiomaticity of support verb constructions in statistical machine translation. Master's thesis, University of Stuttgart.

Kishore A. Papineni, Salim Roukos, Todd Ward, and Wei-Jing Zhu. 2001. BLEU: A method for automatic evaluation of Machine Translation. Technical Report RC22176 (W0109-022), IBM Research Division, Thomas J. Watson Research Center.

Carlos Ramisch, Aline Villavicencio, Leonardo Moura, and Marco Idiart. 2008. Picking them up and figuring them out: Verb-particle constructions, noise and idiomaticity. In *Proceedings of the 12th Conference on Computational Natural Language Learning*, pages 49–56. Association for Computational Linguistics.

Siva Reddy, Diana McCarthy, and Suresh Manandhar. 2011. An empirical study on compositionality in compound nouns. In *Proceedings of the 5th International Joint Conference on Natural Language Processing*, pages 210–218, Chiang Mai, Thailand.

Zhixiang Ren, Yajuan Lü, Jie Cao, Qun Liu, and Yun Huang. 2009. Improving statistical machine translation using domain bilingual multiword expressions. In *Proceedings of the Workshop on Multiword Expressions: Identification, Interpretation, Disambiguation and Applications*, pages 47–54.

Ivan A Sag, Timothy Baldwin, Francis Bond, Ann Copestake, and Dan Flickinger. 2002. Multiword expressions: A pain in the neck for NLP. In *Computational Linguistics and Intelligent Text Processing*, pages 1–15. Springer.

Silke Scheible, Sabine Schulte im Walde, Marion Weller, and Max Kisselew. 2013. A compact but linguistically detailed database for German verb subcategorisation relying on dependency parses from a web corpus. In *Proceedings of the 8th Web as Corpus Workshop*, Lancaster, UK.

Sabine Schulte im Walde, Stefan Müller, and Stephen Roller. 2013. Exploring Vector Space Models to Predict the Compositionality of German Noun-Noun Compounds. In *Proceedings of the 2nd Joint Conference on Lexical and Computational Semantics*, pages 255–265, Atlanta, GA.

Aline Villavicencio, Francis Bond, Anna Korhonen, and Diana McCarthy. 2005. Introduction to the special issue on multiword expressions: Having a crack at a hard nut. *Computer Speech & Language*, 19(4):365–377.

Aline Villavicencio. 2003. Verb-particle constructions and lexical resources. In *Proceedings of the ACL Workshop on Multiword Expressions: Analysis, Acquisition and Treatment*, pages 57–64, Sapporo, Japan.

Eric Wehrli. 2014. The relevance of collocations for parsing. In *Proceedings of the 10th Workshop on Multiword Expressions*, pages 26–32, Gothenburg, Sweden.

Marion Weller, Fabienne Cap, Stefan Müller, Sabine Schulte im Walde, and Alexander Fraser. 2014. Distinguishing degrees of compositionality in compound splitting for Statistical Machine Translation. In *Proceedings of the 1st Workshop on Computational Approaches to Compound Analysis*, pages 81–90, Dublin, Ireland.

Heike Zinsmeister and Ulrich Heid. 2004. Collocations of complex nouns: Evidence for lexicalisation. In *Proceedings of Konvens*, Vienna, Austria.

A Multiword Expression Data Set: Annotating Non-Compositionality and Conventionalization for English Noun Compounds

Meghdad Farahmand
University of Geneva
Geneva, Switzerland

Aaron Smith
Uppsala University
Uppsala, Sweden

Joakim Nivre
Uppsala University
Uppsala, Sweden

firstname.lastname@unige.ch firstname.lastname@lingfil.uu.se

Abstract

Scarcity of multiword expression data sets raises a fundamental challenge to evaluating the systems that deal with these linguistic structures. In this work we attempt to address this problem for a subclass of multiword expressions by producing a large data set annotated by experts and validated by common statistical measures. We present a set of 1048 noun-noun compounds annotated as non-compositional, compositional, conventionalized and not conventionalized. We build this data set following common trends in previous work while trying to address some of the well known issues such as small number of annotated instances, quality of the annotations, and lack of availability of true negative instances.

1 Introduction

The lack of practical data sets that can be used in the training and evaluation of multiword expression (MWE) related systems is a notorious problem (McCarthy et al., 2003; Hermann et al., 2012). It is partly due to the heterogeneous nature of MWEs, partly due to their frequency, and partly due to the unclear boundaries between MWEs and regular phrases. These issues have made the compilation of useful MWE data sets challenging, and any effort to create them invaluable.

In this work we present a data set of two-word English noun-noun compounds which are annotated for two properties: non-compositionality and conventionalization. Although non-compositionality can apply at different levels, from syntactic to semantic, by non-compositionality we strictly mean semantic non-compositionality. Semantic non-compositionality in simple terms is the property of a compound whose meaning can not be readily interpreted from the meanings of its components.

Conventionalization meanwhile refers to the situation where a sequence of words that refer to a particular concept is commonly accepted in such a way that its constituents cannot be substituted for their near-synonyms, according to some cultural or historical convention. Conventionalization can also be referred to as institutionalization or statistical idiosyncrasy (Sag et al., 2002), and is closely related to the concept of collocation (Baldwin and Kim, 2010). Conventionalization is a very broad concept and can apply to a wide range of compounds. Although a large fraction of compounds are to some extent conventionalized, we are interested in and annotate only clear and well-known conventionalizations, which we refer to as "marked conventionalization". For instance, although *exit door* and *floor space* have some elements of conventionalization, this property is more conspicuous in *weather forecast*, *car wash*, and *traffic light*. We assume that non-compositional compounds are by definition conventionalized and annotate this property only when a compound is compositional.

Our data set comprises 1048 compounds which are annotated with binary decisions about whether they are (i) non-compositional and (ii) conventionalized. Although non-compositionality can be a grey area and a non-binary decision may be more precise, eventually this decision must be reduced to a binary

Proceedings of NAACL-HLT 2015, pages 29–33,
Denver, Colorado, May 31 – June 5, 2015.

one: whether or not a compound should be lexicalized due to its non-compositionality.

The main contributions of this work can be described as follows: coverage for two major properties of MWEs (non-compositionality and conventionalization); providing both positive and negative instances of non-compositional and conventionalized classes, allowing the evaluation of MWE identification/extraction systems in terms of both true positive and true negative rates; incorporating a larger number of annotated instances compared to related data sets.

2 Related work

The most important related work is that of Reddy et al. (2011), which provides 90 compounds with a mean compositionality score between 0 and 5. They acquired their annotations using Amazon Mechanical Turk from 30 turkers. They detect and discard poor annotations using Spearman Coefficient Correlation. The number of instances in their final data set, however, might not be enough for evaluation purposes. Moreover, it might not be a trivial task to adapt an identification/extraction system to produce a similar non-compositionality ranking. Korkontzelos and Manandhar (2009) present a data set that comprises 19 non-compositional and 19 compositional instances. In this work the size of the data set is small and compound selection process and the rationale behind decisions about non-compositionality is not expounded. Other related but slightly different works are Biemann and Giesbrecht (2011) who present a set of adjective-noun, verb-subject, and verb-object pairs and their non- compositionality judgments, and McCarthy et al. (2003) who present a set of 116 phrasal verbs and rank their non-compositionality between 0 and 9.

Data sets that incorporate conventionalization are rather difficult to come by. The closest are collocation sets which are also scarce in their own right. Most collocation sets that we could find were either commercial or not publicly available. Moreover, since collocation can refer to a wide range of MWEs and human agreement on statistical idiosyncrasy is not high enough, it is hard to find an annotated collocation set. Instead, extraction systems have been used to automatically produce such sets and the outcomes have been commonly evaluated by either manual evaluation (Smadja, 1993), or by ranking the collocation candidates and calculating precision and recall of the extraction system for the set of n highest ranking candidates (Evert, 2005).

Schneider et al. (2014) is another related work in which generic MWEs are annotated in a 55K-word English web corpus. Their work covers a broad range of "multiword phenomena" with emphasis on heterogeneity, gappy grouping and expression strength which represents the level of idiomaticity of a MWE. They build a corpus of MWEs without restricting themselves to any syntactic categories and they argue that this can to some extent address the problem of heterogeneity of MWEs.

3 Data Preparation

We downloaded English Wikipedia, removed the tags and segmented it into sentences. We then filtered very short and very long sentences, sentences which were not in English, and sentences which contained only numbers and non-alphanumeric characters. This resulted in a clean corpus with 24 million sentences (512 million words). We tagged this corpus using Stanford POS tagger and extracted a list of distinct contiguous noun-noun pairs ($\approx$ 2.6 million) and their frequencies. We filtered out low frequency pairs by removing the pairs whose frequency of occurrence in the corpus was below 10. This led to a set of 169, 000 pairs (`filtered_list` hereafter). We divided this set into 5 frequency classes and randomly extracted 250 pairs from each of those frequency classes (`selected_list` hereafter) in line with McCarthy et al. (2003). Frequency classes were chosen in a way that each class holds approximately the same number of pairs.

Compositional compounds tend to be much more frequent than non-compositional ones: this might lead the data set to be inundated with compositional compounds. To mitigate this problem we asked two experts with backgrounds in corpus linguistics to each provide us with 50[1] examples that they thought were partly or fully non-compositional. These examples were mainly extracted from two non-overlapping random divisions

[1]The choice of this number was made taking into account our time and financial constraints.

of filtered_list, whilst also ensuring that there was no overlap with selected_list. Furthermore, the experts were provided with, and allowed to extract the examples from a set of frequent adjective-noun pairs which incorporate a relatively large number of non-compositional compounds such as *hard disk* and *big shot*. These 100 examples were then added to selected_list. The linguists who performed this selection did not participate in the annotation task.

Finally, we manually removed pairs with foreign or inappropriate/offensive words, those with incorrect POS tags, and the few pairs used to help describing the task to the annotators (see Section 4), from selected_list. We also removed those pairs for which a unified form was more common in the corpus (e.g. ice berg, paper work and life style for which iceberg, paperwork and lifestyle were more frequently occurring).

4 Annotations

We assigned the annotation task to three native and two non-native but fluent speakers of English. We chose to hire experts to perform the annotation task rather than using crowd-sourcing systems such as Amazon Mechanical Turk, where the results can be flawed for various reasons including scammers and low quality of the annotations (Biemann and Giesbrecht, 2011; Reddy et al., 2011). All of our annotators had advanced knowledge of English grammar and the majority had a background in linguistics. We provided the annotators with a detailed set of instructions about non-compositionality and conventionalization. The instructions were extensively exemplified by examples from Reddy et al. (2011), Hermann et al. (2012) and Baldwin and Kim (2010).

For each compound, we asked the annotators to make binary decisions about non-compositionality and marked conventionalization. We explained non-compositionality as being the property of compounds whose meanings cannot be readily interpreted from the meaning of their constituents. The annotators were asked to use the label 0 when they thought a compound was more compositional than non-compositional, and 1 when they thought the compound was more non-compositional than compositional.

Conventionalization, meanwhile, was defined as the main property of compounds that are collocational and whose constituents co-occur more than expected by chance. We introduced the annotators to the non-substitutability test which can help to decide if a compound is conventionalized: if neither of the constituents of the word pair can be substituted for their near synonyms (Manning and Schütze, 1999) we have a conventionalization. Taking *weather forecast* as an example, although *weather prediction* and *climate forecast* are syntactically correct and semantically plausible alternatives, they are not considered proper English compounds. The non-substitutability test often fails in compounds with less noticeable conventionalization; for instance we can still say *exit gate* instead of *exit door* or *floor area* instead of *floor space*. Identifying conventionalization is not a trivial task and human agreement on this property can be relatively low (Krenn et al., 2001). Therefore, we emphasized that we were only interested in marked conventionalization and that this property should be annotated only when the annotator was certain about its presence.

We asked the annotators to make decisions about marked conventionalization only when they annotated a compound as compositional: we assumed that non-compositional compounds are by definition conventionalized. In practice however, in order to avoid overestimated scores and loose overall judgements, we do not regard conventionalization based on non-compositionality and conventionalization annotated on a compositional compound as equal. Instead we define a third label X and assign it to the marked conventionalization field whenever a compound is annotated as non-compositional. This means the marked conventionalization field in fact has three possible labels (0, 1, and X). Throughout the paper, the scores and data set statistics for marked conventionalization are calculated based on these three labels. Nevertheless, the user of the data set retains the option of merging X and 1 and benefiting from a larger set of markedly conventionalized instances for particular tasks.

5 Validation of the Annotations

To ensure that the annotations are sound and in order to eradicate possible problems caused by human error, we calculated Spearman Correlation Coefficient (ρ) between all the annotations and took the average Spearman ρ for each annotator. This was done separately for non-compositionality and marked conventionalization. The results are shown in Table 1.

	average ρ (non-comp.)	average ρ (marked conv.)
annotator1	0.58	0.60
annotator2	0.34	0.46
annotator3	0.52	0.57
annotator4	0.54	0.63
annotator5	0.59	0.64

Table 1: The average Spearman ρ for non-compositionality and conventionalization.

We used Spearman ρ as a means to filter the less reliable annotations (Reddy et al., 2011) by discarding the annotations that had an average Spearman ρ of below 0.50. This left us with four sets of annotations for each property.

6 Inter-Annotator Agreement

We calculated inter-annotator agreement in terms of Fleiss' kappa between the four remaining annotations. A summary of Fleiss' kappa scores and their interpretation according to Landis and Koch (1977) is presented in Table 2.

	non-comp.	marked conv.
Fleiss's kappa	0.62	0.55
kappa error	0.012	0.009
interpretation	substantial agreement	moderate agreement

Table 2: Inter-annotator agreement in terms of Fleiss' kappa for non-compositionality and conventionalization.

The observered moderate agreement on conventionalization is consistent with the findings of Krenn et al. (2001), and in accordance with our claim that conventionalization can be more difficult than non-compositionality for humans to distinguish.

7 Results

Our final data set contains a list of 1048 compounds and, for each compound, four judgements about non-compositionality and four judgments about marked conventionalization. Essentially, our data set consists of three classes of compounds: (i) non-compositional (ii) compositional but markedly conventionalized (iii) compositional and non-conventionalized. These three classes can be described as follows in the context of training and evaluation tasks: (i) positive instances of non-compositional compounds (ii) negative instances of non-compositional but positive instances of conventionalized compounds, and (iii) negative instances of both previous types. We make the data set available as a set of compounds and (2×4) judgments for each (`raw_dataset` hereafter). `raw_dataset` can be used in various formats. For instance we generated a set of compounds that were judged to be non-compositional and conventionalized based on the decision of the majority (3 or more out of 4) and extracted several examples of different classes which are presented in Table 3.

non-compositional	**compositional but conventionalized**	**compositional and not conventionalized**
battle cry	bulletin board	area director
flag stop	cable car	art collection
gun dog	car chase	ankle injury
jet lag	food court	animal life
lead time	wish list	bus service
face value	speed limit	computer usage
mind map	background check	wrestling fan

Table 3: Examples of different classes of compounds that were classified based on the decision of the majority.

One can also generate a set of judgements based on the unanimous decision of the annotators. In each of these two formats, however, some good examples of MWEs are missed due to the fact that half of the annotators marked them as conventionalized due to non-compositionality (label X) while the other half marked them as conventionalized compositional nouns (label 1). One can therefore generate another format that covers such compounds. In such cases it is up to the user of the data set to decide whether they want to regard such instances as non-compositional, as solely conventionalized, or simply as an instance of an MWE. Table 4 presents the key statistics relating to the data set.

Non-Compositionality	
Annotated as non-comp. by the majority	140 (out of which 82 are unanimous)
Annotated as comp. by the majority	840 (out of which 763 are unanimous)
Annotated as comp. by half and non-comp. by the other half	62
Marked Conventionalization	
Annotated as comp. but conv. by the majority	155 (55 of which are unanimous)
Annotated as comp. and non conv. by the majority	570 (467 of which are unanimous)
Annotated as conv. by half and non-conv. by the other half	76
Other[2]	241

Table 4: Data set statistics.

8 Conclusion

We presented a data set of English noun-noun compounds which are judged for two major properties of MWEs: non-compositionality and conventionalization (statistical idiosyncrasy). The data set consists of both positive and negative instances of non-compositional and conventionalized MWEs and can effectively be used in evaluation and training of MWE identification and extraction systems. We recruited expert annotators and validated the reliability of their judgments using common statistical measures. We calculated inter-annotator agreement in terms of Fleiss' kappa, showing moderate and substantial agreements between the annotators for the two properties. The strengths of this data set are its granularity, incorporating both positive and negative instances of MWEs, and the credibility of the judgements as a result of recruiting expert annotators and using statistical validations.

[2] As mentioned before, non conv. in practice has three labels (0, 1, X). "Other" means either the compound was annotated as conv. (1) by half and non-comp. (X) by the other half, or the majority annotated these instances as non-compositional (X), however a minority annotated them as something else (0, 1), or the annotation for these instances includes all labels (0, 1, X) so that none of the labels are the majority.

References

Timothy Baldwin and Su Nam Kim. 2010. Multiword expressions. *Handbook of Natural Language Processing, second edition. Morgan and Claypool.*

Chris Biemann and Eugenie Giesbrecht. 2011. Distributional semantics and compositionality 2011: Shared task description and results. In *Proceedings of the Workshop on Distributional Semantics and Compositionality*, DiSCo '11, pages 21–28, Stroudsburg, PA, USA. Association for Computational Linguistics.

Stefan Evert. 2005. *The statistics of word cooccurrences*. Ph.D. thesis, Dissertation, Stuttgart University.

Karl Moritz Hermann, Phil Blunsom, and Stephen Pulman. 2012. An unsupervised ranking model for noun-noun compositionality. In *Proceedings of the First Joint Conference on Lexical and Computational Semantics*, pages 132–141. Association for Computational Linguistics.

Ioannis Korkontzelos and Suresh Manandhar. 2009. Detecting compositionality in multi-word expressions. In *Proceedings of the ACL-IJCNLP 2009 Conference Short Papers*, pages 65–68. Association for Computational Linguistics.

Brigitte Krenn, Stefan Evert, et al. 2001. Can we do better than frequency? a case study on extracting pp-verb collocations. In *Proceedings of the ACL Workshop on Collocations*, pages 39–46.

J Richard Landis and Gary G Koch. 1977. The measurement of observer agreement for categorical data. *biometrics*, pages 159–174.

Christopher D Manning and Hinrich Schütze. 1999. *Foundations of statistical natural language processing*. MIT press.

Diana McCarthy, Bill Keller, and John Carroll. 2003. Detecting a continuum of compositionality in phrasal verbs. In *Proceedings of the ACL-SIGLEX Workshop on Multiword Expressions: Analysis, Acqusation and Treatment*, pages 73–80.

Siva Reddy, Diana McCarthy, and Suresh Manandhar. 2011. An empirical study on compositionality in compound nouns. In *IJCNLP*, pages 210–218.

Ivan A Sag, Timothy Baldwin, Francis Bond, Ann Copestake, and Dan Flickinger. 2002. Multiword expressions: A pain in the neck for nlp. In *Computational Linguistics and Intelligent Text Processing*, pages 1–15. Springer.

Nathan Schneider, Spencer Onuffer, Nora Kazour, Emily Danchik, Michael T Mordowanec, Henrietta Conrad, and Noah A Smith. 2014. Comprehensive annotation of multiword expressions in a social web corpus. *Proc. of LREC. Reykjavík, Iceland.*

Frank Smadja. 1993. Retrieving collocations from text: Xtract. *Computational Linguistics*, 19:143–177.

Modeling the Statistical Idiosyncrasy of Multiword Expressions

Meghdad Farahmand
University of Geneva
Geneva, Switzerland
meghdad.farahmand@unige.ch

Joakim Nivre
Uppsala University
Uppsala, Sweden
joakim.nivre@lingfil.uu.se

Abstract

The focus of this work is statistical idiosyncrasy (or collocational weight) as a discriminant property of multiword expressions. We formalize and model this property, compile a 2-class data set of MWE and non-MWE examples, and evaluate our models on this data set. We present a possible empirical implementation of collocational weight and study its effects on identification and extraction of MWEs. Our models prove to be more effective than baselines in identifying noun-noun MWEs.

1 Introduction

Multiword Expressions (MWEs) are sequences of words that show some level of idiosyncrasy. For instance they can be semantically idiosyncratic (i.e., their meaning cannot be readily inferred from the meaning of their components, e.g., *flea market*), syntactically idiosyncratic (their syntax cannot be extracted from the syntax of their components, e.g., *at large*), statistically idiosyncratic (their components tend to co-occur more often than expected by chance, e.g., *drug dealer*), or have other forms of idiosyncrasy. MWEs comprise several types and sub-types. Although it is not always clear where to draw the line between various types of MWEs, the two broadest categories are lexicalized MWEs and institutionalized MWEs (Sag et al., 2002). The main property of lexicalized MWEs is syntactic or semantic idiosyncrasy and the main property of institutionalized MWEs is statistical idiosyncrasy. Semantic idiosyncrasy is closely related to the concept of non-compositionality. It is important to note that a MWE is often idiosyncratic in more than one way (Baldwin and Kim, 2010). This means lexicalized MWEs can be statistically idiosyncratic, and institutionalized MWEs can be semantically idiosyncratic. Institutionalized MWEs are closely related to collocations.[1] They can be compositional (*seat belt*) or non-compositional (*hard drive*), but statistically they co-occur more often than expected by chance.

Efficient extraction and identification of MWEs can positively influence some important Natural Language Processing (NLP) tasks such as parsing (Nivre and Nilsson, 2004) and Statistical Machine Translation (Ren et al., 2009). Identification and extraction of MWEs are therefore important research questions in the area of NLP.

In this work we refer to statistical idiosyncrasy as collocational weight and present a method of modeling this property for noun-noun compounds. Comparative evaluation reveals better performance of proposed models compared to that of the baselines.

In previous work, it has often been suggested that collocations can be identified by their non-substitutability. This means we cannot replace a collocation's components with their near synonyms (Manning and Schütze, 1999). For instance we cannot say *brief film* instead of *short film*. Pearce (2001) defines collocations as pairs of words where "one of the words significantly prefers a particular lexical re-

[1] Although the major property of collocations is known to be statistical idiosyncrasy, in many works, semantically idiosyncratic multiword expressions have also been regarded as collocation.

Proceedings of NAACL-HLT 2015, pages 34–38,
Denver, Colorado, May 31 – June 5, 2015.

alization of the concept the other represents." To the best of our knowledge, however, non-substitutability (with near synonyms) or in other words collocational weight has never been explicitly and empirically tested. In this work, we present two models that partially, and fully, model collocational weight, and investigate its effects on extraction of MWEs.

2 Related work

Extraction of MWEs has been widely researched from different perspectives. Various models from rule-based to statistical have been employed to address this problem.

Examples of rule-based models are Seretan (2011) and Jacquemin et al. (1997) who base their extraction on linguistic rules and formalism in order to identify and filter MWE candidates, and Baldwin (2005) who aims at extracting verb particle constructions based on their linguistic properties using a chunker and dependency grammar.

Examples of statistical models are Pecina (2010), Evert (2005), Lapata and Lascarides (2003), and the early work **Xtract** (Smadja, 1993). Farahmand and Martins (2014) present a method of extracting MWEs based on their statistical contextual properties and Hermann et al. (2012) employ distributional semantics to model non-compositionality and use it as a way of identifying lexicalized compounds.

There are also hybrid models in the sense that they benefit from both statistical and linguistic information (Seretan and Wehrli, 2006; Dias, 2003). Ramisch (2012) implements a flexible platform that accepts both statistical and deep linguistic criteria in order to extract and filter MWEs.

There are also bilingual models which are mostly based on the assumption that a translation of a source language MWE exists in a target language (Smith, 2014; Caseli et al., 2010; Ren et al., 2009).

A similar work to ours is Pearce (2001) who uses WordNet in order to produce anti-collocations from synonyms of the components of a MWE candidate, and decides about "MWEhood" based on these anti-collocations. Another similar work is Ramisch et al. (2008) who use WordNet Synsets as one of their resources in order to calculate the entropy between the components of verb particle constructions.

3 Method

Following previous work by Manning and Schütze (1999), and Pearce (2001), we define collocational weight -a discriminant property of mainly institutionalized but also lexical MWEs, for noun-noun pairs according to the following hypotheses:

Simplified Hypothesis *For a given two-word compound, the head word is more likely to co-occur with the modifier than with synonyms of the modifier.*

Main Hypothesis *For a given two-word compound, the head word is more likely to co-occur with the modifier than with synonyms of the modifier, and the modifier is more likely to co-occur with the head than with synonyms of the head.*

We formalize these hypotheses in the form of M_1 and M_2 models which implement the simplified and main hypotheses and are described by equations (1) and (2), respectively.

$$M_1 : P(w_2|w_1) > \alpha P(w_2|Syns(w_1)) \quad (1)$$

where:

$$P(w_2|w_1) = \frac{\#(w_1 w_2)}{\#(w_1)}$$

and

$$P(w_2|Syns(w_1)) = \frac{\sum_{w_1' \in Syns(w_1)} \#(w_1' w_2)}{\sum_{w_1' \in Syns(w1)} \#(w_1' + \mathcal{L})}$$

$w_1 w_2$ represents a compound. $Syns(w)$ represents a set of synonyms of w, and in order to obtain such a set we use WordNet's $synset()$ function. $\mathcal{L}$ is the smoothing factor, which is set to 0.1, and α is a parameter that we altered between $[1 - 30]$. $\mathcal{L}$ and α are also present in M_2 and are assigned the same values as in M_1.

$$M_2 : P(w_2|w_1) > \alpha P(w_2|Syns(w_1)) \quad (2)$$

$$\&\& \; P(w_1|w_2) > \alpha P(w_1|Syns(w_2))$$

where:

$$P(w_2|w_1) = \frac{\#(w_1 w_2)}{\#(w_1)}$$

$$P(w_1|w_2) = \frac{\#(w_1 w_2)}{\#(w_2)}$$

and

$$P(w_2|Syns(w_1)) = \frac{\sum_{w'_1 \in Syns(w_1)} \#(w'_1 w_2)}{\sum_{w'_1 \in Syns(w1)} \#(w'_1) + \mathcal{L}}$$

$$P(w_1|Syns(w_2)) = \frac{\sum_{w'_2 \in Syns(w_2)} \#(w_1 w'_2)}{\sum_{w'_2 \in Syns(w2)} \#(w'_2) + \mathcal{L}}$$

4 Experiments

In order to test our hypotheses, we implement the two models described above and two baselines, and run a comparative evaluation. We divide our data into two subsets: development and test sets. The evaluation is carried out in two phases. In the first phase we perform model selection and find the optimal parameters for various models on the development set. In the second phase we evaluate the selected models with optimal parameters on the test set, which remains unseen by the models up to this phase.

4.1 Data

Although there exist a few data sets for English compounds (Baldwin and Kim, 2010; Reddy et al., 2011), to the best of our knowledge there is no data set with annotations for both MWE and non-MWE classes. We required this for the evaluation of our models therefore we compiled our own data set. We randomly extracted a set of 3000 noun-noun pairs that had the frequency of greater than 10 from across POS-tagged English Wikipedia. We kept only the pairs whose both head and modifier had more than one synonym according to WordNet. In cases were a given compound had different POS tags, we selected the most frequent tags. We asked two computational linguists with background in MWE research to annotate the pairs as MWE and non-MWE. Pairs which were either semantically or statistically idiosyncratic, or both were annotated as MWE. Pairs which were neither semantically nor syntactically nor statistically idiosyncratic were annotated as non-MWE. To asses the inter annotator agreement we calculated Cohen's kappa (κ) and to measure the pairwise correlation among the annotators we calculated Spearman's rank correlation coefficient (ρ). The Spearman ρ was equal to 0.66. The Cohen's kappa was equal to 0.64 (with the error of 0.02) which can be interpreted as "substantial agreement" according to Landis and Koch (1977). In the final data set, the instances which were judged as MWE by both annotators were regarded as MWE and the instances which were judged as non-MWE by both annotators were regarded as non-MWE. This resulted in a set of 262 instances of MWE and 560 instances of non-MWE classes. To avoid the possible bias of the results towards non-MWE class, we reduced the size of non-MWE class to 262 by randomly removing 298 instances. Afterward we divided the data into development ($2/3$) and test ($1/3$) sets, which contain the same proportion of MWE and non-MWE instances. An overview of the data set is presented in Table 1.

Set	MWE	non-MWE
original set	262	262
dev. set	174	174
test set	88	88
examples	gold rush, role model, family tree, city center, bow saw, life cycle	chess talent, bus types, attack damage, player skill, oil storage, lobby area

Table 1: Dataset statistics.

4.2 Evaluation

We implement the following two baselines: (1) Multinomial likelihood (Evert, 2005), which calculates the probability of the observed contingency table for a given pair under the null hypothesis of independence. (2) Mutual information (Church and Hanks, 1990), which calculates the mutual dependency of words of a co-occurrence, and has been proved efficient in identification and extraction of MWEs (Pecina, 2010; Evert, 2005). With respect to the range of scores, we set and alter a threshold for multinomial likelihood ($M.N.L$ hereafter) and mutual information ($M.I.$ hereafter). Pairs that obtain a score above the threshold are considered MWE, and pairs that obtain a score below the threshold are considered non-MWE. Figure 1 illustrates the precision-recall curve for our models and the baselines on the development set.

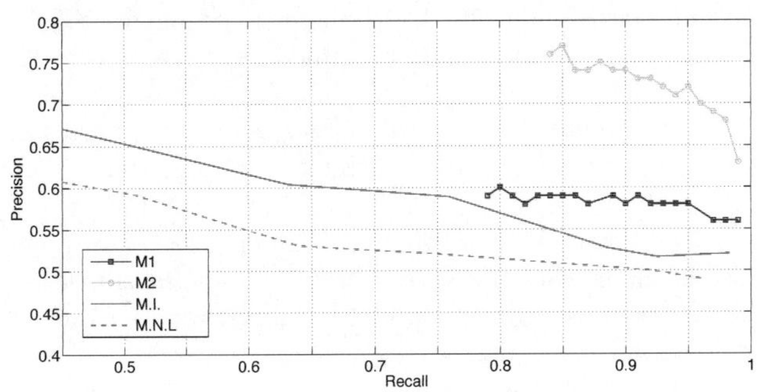

Figure 1: Precision-recall curve for various models.

The two baseline models i.e., $M.N.L.$ and $M.I.$ reach a high precision only at the cost of a dramatic loss in recall. They behave similarly, however, $M.I.$ in general performs better. M_2 clearly performs better compare to all other models. It reaches a high precision and recall, however, its precision declines rather quickly when recall increases. M_1 shows a more steady behaviour in the sense that reaching a higher recall doesn't significantly impact its precision. Figure 2 shows how F_1 score changes for various models when changing parameters in order to go from high precision to high recall. M_1 and M_2 constantly have a higher F_1 score, where $M.I.$ and $M.N.L.$ start off with a low score and reach a score which is comparable with that of the other models.

Out of the four tested models, with respect to F_1 scores, we select M_1, M_2, and $M.I.$ for further experiments. We set the relevant parameters to optimal values[2] (obtained by looking at the highest F_1 scores) and run the next experiments on the test set, which has remained unseen by the models up to this point. Table 2 shows the result of these experiments. The performance of all three models on the test set is consistent with their performance on the development set. M_2 reaches the highest precision and F_1 score. $M.I.$ has the highest recall but a low precision, and M_1 has a high recall and a reasonable but not very high precision.

[2]Optimal values of the parameters are as follows: α in M_1 : 15, α in M_2 : 20 and threshold for $M.I.$: 0.2

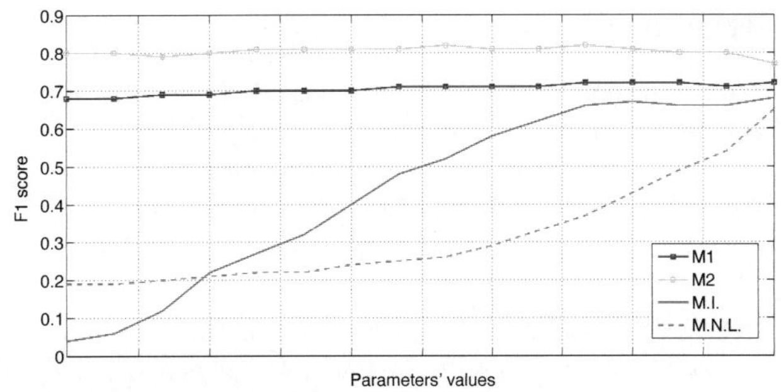

Figure 2: F_1 score for various models.

model	precision	recall	F_1
M_1	0.57	0.88	0.69
M_2	0.75	0.86	0.80
$M.I.$	0.51	0.95	0.66

Table 2: Evaluation results in terms of precision, recall and F_1 score for the three selected models.

5 Conclusions

We showed that statistical idiosyncrasy can play a significant role in identification and extraction of MWEs. We showed that this property can be used efficiently to extract idiosyncratic noun compounds which constitute the largest subset of English MWEs. We referred to statistical idiosyncrasy as collocational weight and formalized this property and implemented two corresponding models. We empirically tested the performance of these models against two baselines and showed that one of our models constantly outperforms the baselines and reaches an F_1 score of 0.80 on the test set.

Acknowledgments

We would like to thank James Henderson and Aaron Smith for discussions of various points and their help in carrying out this work.

References

Timothy Baldwin and Su Nam Kim. 2010. Multiword expressions. *Handbook of Natural Language Processing, second edition. Morgan and Claypool.*

Timothy Baldwin. 2005. Deep lexical acquisition of verb–particle constructions. *Computer Speech & Language*, 19(4):398–414.

Helena de Medeiros Caseli, Carlos Ramisch, Maria das Graças Volpe Nunes, and Aline Villavicencio. 2010. Alignment-based extraction of multiword expressions. *Language resources and evaluation*, 44(1-2):59–77.

Kenneth Ward Church and Patrick Hanks. 1990. Word association norms, mutual information, and lexicography. *Comput. Linguist.*, 16(1):22–29, March.

Gaël Dias. 2003. Multiword unit hybrid extraction. In *Proceedings of the ACL 2003 workshop on Multiword expressions: analysis, acquisition and treatment-Volume 18*, pages 41–48. Association for Computational Linguistics.

Stefan Evert. 2005. *The statistics of word cooccurrences*. Ph.D. thesis, Dissertation, Stuttgart University.

Meghdad Farahmand and Ronaldo Martins. 2014. A supervised model for extraction of multiword expressions based on statistical context features. In *Proceedings of the 10th Workshop on Multiword Expressions (MWE)*, pages 10–16. Association for Computational Linguistics.

Karl Moritz Hermann, Phil Blunsom, and Stephen Pulman. 2012. An unsupervised ranking model for noun-noun compositionality. In *Proceedings of the First Joint Conference on Lexical and Computational Semantics*, pages 132–141. Association for Computational Linguistics.

Christian Jacquemin, Judith L Klavans, and Evelyne Tzoukermann. 1997. Expansion of multi-word terms for indexing and retrieval using morphology and syntax. In *Proceedings of the eighth conference on European chapter of the Association for Computational Linguistics*, pages 24–31. Association for Computational Linguistics.

J Richard Landis and Gary G Koch. 1977. The measurement of observer agreement for categorical data. *biometrics*, pages 159–174.

Mirella Lapata and Alex Lascarides. 2003. Detecting novel compounds: The role of distributional evidence. In *Proceedings of the tenth conference on European chapter of the Association for Computational Linguistics-Volume 1*, pages 235–242. Association for Computational Linguistics.

Christopher D Manning and Hinrich Schütze. 1999. *Foundations of statistical natural language processing*. MIT press.

Joakim Nivre and Jens Nilsson. 2004. Multiword units in syntactic parsing. In *In Workshop on Methodologies and Evaluation of Multiword Units in Real-World Applications*.

Darren Pearce. 2001. Synonymy in collocation extraction. In *Proceedings of the Workshop on WordNet and Other Lexical Resources, Second meeting of the North American Chapter of the Association for Computational Linguistics*, pages 41–46. Citeseer.

Pavel Pecina. 2010. Lexical association measures and collocation extraction. *Language resources and evaluation*, 44(1-2):137–158.

Carlos Ramisch, Aline Villavicencio, Leonardo Moura, and Marco Idiart. 2008. Picking them up and figuring them out: Verb-particle constructions, noise and idiomaticity. In *Proceedings of the Twelfth Conference on Computational Natural Language Learning*, pages 49–56. Association for Computational Linguistics.

Carlos Ramisch. 2012. A generic framework for multiword expressions treatment: from acquisition to applications. In *Proceedings of ACL 2012 Student Research Workshop*, pages 61–66. Association for Computational Linguistics.

Siva Reddy, Diana McCarthy, and Suresh Manandhar. 2011. An empirical study on compositionality in compound nouns. In *IJCNLP*, pages 210–218.

Zhixiang Ren, Yajuan Lü, Jie Cao, Qun Liu, and Yun Huang. 2009. Improving statistical machine translation using domain bilingual multiword expressions. In *Proceedings of the Workshop on Multiword Expressions: Identification, Interpretation, Disambiguation and Applications*, pages 47–54. Association for Computational Linguistics.

Ivan A Sag, Timothy Baldwin, Francis Bond, Ann Copestake, and Dan Flickinger. 2002. Multiword expressions: A pain in the neck for nlp. In *Computational Linguistics and Intelligent Text Processing*, pages 1–15. Springer.

Violeta Seretan and Eric Wehrli. 2006. Accurate collocation extraction using a multilingual parser. In *Proceedings of the 21st International Conference on Computational Linguistics and the 44th annual meeting of the Association for Computational Linguistics*, pages 953–960. Association for Computational Linguistics.

Violeta Seretan. 2011. *Syntax-based collocation extraction*, volume 44. Springer.

Frank Smadja. 1993. Retrieving collocations from text: Xtract. *Computational Linguistics*, 19:143–177.

Aaron Smith. 2014. Breaking bad: Extraction of verb-particle constructions from a parallel subtitles corpus. In *Proceedings of the 10th Workshop on Multiword Expressions (MWE)*, pages 1–9. Association for Computational Linguistics.

Clustering-based Approach to Multiword Expression Extraction and Ranking

Elena Tutubalina
Higher Institute for Information Technology and Information Systems
Kazan Federal University
Kazan, Russia
tutubalinaev@gmail.com

Abstract

We present a domain-independent clustering-based approach for automatic extraction of multiword expressions (MWEs). The method combines statistical information from a general-purpose corpus and texts from Wikipedia articles. We incorporate association measures via dimensions of data points to cluster MWEs and then compute the ranking score for each MWE based on the closest exemplar assigned to a cluster. Evaluation results, achieved for two languages, show that a combination of association measures gives an improvement in the ranking of MWEs compared with simple counts of co-occurrence frequencies and purely statistical measures.

1 Introduction

Extraction of multiword expressions (MWEs) is a challenging and well-known task, aimed at identifying lexical items with idiosyncratic interpretations that can be decomposed into single words (Sag et al., 2002). In this study, we primarily focus on the extraction of two-word expressions in Russian.

A number of lexical association measures and their combinations have been employed in previous studies about extraction of general-purpose collocations and domain-specific terms (Krenn and Evert, 2001; Pearce, 2002; Evert, 2004; Pecina and Schlesinger, 2006; Hoang et al., 2009; Hartmann et al., 2012). Ranked collocations with higher association scores are selected into the n-best list. These simple approaches are limited by the size of corpora and the effect of low frequency on ranking (Krenn and Evert, 2001; Evert and Krenn, 2005; Bouma, 2009). Most studies regard MWE as a classification task and based on supervised methods to predict the class (collocations or non-collocations) to which an MWE candidate relates (Pecina and Schlesinger, 2006; Ramisch, 2015). There is no labeled training set in Russian for these approaches, and data annotation is time-consuming. The task could be seen as a ranking task: ranking model group comparable entities into queries by criteria and constructing a ranking model using training data with exemplars to predict a ranking score. However, there are no formal principles on how to detect comparable MWEs from general-purpose corpora for Russian. Therefore, in this study we focus on clustering semantically similar MWE candidates using association measures, calculated on a general-purpose corpora and Wikipedia.

A particular general-purpose corpus, such as the Russian National Corpus or the British National Corpus, provides only a partial coverage of the modern language. Although association measures have been widely applied, they have a limitation: the computed probabilities may be small in the particular corpus, which gives a lower rank for MWE in the n-best list. To avoid this situation, we incorporate the standard statistical measure, computed from the general-purpose corpus, with Wikipedia, that contains a vast amount of knowledge (e.g., named entities, domain-specific terms, and disambiguation of word senses).

Given a small number of most representative MWEs as exemplars, our primary goal is to identify MWE noun candidates, considering similarity between a candidate and the exemplars, based on association scores in both resources. Our method consists of three steps: (i) extracting bigrams that serve as MWE candidates, adopting Wikipedia arti-

Proceedings of NAACL-HLT 2015, pages 39–43,
Denver, Colorado, May 31 – June 5, 2015.

cles, and using predefined morphosyntactic patterns; (ii) grouping the candidates using clustering techniques; and (iii) ranking MWE candidates by a score, which is computed based on the distance between the candidate and the closest exemplar multiplied by the percent of exemplars in the cluster. The third step relies on the intuition that MWEs are highly ranked in clusters with a higher number of exemplars due to strong similarity between these expressions.

We demonstrate that combining association measures from two resources is effective, and improvement according to precision-recall curves can be achieved by a small number of measures combined.

2 Related Work

Over the last few decades, a large number of works in computational corpus linguistics have been published concerning the extraction of multiword terms, collocations, and keyphrases that is well described in Evert (2004), Gries, (2013), Hasan and Ng (2014), and Ramisch (2015). The research area covers several different methods, for example, ranking MWEs by association measures (Krenn and Evert, 2001; Pearce, 2002; Evert, 2004; Braslavski and Sokolov, 2006); contrastive filtering of domain-specific MWEs (Bonin et al., 2010); methods that combine statistic measures to find complex ranking functions, using clustering algorithms and neural networks (Pecina and Schlesinger, 2006; Antoch et al., 2013); machine learning approaches to classify MWEs into predefined categories (Pecina and Schlesinger, 2006; Ramisch, 2015); and Wikipedia-based approaches (Medelyan et al., 2009a; Medelyan et al., 2009b).

Many methods combine the different properties of two or more association measures to find high-ranking collocations with a strong association based on these measures (Church et al., 1991; Pecina and Schlesinger, 2006; Liu et al., 2009). Church et al. (1991) used an association measure constructed from mutual information (MI) and t-score formulae with scaling functions for collocation identification. Pecina and Schlesinger (2006) presented supervised methods based on 82 association measures to define a ranker function. They did not select the "best universal method" for combining association measures because the task depends on many factors, such as language and data, among others. Liu et al. (2009) adopted Wikipedia to compute term relatedness based on a vector of Wikipedia concepts for keyphrase extraction. They selected four measures to group terms of a given document based on the semantic relatedness between them. These measures are cosine similarity, Euclidean distance, pointwise mutual information (PMI), and normalized similarity distance. Antoch et al. (2013) combined association measures considered as binary classifiers using receiver operating characteristic curves. They used a hierarchical clustering algorithm to achieve better results by clustering these measures. The authors observed that high efficiency of combining representatives of the clusters of equivalent association measures depends on a dataset. Jain (2010) proposed that there is no single clustering algorithm that is able to outperform other algorithms across all applications.

3 The Clustering-based Approach for Ranking MWEs

In this section, we describe the proposed clustering-based approach. In contrast to classification methods that predict whether a MWE is a true collocation or not, the goal is to determine which MWE candidates are best statistically similar to a small set of exemplars. Exemplars are MWEs (e.g., from the gold standard set) with a rather high degree of association between the word components. We employ Wiktionary to extract MWE exemplars. We perform the clustering of the extracted MWEs using a k-means algorithm and log-likelihood measure.

The proposed approach is composed of three steps: (i) extracting a list of MWEs from Wikipedia article titles, (ii) computing the log-likelihood of the MWE data given the general-purpose corpus and texts from Wikipedia, and (iii) grouping MWE candidates by the k-means clustering algorithm and then ranking cluster points by measuring the distance from these points to the closest exemplar multiplied by the percent of exemplars in the cluster.

3.1 Selecting MWE Candidates

We selected MWE candidates from Wikipedia article titles due to the following reasons: (i) the Russian sentence structure is very flexible, and extraction of bigrams by the patterns, where words are considered neighbors (adjacent words), is insufficient; and (ii) Wikipedia article titles have explicit phrase boundaries, marked by human editors in Wikipedia markup (Hartmann et al., 2012). The following filter was applied to all the two-word sequences: the candidates were not allowed to contain punctuation marks except hyphenated expressions, and the candidates were not allowed to contain proper names and common geographic locations. The extracted candidates were then filtered by predefined morphosyntactic patterns (e.g., adjective + noun, noun + noun). The morphosyntactic analyzer Mystem[1] and NLTK library are applied for Russian and English, respectively. We used a list of patterns from Braslavski and Sokolov's (2008) and Manning's papers (1999) for texts in Russian and English, respectively.

3.2 Clustering MWE Candidates and Ranking

The proposed approach assigns MWE candidates to the clusters based on the distribution of statistical measures associated with each candidate in general-purpose corpora. The clustering method we apply is k-means that has been widely used with the Euclidean metric for computing the distance between points and cluster centers (Jain, 2010). As indicated from the results, reported in Section 4 of this paper and recent studies (Evert, 2004; Evert and Krenn; 2005), log-likelihood achieves better results than ranking by other statistical measures, such as t-score and MI. Therefore, we compute log-likelihood as statistical characteristics of MWE candidates, based on two different resources of texts.

In this approach, MWE candidates are represented as points in a two-dimensional space, where each dimension represents by log-likelihood. We make assumption that (i) the distribution over all exemplars is similar to a distribution over all words in the corpus, and (ii) MWEs are independently distributed and probabilities are estimated as frequency ratios, which is similar to the naive Bayes assumption (Baker and McCallum, 1998). MWE candidates are ranked by the following formula, that shows the ranking score of MWE j in cluster cl:

$$score(mwe = j) = (1 - \frac{\min_{i=1,\ldots,n_{cl}} d(j, gs_i)}{r_{cl}}) * np_{cl} \quad (1)$$

[1] Mystem is available at https://tech.yandex.ru/mystem/.

where n_{cl} indicates the number of exemplars in cluster cl, np_{cl} denotes n_{cl} in percent, $d(j, gs_i)$ denotes Euclidean distance between MWE j and the exemplar gs_i in cluster cl, r_{cl} denotes radius of cluster cl.

4 Evaluation

We use the Russian National Corpus (RNC) and the British National Corpus (BNC) as the general-purpose corpus of the Russian language and the English language, respectively. For corpora in Russian, we generated frequency lists of bigrams in singular and plural forms. We adopt n-gram data of English Wikipedia and the BNC, extracted by Lin et al. (2010) and Leech and Rayson (2014). We suppose that all MWE candidates occur at least once in corpora due to frequency thresholds in the lists. Table 1 shows MWEs that are top-ranked by our approach.

Russian MWEs	**English MWEs**
мировая война (*mirovaya voyna*) 'world war'	world war
советский союз (*sovetskiy soyuz*) 'soviet union'	soviet union
настоящее время (*nastoyashchee vremya*) 'present time'	feature film
чемпионат мира (*chempionat mira*) 'world cup'	binomial name
населенный пункт (*naselennyy punkt*) 'human settlement'	world champion
водные ресурсы (*vodnye resursy*) 'water resources'	popular culture

Table 1: Sample of top-ranked collocations.

We adopt Wiktionary as the gold standard dataset for Russian and English due to use of Russian Wiktionary as a data source for WordNet-like resources. The single-word nouns from Wiktionary were used as "raw materials" for the Yet Another RussNet (YARN) project (Braslavski et al., 2014). Comparison of vocabularies in the English and Russian editions of Wiktionary is described in (Krizhanovsky and Smirnov, 2013). The gold standard set for Russian was filtered to remove non-collocations. Table 2 shows a summary of MWEs for two languages.

We compute the precision-recall curves of the n-best lists to evaluate our approach. For comparison, we use n-best lists that are ranked by popular association measures: t-score, log-likelihood, and MI. Wermter and Hahn (2006) proposed that purely association measures could not reveal any significant improvement over co-occurrence frequency. We have also used frequencies of MWEs as a baseline measure for ranking. The types of corpus are followed by a subscript: 1 refers to the general-purpose corpus, and 2 refers to texts from Wikipedia articles.

Language	Russian	English
No. of tokens in the general-purpose corpus	364,881,378	110,691,482
No. of Wikipedia articles	1,172,000+	4,675,000+
No. of MWE candidates	164,805	135,659
No. of MWEs, extracted from Wiktionary	7433	40996
No. of MWEs, selected for the gold standard	3670	40996
Intersection of the sets	2216	6342

Table 2: Summary of the list of MWE candidates.

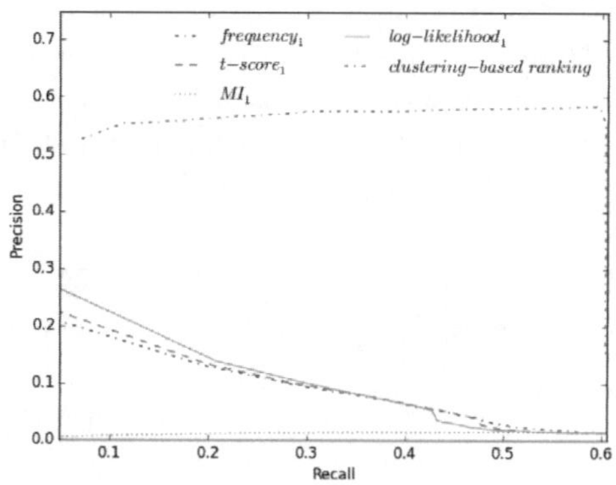

Figure 1: Precision-recall curves of the proposed approach and association measures (for Russian).

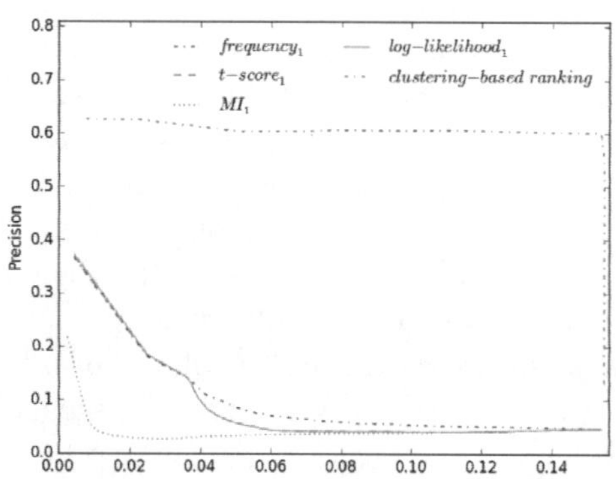

Figure 2: Precision-recall curves of the proposed approach and association measures (for English).

The results, shown in Figures 1 and 2, indicate that the proposed approach outperforms baseline ranking by association measures, but the precision of the n-best list is significantly decreased with increase of recall. In order to evaluate the impact of a varied number of clusters, we conduct experiments on the

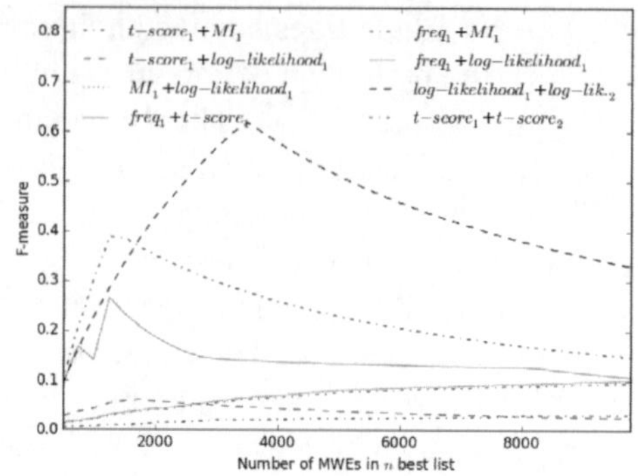

Figure 3: Comparison of F-measure curves of the proposed approach based on different statistical measures.

dataset in Russian using log-likelihood. We change the number of clusters from 5 to 30 to achieve the maximum F-measure with the minimum number of n-best ranked MWEs. Results, shown in Table 3, indicate that n equals 3,500 for each experiment, and the number of clusters is 5.

No. of clusters	P@n	R@n	F-measure
5	0.553	0.6029	0.5769
10	0.5438	0.5928	0.5672
15	0.568	0.5418	0.5546
20	0.5634	0.5374	0.5501
25	0.5431	0.5181	0.5303
30	0.5371	0.5124	0.5245

Table 3: Evaluation results with a varied number of clusters, n equals to 3,500 (for Russian).

To confirm that a combination of association measures from two resources significantly helps in the task of extracting MWEs, we compare our results with different combinations of measures according to F-measure. Figure 3 shows that the combination of log-likelihood, based on two corpora in Russian, gives the best results compared with others.

5 Conclusion and Future Work

In this paper, we proposed a clustering-based approach for the extraction of multiword expressions (MWEs). We incorporated association measures, computed from two corpora, by representing each MWE as a two-dimensional data point. The method assigned MWEs to clusters using k-means clustering and then ranked MWEs by Euclidean distance to the nearest exemplar from the gold standard set. The efficiency of our approach depends on MWE probabilities in two corpora, and the small set of multiword exemplars is required. For future works, we plan to split MWE candidates into small queries of comparable MWEs by linguistic criteria and then use query-dependent ranking for each query-MWE pair.

Acknowledgments

This work was partially supported by Russian Foundation for Basic Research (Project № 13-07-00773).

References

Antoch J., Prchal L., and Sarda P. 2013. *Combining Association Measures for Collocation Extraction Using Clustering of Receiver Operating Characteristic Curves*. Journal of classification, 30(1):100-123.

Baker L. D. and McCallum A. K. 1998. *Distributional clustering of words for text classification*. Proceedings of the ACM SIGIR conference on Research and development in information retrieval, pp. 96-103.

Bonin F., Dell'Orletta F., Venturi G., & Montemagni S. 2010. *Contrastive filtering of domain-specific multiword terms from different types of corpora*. Proceedings of 23rd International Conference on Computational Linguistics, p. 77

Bouma G. 2009. *Normalized (pointwise) mutual information in collocation extraction*. Proceedings of GSCL, pp. 31-40

Braslavski P. and Sokolov E. 2008. *Comparison of five methods for variable length term extraction*. In Computational Linguistics and Intellectual Technologies: Proceedings of the International Conference "Dialog", №. 7, pp. 14. (In Russian)

Braslavski P., Ustalov D., and Mukhin M. 2014. *A spinning wheel for YARN: user interface for a crowdsourced thesaurus*. Proceedings of the 14th Conference of the European Chapter of the Association for Computational Linguistics, pp. 101-104.

Evert S. and Krenn B. 2001. *Multiword expressions: A pain in the neck for NLP*. Proceedings of the 39th Annual Meeting on Association for Computational Linguistics, pp. 188-195

Evert S. 2004. *The statistics of word cooccurrences: word pairs and collocations*.

Evert S. and Krenn B. 2005. *Using small random samples for the manual evaluation of statistical association measures*. Computer Speech & Language, № 4.

Gries S. T. 2013. *50-something years of work on collocations: what is or should be next*. International Journal of Corpus Linguistics, 18(1):137-166.

Gusfield D. 1997. *Algorithms on Strings, Trees and Sequences*. Cambridge University Press, UK.

Pearce D. 2002. *A Comparative Evaluation of Collocation Extraction Techniques*. LREC.

Pecina P. and Schlesinger P. 2006. *Combining association measures for collocation extraction*. Proceedings of the COLING/ACL on Main conference poster sessions, pp. 651-658.

Hasan Kazi Saidul and Ng Vincent 2014. *Automatic keyphrase extraction: A survey of the state of the art*. Proceedings of the Association for Computational Linguistics (ACL).

Hartmann S., Szarvas G., & Gurevych I. 2012. *Mining multiword terms from Wikipedia. Semi-Automatic Ontology Development: Processes and Resources*. Semi-Automatic Ontology Development: Processes and Resources, pp. 226-258.

Hoang H. H., Kim S. N., & Kan M.-Y. 2009. *A re-examination of lexical association measures*. Proceedings of the ACL 2009 Workshop on Multiword Expressions: Identification, Interpretation, Disambiguation and Applications, pp. 31–39.

Jain A. K. 2010. *Data clustering: 50 years beyond K-means*. Pattern recognition letters, 31(8):651-666.

Lin, D., Church, K. W., Ji, H., Sekine, S., Yarowsky, D., Bergsma, S., & Narsale, S. 2010. *New Tools for Web-Scale N-grams*. LREC.

Krizhanovsky A. A. and Smirnov A. V. 2013. *An approach to automated construction of a general-purpose lexical ontology based on Wiktionary*. Journal of Computer and Systems Sciences International, 52(2):215-225.

Leech G. & Rayson P. 2014. *Word frequencies in written and spoken English: Based on the British National Corpus*. Routledge.

Manning C. D. 1999. *Foundations of statistical natural language processing*. MIT press.

Medelyan Olena, Frank Eibe, and Witten Ian H. 2009a. *Human-competitive tagging using automatic keyphrase extraction*. Proceedings of the 2009 Conference on EMNLP, pp. 1318–1327.

Medelyan Olena, Milne David, Legg Catherine, and Witten Ian H. 2009b. *Mining meaning from Wikipedia*. International Journal of Human-Computer Studies, № 9 (2009), pp. 716-754.

Ramisch, C. 2015. *Evaluation of MWE Acquisition*. Multiword Expressions Acquisition, pp. 105-125.

Sag Ivan A., Baldwin Timothy, Bond Francis, Copestake Ann, and Flickinger Dan 2002. *Multiword expressions: A pain in the neck for NLP*. Computational Linguistics and Intelligent Text Processing, pp. 38-43

Wermter J. and Hahn U. 2006. *You can't beat frequency (unless you use linguistic knowledge): a qualitative evaluation of association measures for collocation and term extraction*. The 21st International Conference on Computational Linguistics, pp. 785-792

How Constructions Mean
(Invited Talk Abstract)

Paul Kay
ICSI, UC Berkeley
paulkay@berkeley.edu

Laura A. Michaelis
Department of Linguistics
University of Colorado Boulder
Laura.Michaelis@Colorado.EDU

One of the major motivations for a construction-based approach to syntax is that a given rule of syntactic formation can often be associated with more than one semantic specification. For example, a pair of expressions like purple plum and alleged thief call on different rules of semantic combination. The first involves something related to intersection of sets: a purple plum is a member of the set of purple things and of the set of plums. But an alleged thief is not a member of the intersection of the set of thieves and the set of alleged things. Indeed, that intersection is empty, since only a proposition can be alleged and a thief is never a proposition. Constructional approaches recognize as instances of compositionality cases in which two different meanings for the same syntactic form are licensed by two different collections of form-meaning licensors, i.e., by two different collections of constructions. Construction-based grammars are nevertheless compositional in the usual sense: if you know the meanings of the words and you know all the rules that combine words and phrases into larger formal units, while simultaneously combining the meanings of the smaller units into the meanings of the larger ones, then you know the forms and meanings of all the larger units, including all the sentences. Constructional approaches focus on the fact that there are many such rules, and especially on the rules that assign meanings to complex structures. Such approaches do not draw a theoretical distinction between those rules thought to be in the core and those considered peripheral. The construction grammarian conceives of a language as a continuum of generality of expressions; a construction grammar models this continuum with an array of constructions of correspondingly graded generality (Fillmore et al. 1988).

This paper surveys the various ways meanings can be assembled in a construction-based grammar, with a focus on the continuum of idiomaticity, a gradient of lexical fixity stretching from frozen idioms, like the salt of the, earth, in the doghouse and under the weather, on the one hand, to fully productive rules on the other, e.g., the rule licensing Kim blinked (the Subject-Predicate construction). The semantics of constructions is the semantics to be discovered along the full length of this gamut. Meanings discussed include: literal meaning, the meanings of constructions that regulate argument expression, context indexation, less commonly recognized illocutionary forces, metalinguistic commentary and topic-focus alignment. We conclude that the seamless integration of relatively idiomatic constructions with more productive ones in actual sentences undermines the notion of a privileged core grammar.

Proceedings of NAACL-HLT 2015, page 44,
Denver, Colorado, May 31 – June 5, 2015.

Never-Ending Multiword Expressions Learning

Alexandre C. Rondon
Federal Univ. of São Carlos
São Carlos, Brazil
alex.crondon@gmail.com

Helena de Medeiros Caseli
Federal Univ. of São Carlos
São Carlos, Brazil
helenacaseli@dc.ufscar.br

Carlos Ramisch
Aix Marseille Université
Marseille, France
carlos.ramisch@lif.univ-mrs.fr

Abstract

This paper introduces NEMWEL, a system that performs Never-Ending MultiWord Expressions Learning. Instead of using a static corpus and classifier, NEMWEL applies supervised learning on automatically crawled news texts. Moreover, it uses its own results to periodically retrain the classifier, bootstrapping on its own results. In addition to a detailed description of the system's architecture and its modules, we report the results of a manual evaluation. It shows that NEMWEL is capable of learning new expressions over time with improved precision.

1 Introduction

Multiword expressions (MWEs) are combinations of two or more lexemes which present some lexical, syntactic, semantic, pragmatic or statistical idiosyncrasies with respect to regular combinations (Baldwin and Kim, 2010). Examples include idioms (*saw logs* as *to snore*), phrasal verbs (*pull over*, *give up*), noun compounds (*machine learning*, *support vector machine*) and complex function words (*as well as*, *with respect to*).

In human languages, such constructions are very frequent, as native speakers rarely realize how often they employ them (Sag et al., 2002; Jackendoff, 1997b). However, they are not frequent in NLP resources such as lexicons and grammars, and this represents a bottleneck for building robust and accurate NLP applications.

Since the construction of such resources is onerous and demands highly qualified linguistic expertise, *automatic MWE lexicon extraction* is an attractive alternative which has been one of the most active topics in the MWE research community. Proposed methods are often based on supervised and unsupervised learning of MWE lists from textual corpora (Evert and Krenn, 2005; Pecina, 2008). In spite of the availability of very large corpora like the Gigaword or WaC (Baroni et al., 2009), these methods are still limited by the coverage of the texts in the source corpus.

This paper presents NEMWEL, a machine learning system able to learn MWEs following the never-ending approach (Mitchell et al., 2015). NEMWEL automatically extracts MWE candidates from a corpus periodically crawled from a Brazilian online news portal. Then, based on supervised training, NEMWEL classifies the candidates and promotes some of them to the status of "true MWEs", which are used to retrain the classifier. This process is repeated endlessly, taking into consideration the true MWEs learned in previous steps. By doing so, NEMWEL tries to resemble the way human beings learn.

We have developed a prototype that implements this idea. To the best of our knowledge, this is the first attempt to build MWE lexicons using a never-ending learning approach. We have manually evaluated the extracted MWEs and we show that the precision of the learner seems to increase with time.

Proceedings of NAACL-HLT 2015, pages 45–53,
Denver, Colorado, May 31 – June 5, 2015. ©2015 Association for Computational Linguistics

The remainder of this paper is structured as follows: we discuss related work on MWE extraction (Section 2) and never-ending learning methods (Section 3). Then, we present the architecture and detail the modules in NEMWEL (Section 4). Finaly, we present the results of automatic and manual evaluation in Brazilian Portuguese (Section 5) and ideas for future work (Section 6).

2 MWE Extraction

Automatic unsupervised MWE learning from corpora has been proposed based on pairwise association measures (Church and Hanks, 1990; Smadja, 1993; Pedersen et al., 2011), string matching (Duan et al., 2006), extraction patterns based on expert linguistic knowledge and automatic analysis (Justeson and Katz, 1995; Seretan and Wehrli, 2009) or a combination of these methods (Araujo et al., 2011).

Supervised machine learning methods have also been used for MWE lexicon learning.[1] Pecina (2008) proposes a logistic regression classifier which uses as features a set of 84 different lexical association measures. Ramisch et al. (2008) use decision trees for classifying MWEs based on standard association measures as well, but they add variation entropy. In terms of classifiers, many alternatives have been tested like bayesian networks (Dubremetz and Nivre, 2014) and support vector machines (Farahmand and Martins, 2014). Zilio et al. (2011) use a stable set of features, but compare several classification algorithms implemented in Weka. Furthermore, in-context MWE tagging has been performed using sequence learning models like conditional random fields (Constant and Sigogne, 2011) and structured perceptron (Schneider et al., 2014).[2]

Many alternative sources and methods have been tested for MWE extraction, like parallel texts (Caseli et al., 2010; Tsvetkov and Wintner, 2010), bilingual lexicons (Salehi and Cook, 2013), Wikipedia interlingual links (Attia et al., 2010), WordNet synonyms (Pearce, 2001) and distributional neighbors (Reddy et al., 2011). The web has also been considered as a source for MWE learning, often using page hit counts from search engines (Lapata and Keller, 2005; Kim and Nakov, 2011). However, in related work, candidates are not extracted from web texts, but from traditional corpora.

Differently from previous corpus-based or web-based learning approaches, our goal is not to build one static MWE lexicon. Instead, we propose to build a system that continuously learns new expressions from the web. It populates and enriches the lexicon with new MWEs every day. Our proposal is to employ bootstrapping on a traditional supervised machine learning setting, enriched with new features and dynamically crawled corpora. At any given time, a snapshot of the database will include the current MWE lexicon, which can be exported, evaluated and used to retrain the classifier. To the best of our knowledge, this is the first time never-ending learning is applied to MWE lexicon discovery.

3 Never-Ending Learning

In traditional machine learning, an algorithm is usually applied to learn a model from a fixed amount of labeled training data. Although effective in many applications, this way of learning is very limited and also far from the way that human beings learn. Never-ending learning is an approach that tries to resemble the way humans learn, taking into account different sources of information and using previous experience to guide subsequent learning (Mitchell et al., 2015). It can be classified as a bootstrapping algorithm. It requires a small set of annotated items, used to initialize the model, and then it uses its own results to retrain the classifier in future iterations.

The main system developed following the never-ending learning approach is the Never-Ending Language Learner (NELL) of Carlson et al. (2010). NELL is the learning system of the Read the Web project[3] and it is running 24 hours/day since 2010. NELL's goals are (1)

[1] Usually, such methods require a list of candidate expressions annotated as true or false MWEs.

[2] Such models require corpora where sentences are annotated with the MWE sequences they contain.

[3] `http://rtw.ml.cmu.edu/rtw/`

to read the web extracting beliefs (true facts) that populate a knowledge base and (2) to learn better day by day. To do so, NELL is able to perform different learning tasks (category classification, relation classification, etc.) and combine different learning functions to make decisions and improve its learning methods (Mitchell et al., 2015).

In this paper we describe the Never-Ending MultiWord Expressions Learner (NEMWEL). Different from NELL, NEMWEL is in its first year of life and is intended only to learn MWEs. But, following the main never-ending learning premise, NEMWEL uses its previously learned knowledge to better learn new MWEs.

According to Jackendoff (1997a), there are as many MWEs in a lexicon as single words. For Sag et al. (2002) this is an underestimation and the real number of MWEs grows with language evolution. These findings corroborate our idea that a never-ending learning system is a good solution to tackle the MWE extraction problem.

4 The Never-Ending MWE Learner

The NEMWEL was developed in Java and is divided into four modules – crawler, extractor, processor and promoter – explained in the next subsections. These four modules are applied in sequence and repeatedly in each iteration of NEMWEL.

4.1 Crawler

The first module, the Crawler, is responsible for collecting texts from the web to build a corpus. In our current prototype, in each iteration, 40 different articles from the G1 news portal[4] are downloaded randomly, cleaned by removing HMTL markup and boilerplate content, and concatenated in one unique file. Figure 1 shows an excerpt of a text from one iteration of the Crawler module.

4.2 Extractor

After collecting and cleaning the texts, the Extractor annotates the tokens in each text with its surface form, part-of-speech tag and lemma. To do so, we used the TreeTagger (Schmid, 1994) with a model trained for Portuguese[5]. Tagging the corpus is required because we evaluate our learner using nominal MWEs, thus we need to be able to identify nouns and their complements. The TreeTagger was chosen because it is free, easy to use and fast, enabling us to quickly process large amounts of crawled texts. The same excerpt of Figure 1 processed by the Extractor is shown in Figure 2.

Mais de 100 famílias de baixa renda ocuparam casas de um **conjunto habitacional**, em Paulínia (SP), na madrugada desta quarta-feira (19). *More than 100 low-income families occupied houses of a* ***housing development*** *in Paulinia (SP) in the early hours of this Wednesday (19).*

Figure 1: Excerpt of a text crawled from the news portal. Original text (in Brazilian Portuguese) and its English translation (manually prepared for this paper).

The sequences of tagged tokens in the crawled texts are processed by the *mwetoolkit* (Ramisch, 2015), which is the core of our Extractor and Processor modules. In the Extractor, a list of MWE candidates is obtained by matching a multilevel regular-expression pattern (Figure 3) against the tagged corpus. Figure 4 shows an example of MWE candidate extracted from our example sentence, using the pattern of Figure 3. The pattern is based on intuitive noun phrase descriptions, but it also captures more candidates, that are not necessarily nominal compounds. Further filters must be applied to remove regular noun phrases and keep only nominal MWEs.

4.3 Processor

In this module, the mwetoolkit calculates some association measures that will be used by the Promoter in the next step. These measures are calculated based on the number of occurrences of the MWE candidate and of the words that

[4] http://g1.globo.com

[5] http://gramatica.usc.es/~gamallo/tagger_intro.htm

Mais	ADV	mais
de	PRP	de
100	CARD	@card@
...		
casas	NOM	casa
de	PRP	de
um	DET	um
conjunto	**NOM**	**conjunto**
habitacional	**ADJ**	**habitacional**
,	VIRG	,
em	PRP	em
Paulínia	NOM	paulínia
(	QUOTE	(
SP	NOM	SP
)	QUOTE	)
,	VIRG	,
na	PRP	em
madrugada	NOM	madrugada
desta	PRP	de
quarta-feira	NOM	quarta-feira
(	QUOTE	(
19	CARD	@card@
)	QUOTE	)
.	SENT	.

Figure 2: The excerpt from Figure 1 after part-of-speech tagging by TreeTagger.

```
<patterns>
  <pat>
    <w pos="NOM"/>
    <pat repeat="{1,3}"/>
      <either>
        <pat>
          <w pos="PRP*" lemma="de"/>
          <w pos="NOM"/>
        </pat>
        <pat>
          <w pos="ADJ"/>
        </pat>
      </either>
    </pat>
  </pat>
</patterns>
```

Figure 3: List of part-of-speech sequences describing nominal multiword expressions in Brazilian Portuguese. They correspond to a noun followed by 1 to 3 complements, which can be either an adjective or a prepositional phrase introduced by *de*.

```
<cand candid="684">
  <ngram>
    <w lemma="conjunto">
      <freq name="g1" value="10"/>
      <freq name="plnbr" value="3005"/>
    </w>
    <w lemma="habitacional">
      <freq name="g1" value="3"/>
      <freq name="plnbr" value="359"/>
    </w>
    <freq name="g1" value="3"/>
    <freq name"plnbr" value="86"/>
  </ngram>
  ...
</cand>
```

Figure 4: MWE candidate extracted from the sentence of Figure 1 using the pattern of Figure 3.

compose it. In our experiments, these numbers of occurrences were calculated using the G1 corpus and also the PLN-BR corpus[6], which contains around 29 million words of news articles from the *Folha de São Paulo* newspaper, from 1994 to 2004. The use of the larger, static corpus may help because it provides more accurate association measures as features. For instance, in Figure 4, we can see that G1 returns 3 occurrences for *conjunto habitacional*, and 10 and 3 occurrences for the individual words. It is known that association measures are sensitive to low-frequency data, so it is probably a good idea to complement this with a measure calculated on PLN-BR, where the frequencies are of 86 occurrences for the expression, 3006 occurrences for the first words and 359 occurrences for the second word.

4.3.1 Features

The next module, the Promoter, uses supervised training performed using the 17 features defined below.

- **Association measures** – measure of the strength of the association between the frequency of an n-gram and the frequency of each word that forms the n-gram. In our experiments, four measures were used: normalized frequency, Student's t score, point-

[6] http://www.nilc.icmc.usp.br/plnbr

wise mutual information and Dice's coefficient. All of these measures were calculated by the mwetoolkit in the two corpora: G1 and PLN-BR. Thus, in total, we have eight features based on association measures.

- **Translatability** – measure based on the non-translatability property of true MWEs. First, we estimate the probability of a content word w[7] to be translated into a word x in English (`en`) and then back to Portuguese (`pt`), using a bilingual weighted lexicon:

  $$T(w) = \sum_x P_{pt \to en}(w, x) \times P_{en \to pt}(x, w)$$

  Two new features were proposed based on this probability:

  $$\texttt{translatability\_mult} = \prod_{i=1}^{n} T(w_i)$$

  $$\texttt{translatability\_mean} = \frac{1}{n} \sum_{i=1}^{n} T(w_i)$$

  Figure 5 shows an example of these features for the candidate expression *taxa de juros* (*interest rate*).

- **POS context** – the part of speech of the three previous and the three next tokens around the MWE candidate. We also use the concatenated parts of speech of the words that form the MWE candidate. When there are more than one possible contexts, the most frequent one is chosen. Thus, seven features are based on the POS context, three in each direction and the POS sequence of the target candidate.

The new features proposed in this paper, based on translatability, are based on linguistic tests that show that MWEs have limited variability and thus, in most cases, cannot be translated word by word. It is calculated using two probabilistic bilingual dictionaries generated by NATools[8] from the FAPESP parallel corpus corpus[9]. This corpus contains a set of sentence-aligned Portuguese-English and English-Portuguese articles about research projects. From this corpus, NATools outputs, for each source word, a list of up to 10 best translations accompanied by its probability.

$$\begin{aligned}
T(\text{taxa}) &= P_{pt \to en}(\text{taxa}, \text{rate}) \times \\
&\quad P_{en \to pt}(\text{rate}, \text{taxa}) + \\
&\quad P_{pt \to en}(\text{taxa}, \text{level}) \times \\
&\quad P_{en \to pt}(\text{level}, \text{taxa}) + \\
&\quad P_{pt \to en}(\text{taxa}, \text{interest}) \times \\
&\quad P_{en \to pt}(\text{interest}, \text{taxa}) \\
&= 0.583 \times 0.537 + 0.251 \times 0.096 + \\
&\quad 0.008 \times 0 \\
&= 0.3372 \\
T(\text{juros}) &= P_{pt \to en}(\text{juros}, \text{interest}) \times \\
&\quad P_{en \to pt}(\text{interest}, \text{juros}) + \\
&\quad P_{pt \to en}(\text{juros}, \text{rates}) \times \\
&\quad P_{en \to pt}(\text{rates}, \text{juros}) + \\
&= 0.628 \times 0.032 + 0.372 \times 0.114 \\
&= 0.0625 \\
\texttt{translatability_mult} & \\
&= T(\text{taxa}) \times T(\text{juros}) \\
&= 0.0211 \\
\texttt{translatability_mean} & \\
&= \tfrac{1}{2} T(\text{taxa}) + T(\text{juros}) \\
&= 0.1998
\end{aligned}$$

Figure 5: Example of the two features based on translatability of the MWE candidate *taxa de juros* (*interest rate*).

To the best of our knowledge, this is the first time that translatability is implemented for MWE automatic extraction using automatically built bilingual lexicons. Related methods are based on non weighted, standard bilingual lexicons like PanLex or Wikipedia titles (Salehi and Cook, 2013; Attia et al., 2010).

4.4 Promoter

The last module, the Promoter, analyses the MWE candidates and promotes to *beliefs* the ones with the best scores. Beliefs are candidates that were classified as true MWEs in a previous iteration of the learner.

The Promoter applies a classification model trained using Weka (Hall et al., 2009) as a wrapper and LibSVM (Chang and Lin, 2011) as the

[7] In our experiments, content words are nouns and adjectives.

[8] `http://corpora.di.uminho.pt/natools`

[9] `http://www.nilc.icmc.usp.br/nilc/tools/FapespCorpora.htm`

core. The result is a support vector machine that distinguishes true MWEs from ordinary noun phrases. As training data, it uses previously annotated instances. The Promoter is generated based on examples that were already classified, either manually, for the Promoter-0, or manually+automatically, for the Promoters built in subsequent iterations.

SVM was the chosen classifier because it has presented good performance on diverse NLP tasks such as text categorization (Sassano, 2003), sentiment analysis (Mullen and Collier, 2004) and named entity recognition (Li et al., 2008), as well as standard corpus-based MWE extraction (Farahmand and Martins, 2014).

5 Evaluation

An initial training corpus was generated from texts of the G1 news portal. From this corpus, NEMWEL extracted 1,100 candidate MWEs which were manually annotated by two native speakers of Brazilian Portuguese: 600 candidates for each one with an intersection of 100 candidates. The annotation interface showed the candidate and the sentences from the G1 corpus from which the candidate was extracted (see Figure 6). The annotators had to perform a binary choice as to whether the candidate was a true MWE ("Sim") or not ("Não"). Each annotator cross-checked the other one's items. This last cross-checking step was crucial because, even though some guidelines were provided, some cases were hard to decide and required discussion. From this first annotation, 19% of the candidates were evaluated as true MWEs. The kappa agreement (Cohen, 1960) was 0.85, which indicates a very good agreement.

The annotated set was used to train our Promoter-0 as explained in section 4.4. NEMWEL, then, run for 15 iterations and, at each 5 iterations (a generation), a new Promoter was trained using the beliefs and false MWEs classified in the previous iterations.[10] After these 15 iterations, a new sample of 1,200 MWE

	Iterations			
	1-5	6-10	11-15	All
Precision	24.6%	32.2%	34.3%	30.5%
Recall	55.6%	65.5%	52.3%	57.0%
F1	34.1%	43.2%	41.4%	39.7%
Accuracy	85.5%	87.5%	83.8%	85.6%

Table 1: Results of NEMWEL's evaluation after 15 iterations and 3 generations of new Promoters.

candidates was manually evaluated by the two native speakers, but with no overlap between the annotators. To allow the analysis of the learning curve over time, this sample contained 400 candidates extracted in each generation, from which each annotator judged half, that is, 600 candidates per annotator, 200 for each generation.

From the 1,200 candidates, 15.6% were classified as true MWE. The results are shown in Table 1 in terms of precision, recall, F-measure and accuracy calculated regarding true positives (TP), false positives (FP), true negatives (TN) and false negatives (FN):

- Precision $= \frac{TP}{TP+FP}$
- Recall $= \frac{TP}{TP+FN}$
- F1 $= 2 \times \frac{P \times R}{P+R}$
- Accuracy $= \frac{TP+TN}{TP+FP+TN+FN}$

As we can notice from Table 1, the precision rises 10 percentage points from the first to the last iteration, indicating that NEMWEL is capable of improving its learning performance, as expected for a never-ending learning system. The decay in recall from 65.5% to 52.3% from the second to the third generation seems to be related to overfitting. Another possible explanation for this decay is that only the candidate MWEs annotated as true by both annotators were taking into account. Furthermore, since the dataset is unbalanced, the classifier

[10] Thus, in our experiments, three Promoters were generated: (1) Promoter-0, trained only with manually annotated data, run from iteration 1 to 5 (first generation); (2) Promoter-1, trained with manually annotated data and the true/false MWEs learned in the first generation, run from iteration 6 to 10; and (3) Promoter-2, trained with manually annotated data and the true/false MWEs learned in the first two generations, run from iteration 11 to 15.

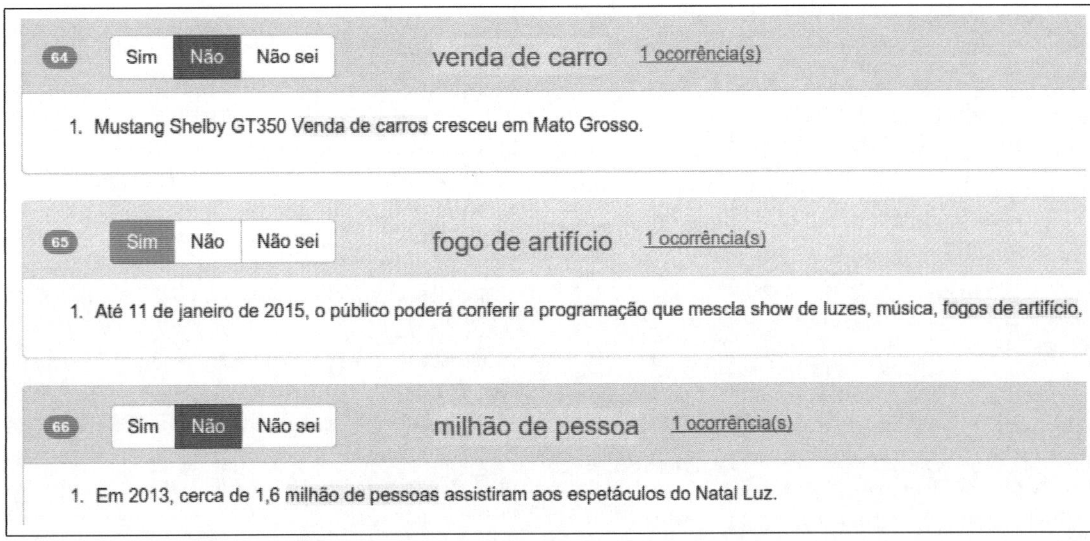

Figure 6: Interface for manual annotation of MWE candidates.

may tend to classify new candidates always as non MWEs. New experiments will be carried out to investigate this decay. Table 2 shows some examples of MWE candidates extracted by NEMWEL.

6 Conclusions

From the results presented in this paper, it is possible to conclude that the never-ending learning approach can be applied to the automatic extraction of MWEs. Although with just a few iterations (15), it was already possible to see that NEMWEL is able to improve its learning based on previously learned knowledge, with an increase of 10 percentage points in precision.

The next steps of this work include running NEMWEL for a long period, ideally 24 hours per day, continuously. It is also our intention to expand NEMWEL to be able to learn other MWEs, from other sources and for different languages, such as English, maybe following a multilingual extraction process. Finally, some new features can be added such as the one that tests the substitutability of a MWE candidate, i.e., the non-replacement of words that form the MWE candidate by synonyms. NEMWEL's source code and search interface will be available soon at: `http://www.lalic.dc.ufscar.br/never-ending/`.

MWE candidate	NEWMEL	Reference
horário comercial *business hours*	F	T
dona de casa *housewife*	F	T
dor de cabeça *headache*	F	T
fogo de artifício *firework*	T	T
empate técnico *technical draw*	T	T
terminal de ônibus *bus terminal*	T	T
estado do Rio *state of Rio*	F	F
ano passado *last year*	F	F
local de exame *test site*	F	F
redução de custo *cost reduction*	T	F
banco traseiro *rear seat*	T	F
processo de seleção *selection process*	T	F

Table 2: Examples of true MWE candidates extracted by NEMWEL, respectively: false negatives, true positives, true negatives and false positives.

Acknowledgments

We would like to thank São Paulo Research Foundation (FAPESP) for the grants #2013/11811-0 and #2013/50757-0 (AIM-WEST project). This work is also part of CAMELEON (CAPES-COFECUB #707/11) and RITA (CAPES #047/14) projects.

References

Vitor De Araujo, Carlos Ramisch, and Aline Villavicencio. 2011. Fast and flexible MWE candidate generation with the mwetoolkit. In Kordoni et al. (Kordoni et al., 2011), pages 134–136.

Mohammed Attia, Antonio Toral, Lamia Tounsi, Pavel Pecina, and Josef van Genabith. 2010. Automatic extraction of Arabic multiword expressions. In Éric Laporte, Preslav Nakov, Carlos Ramisch, and Aline Villavicencio, editors, *Proc. of the COLING Workshop on MWEs: from Theory to Applications (MWE 2010)*, pages 18–26, Beijing, China, Aug. ACL.

Timothy Baldwin and Su Nam Kim. 2010. Multiword expressions. In Nitin Indurkhya and Fred J. Damerau, editors, *Handbook of Natural Language Processing*, pages 267–292. CRC Press, Taylor and Francis Group, Boca Raton, FL, USA, 2 edition.

Marco Baroni, Silvia Bernardini, Adriano Ferraresi, and Eros Zanchetta. 2009. The wacky wide web: a collection of very large linguistically processed web-crawled corpora. *Lang. Res. & Eval.*, 43(3):209–226, Sep.

Andrew Carlson, Justin Betteridge, Bryan Kisiel, Burr Settles, Estevam R. Hruschka Jr., and Tom M. Mitchell. 2010. Toward an architecture for never-ending language learning. In *Proceedings of the Twenty-Fourth Conference on Artificial Intelligence (AAAI 2010)*.

Helena de Medeiros Caseli, Carlos Ramisch, Maria das Graças Volpe Nunes, and Aline Villavicencio. 2010. Alignment-based extraction of multiword expressions. *Lang. Res. & Eval. Special Issue on Multiword expression: hard going or plain sailing*, 44(1-2):59–77, Apr.

C. C. Chang and C. J. Lin. 2011. LIBSVM: A Library for Support Vector Machines. In *ACM Transactions on Intelligent Systems and Technology*.

Kenneth Church and Patrick Hanks. 1990. Word association norms mutual information, and lexicography. *Comp. Ling.*, 16(1):22–29.

J. Cohen. 1960. A coefficient of agreement for nominal scales. *Educational and Psychological Measurement*, 20(1):37–46.

Matthieu Constant and Anthony Sigogne. 2011. MWU-aware part-of-speech tagging with a CRF model and lexical resources. In Kordoni et al. (Kordoni et al., 2011), pages 49–56.

Jianyong Duan, Ruzhan Lu, Weilin Wu, Yi Hu, and Yan Tian. 2006. A bio-inspired approach for multi-word expression extraction. In James Curran, editor, *Proc. of the COLING/ACL 2006 Main Conference Poster Sessions*, pages 176–182, Sidney, Australia, Jul. ACL.

Marie Dubremetz and Joakim Nivre. 2014. Extraction of nominal multiword expressions in french. In *Proceedings of the 10th Workshop on Multiword Expressions (MWE)*, pages 72–76, Gothenburg, Sweden, April. Association for Computational Linguistics.

Stefan Evert and Brigitte Krenn. 2005. Using small random samples for the manual evaluation of statistical association measures. *Comp. Speech & Lang. Special issue on MWEs*, 19(4):450–466.

Meghdad Farahmand and Ronaldo Martins. 2014. A supervised model for extraction of multiword expressions, based on statistical context features. In *Proceedings of the 10th Workshop on Multiword Expressions (MWE)*, pages 10–16, Gothenburg, Sweden, April. Association for Computational Linguistics.

Nicole Grégoire, Stefan Evert, and Brigitte Krenn, editors. 2008. *Proc. of the LREC Workshop Towards a Shared Task for MWEs (MWE 2008)*, Marrakech, Morocco, Jun.

Mark Hall, Eibe Frank, Geoffrey Holmes, Bernhard Pfahringer, Peter Reutemann, and Ian H. Witten. 2009. The weka data mining software: An update. In *SIGKDD Explorations*, volume 11.

Ray Jackendoff. 1997a. *The Architecture of the Language Faculty*. Number 28 in Linguistic Inquiry Monographs. MIT Press, Cambridge, MA, USA. 262 p.

Ray Jackendoff. 1997b. Twistin' the night away. *Language*, 73:534–559.

John S. Justeson and Slava M. Katz. 1995. Technical terminology: some linguistic properties and an algorithm for identification in text. *Nat. Lang. Eng.*, 1(1):9–27.

Su Nam Kim and Preslav Nakov. 2011. Large-scale noun compound interpretation using bootstrapping and the web as a corpus. In Regina Barzilay and Mark Johnson, editors, *Proc. of the 2011 EMNLP (EMNLP 2011)*, pages 648–658, Edinburgh, Scotland, UK, Jul. ACL.

Valia Kordoni, Carlos Ramisch, and Aline Villavicencio, editors. 2011. *Proc. of the ACL Workshop on MWEs: from Parsing and Generation to the Real World (MWE 2011)*, Portland, OR, USA, Jun. ACL.

Mirella Lapata and Frank Keller. 2005. Web-based models for natural language processing. *ACM Trans. Speech and Lang. Process. (TSLP)*, 2(1):1–31.

D. Li, G. Savova, and K. Kipper-Schuler. 2008. Conditional random fields and support vector machines for disorder named entity recognition in clinical texts. In *Proceedings of the workshop on current trends in biomedical natural language processing*, pages 94–95, Columbus, Ohio.

T. Mitchell, W. Cohen, E. Hruschka, P. Talukdar, J. Betteridge, A. Carlson, B. Dalvi, M. Gardner, B. Kisiel, J. Krishnamurthy, N. Lao, K. Mazaitis, T. Mohamed, N. Nakashole, E. Platanios, A. Ritter, M. Samadi, B. Settles, R. Wang, D. Wijaya, A. Gupta, X. Chen, A. Saparov, M. Greaves, and J. Welling. 2015. Never-ending learning. In *Proceedings of the Twenty-Ninth AAAI Conference on Artificial Intelligence (AAAI-15)*.

T. Mullen and N. Collier. 2004. Sentiment analysis using support vector machines with diverse information sources. In *Proceedings of the Conference on Empirical Methods in Natural Language Processing (EMNLP)*, pages 412–418.

Darren Pearce. 2001. Synonymy in collocation extraction. In *WordNet and Other Lexical Resources: Applications, Extensions and Customizations (NAACL 2001 Workshop)*, pages 41–46, Jun.

Pavel Pecina. 2008. Reference data for Czech collocation extraction. In Grégoire et al. (Grégoire et al., 2008), pages 11–14.

Ted Pedersen, Satanjeev Banerjee, Bridget McInnes, Saiyam Kohli, Mahesh Joshi, and Ying Liu. 2011. The *n*-gram statistics package (text::NSP) : A flexible tool for identifying *n*-grams, collocations, and word associations. In Kordoni et al. (Kordoni et al., 2011), pages 131–133.

Carlos Ramisch, Paulo Schreiner, Marco Idiart, and Aline Villavicencio. 2008. An evaluation of methods for the extraction of multiword expressions. In Grégoire et al. (Grégoire et al., 2008), pages 50–53.

Carlos Ramisch. 2015. *Multiword Expressions Acquisition: A Generic and Open Framework*, volume XIV of *Theory and Applications of Natural Language Processing*. Springer.

Siva Reddy, Diana McCarthy, and Suresh Manandhar. 2011. An empirical study on compositionality in compound nouns. In *Proceedings of 5th International Joint Conference on Natural Language Processing*, pages 210–218, Chiang Mai, Thailand, November. Asian Federation of Natural Language Processing.

Ivan Sag, Timothy Baldwin, Francis Bond, Ann Copestake, and Dan Flickinger. 2002. Multiword expressions: A pain in the neck for NLP. In *Proc. of the 3rd CICLing (CICLing-2002)*, volume 2276/2010 of *LNCS*, pages 1–15, Mexico City, Mexico, Feb. Springer.

Bahar Salehi and Paul Cook. 2013. Predicting the compositionality of multiword expressions using translations in multiple languages. In *Second Joint Conference on Lexical and Computational Semantics (*SEM), Volume 1: Proceedings of the Main Conference and the Shared Task: Semantic Textual Similarity*, pages 266–275, Atlanta, Georgia, USA, June. Association for Computational Linguistics.

M. Sassano. 2003. Virtual Examples for Text Classification with Support Vector Machines. In *Proceedings of the Conference on Empirical Methods in Natural Language Processing (EMNLP)*, pages 208–215.

Helmut Schmid. 1994. Probabilistic part-of-speech tagging using decision trees. In *Proceedings of the International Conference on New Methods in Language Processing*, pages 44–49.

Nathan Schneider, Emily Danchik, Chris Dyer, and Noah A. Smith. 2014. Discriminative lexical semantic segmentation with gaps: running the MWE gamut. *Transactions of the Association for Computational Linguistics*, 2:193–206, Apr.

Violeta Seretan and Eric Wehrli. 2009. Multilingual collocation extraction with a syntactic parser. *Lang. Res. & Eval. Special Issue on Multilingual Language Resources and Interoperability*, 43(1):71–85, Mar.

Frank A. Smadja. 1993. Retrieving collocations from text: Xtract. *Comp. Ling.*, 19(1):143–177.

Yulia Tsvetkov and Shuly Wintner. 2010. Extraction of multi-word expressions from small parallel corpora. In Chu-Ren Huang and Dan Jurafsky, editors, *Proc. of the 23rd COLING (COLING 2010) — Posters*, pages 1256–1264, Beijing, China, Aug. The Coling 2010 Organizing Committee.

Leonardo Zilio, Luiz Svoboda, Luiz Henrique Longhi Rossi, and Rafael Martins Feitosa. 2011. Automatic extraction and evaluation of mwe. In *STIL 2011 - Cuiabá, MT, Brasil*.

The Impact of Multiword Expression Compositionality on Machine Translation Evaluation

Bahar Salehi,[♠♣] **Nitika Mathur,**[♠] **Paul Cook**[♡] **and Timothy Baldwin**[♠♣]
♣ NICTA Victoria Research Laboratory
♠ Department of Computing and Information Systems
The University of Melbourne
Victoria 3010, Australia

♡ Faculty of Computer Science
University of New Brunswick
Fredericton, NB E3B 5A3, Canada

{bsalehi,nmathur}@student.unimelb.edu.au, paul.cook@unb.ca, tb@ldwin.net

Abstract

In this paper, we present the first attempt to integrate predicted compositionality scores of multiword expressions into automatic machine translation evaluation, in integrating compositionality scores for English noun compounds into the TESLA machine translation evaluation metric. The attempt is marginally successful, and we speculate on whether a larger-scale attempt is likely to have greater impact.

1 Introduction

While the explicit identification of multiword expressions ("MWEs": Sag et al. (2002), Baldwin and Kim (2009)) has been shown to be useful in various NLP applications (Ramisch, 2012), recent work has shown that automatic prediction of the degree of compositionality of MWEs also has utility, in applications including information retrieval ("IR": Acosta et al. (2011)) and machine translation ("MT": Weller et al. (2014), Carpuat and Diab (2010) and Venkatapathy and Joshi (2006)). For instance, Acosta et al. (2011) showed that by considering non-compositional MWEs as a single unit, the effectiveness of document ranking in an IR system improves, and Carpuat and Diab (2010) showed that by adding compositionality scores to the Moses SMT system (Koehn et al., 2007), they could improve translation quality.

This paper presents the first attempt to use MWE compositionality scores for the *evaluation* of MT system outputs. The basic intuition underlying this work is that we should sensitise the relative reward associated with partial mismatches between MT outputs and the reference translations, based on compositionality. For example, an MT output of *white tower* should not be rewarded for partial overlap with *ivory tower* in the reference translation, as *tower* here is most naturally interpreted compositionally in the MT output, but non-compositionally in the reference translation. On the other hand, a partial mismatch between *traffic signal* and *traffic light* should be rewarded, as the usage of *traffic* is highly compositional in both cases. That is, we ask the question: can we better judge the quality of translations if we have some means of automatically estimating the relative compositionality of MWEs, focusing on compound nouns, and the TESLA machine translation metric (Liu et al., 2010).

2 Related Work

In this section, we overview previous work on MT evaluation and measuring the compositionality of MWEs.

2.1 Machine Translation Evaluation

Automatic MT evaluation methods score MT system outputs based on similarity with reference translations provided by human translators. This scoring can be based on: (1) simple string similarity (Papineni et al., 2002; Snover et al., 2006); (2) shallow linguistic information such as lemmatisation, POS tagging and synonyms (Banerjee and Lavie, 2005; Liu et al., 2010); or (3) deeper linguistic information such as semantic roles (Giménez and Màrquez, 2008; Padó et al., 2009).

In this research, we focus on the TESLA MT eval-

Proceedings of NAACL-HLT 2015, pages 54–59,
Denver, Colorado, May 31 – June 5, 2015.

uation metric (Liu et al., 2010), which falls into the second group and uses a linear programming framework to automatically learn weights for matching n-grams of different types, making it easy to incorporate continuous-valued compositionality scores of MWEs.

2.2 Compositionality of MWEs

Earlier work on MWE compositionality (Bannard, 2006) approached the task via binary classification (compositional or non-compositional). However, there has recently been a shift towards regression analysis of the task, and prediction of a continuous-valued compositionality score (Reddy et al., 2011; Salehi and Cook, 2013; Salehi et al., 2014). This is the (primary) approach we take in this paper, as outlined in Section 3.2.

3 Methodology

3.1 Using compositionality scores in TESLA

In this section, we introduce TESLA and our method for integrating compositionality scores into the method.

Firstly, TESLA measures the similarity between the unigrams of the two given sentences (MT output and reference translation) based on the following three terms for each pairing of unigrams x and y:

$$\begin{aligned} S_{ms} &= \begin{cases} 1 & \text{if } lemma(x) = lemma(y) \\ \frac{a+b}{2} & \text{otherwise} \end{cases} \\ S_{lem}(x,y) &= I(lemma(x) = lemma(y)) \\ S_{pos}(x,y) &= I(POS(x) = POS(y)) \end{aligned}$$

where:

$$\begin{aligned} a &= I(synset(x) \cap synset(y)) \\ b &= I(POS(x) = POS(y)) \end{aligned}$$

$lemma$ returns the lemmatised unigram, POS returns the POS tag of the unigram, $synset$ returns the WordNet synsets associated with the unigram, and $I(.)$ is the indicator function.

The similarity between two n-grams $x = x^{1,2,\ldots,n}$ and $y = y^{1,2,\ldots,n}$ is measured as follows:

$$s(x,y) = \begin{cases} 0 & \text{if } \exists i, s(x^i, y^i) = 0 \\ \frac{1}{n}\sum_{i=1}^{n} s(x^i, y^i)) & \text{otherwise} \end{cases}$$

TESLA uses an integer linear program to find the phrase alignment that maximizes the similarity scores over the three terms (S_{ms}, S_{lem} and S_{pos}) for all n-grams.

In order to add the compositionality score to TESLA, we first identify MWEs in the MT output and reference translation. If an MWE in the reference translation aligns exactly with an MWE in the MT output, the weight remains as 1. Otherwise, we replace the computed weight computed for the noun compound with the product of computed weight and the compositionality degree of the MWE. This forces the system to be less flexible when encountering less compositional noun compounds. For instance, in TESLA, if the reference sentence contains *ivory tower* and the MT output contains *white building*, TESLA will align them with a score of 1. However, by multiplying this weight with the compositionality score (which should be very low for *ivory tower*), the alignment will have a much lower weight.

3.2 Predicting the compositionality of MWEs

In order to predict the compositionality of MWEs, we calculate the similarity between the MWE and each of its component words, using the three approaches detailed below. We calculate the overall compositionality of the MWE via linear interpolation over the component word scores, as:

$$\begin{aligned} comp(mwe) &= \alpha comp_c(mwe, w_1) + \\ &\quad (1-\alpha) comp_c(mwe, w_2) \end{aligned}$$

where mwe is, without loss of generality, made up of component words w_1 and w_2, and $comp_c$ is the compositionality score between mwe and the indicated component word. Based on the findings of Reddy et al. (2011), we set $\alpha = 0.7$.

Distributional Similarity (DS): the distributional similarity between the MWE and each of its components (Salehi et al., 2014), calculated based on cosine similarity over co-occurrence vectors, in the manner of Schütze (1997), using the 51st–1050th most frequent words in the corpus as dimensions. Context vectors were constructed from English Wikipedia.

	All sentences	Contains NC
METEOR	0.277	0.273
BLEU	0.216	0.206
TESLA	0.238	0.224
TESLA-DS	0.238	0.225
TESLA-SS+DS	0.238	0.225
TESLA-0/1	0.238	0.225

Table 1: Kendall's (τ) correlation over WMT 2013 (all-en), for the full dataset and also the subset of the data containing a noun compound in both the reference and the MT output

	All sentences	Contains NC
METEOR	0.436	0.500
BLEU	0.272	0.494
TESLA	0.303	0.467
TESLA-DS	0.305	0.464
TESLA-SS+DS	0.305	0.464
TESLA-0/1	0.308	0.464

Table 2: Pearson's (r) correlation results over the WMT all-en dataset, and the subset of the dataset that contains noun compounds

SS+DS: the arithmetic mean of DS and string similarity ("SS"), based on the findings of Salehi et al. (2014). SS is calculated for each component using the LCS-based string similarity between the MWE and each of its components in the original language as well as a number of translations (Salehi and Cook, 2013), under the hypothesis that compositional MWEs are more likely to be word-for-word translations in a given language than non-compositional MWEs. Following Salehi and Cook (2013), the translations were sourced from PanLex (Baldwin et al., 2010; Kamholz et al., 2014).

In Salehi and Cook (2013), the best translation languages are selected based on the training data. Since, we focus on NCs in this paper, we use the translation languages reported in that paper to work best for English noun compounds, namely: Czech, Norwegian, Portuguese, Thai, French, Chinese, Dutch, Romanian, Hindi and Russian.

4 Dataset

We evaluate our method over the data from WMT 2013, which is made up of a total of 3000 translations for five to-English language pairs (Bojar et al., 2013). As our judgements, we used: (1) the original pairwise preference judgements from WMT 2013 (i.e. which of translation A and B is better?); and (2) continuous-valued adequacy judgements for each MT output, as collected by Graham et al. (2014).

We used the Stanford CoreNLP parser (Klein and Manning, 2003) to identify English noun compounds in the translations. Among the 3000 sentences, 579 sentences contain at least one noun compound.

5 Results

We performed two evaluations, based on the two sets of judgements (pairwise preference or continuous-valued judgement for each MT output). In each case, we use three baselines (each applied at the segment level, meaning that individual sentences get a score): (1) METEOR (Banerjee and Lavie, 2005), (2) BLEU (Papineni et al., 2002), and (3) TESLA (without compositionality scores). We compare these with TESLA incorporating compositionality scores, based on DS ("TESLA-DS") and SS+DS ("TESLA-SS+DS"). We also include results for an exact match method which treats the MWEs as a single token, such that unless the MWE is translated exactly the same as in the reference translation, a score of zero results ("TESLA-0/1"). We did not experiment with the string similarity approach alone, because of the high number of missing translations in PanLex.

In the first experiment, we calculate the segment level Kendall's τ following the method used in the WMT 2013 shared task, as shown in Table 1, including the results over the subset of the data which contains a compound noun in both the reference and the MT output ("contains NC"). When comparing TESLA with and without MWE compositionality, we observe a tiny improvement with the inclusion of the compositionality scores (magnified slightly over the NC subset of the data), but not great enough to boost the score to that of METEOR. We also observe slightly lower correlations for TESLA-0/1 than TESLA-DS and TESLA-SS+DS, which consider degrees of compositionality, for fr-en, de-en and es-en (results not shown).

In the second experiment, we calculate Pearson's r correlation over the continuous-valued adequacy

Language Pair	*comp*	P→N	N→P	Δ
fr-en	DS	17	18	1
	SS+DS	14	16	2
	0/1	30	29	−1
de-en	DS	21	24	3
	SS+DS	14	18	4
	0/1	48	40	−8
es-en	DS	12	18	6
	SS+DS	11	17	6
	0/1	20	25	5
cs-en	DS	21	23	2
	SS+DS	14	16	2
	0/1	46	49	3
ru-en	DS	38	51	13
	SS+DS	29	39	10
	0/1	65	80	15

Table 3: The number of judgements that were ranked correctly by TESLA originally, but incorrectly with the incorporation of compositionality scores ("P→N") and vice versa ("N→P"), and the absolute improvement with compositionality scores ("Δ")

judgements, as shown in Table 2, again over the full dataset and also the subset of data containing compound nouns. The improvement here is slightly greater than for our first experiment, but not at a level of statistical significance (Graham and Baldwin, 2014). Perhaps surprisingly, the exact compositionality predictions produce a higher correlation than the continuous-valued compositionality predictions, but again, even with the inclusion of the compositionality features, TESLA is outperformed by METEOR. The correlation over the subset of the data containing compound nouns is markedly higher than that over the full dataset, but the r values with the inclusion of compositionality values are actually all slightly below those for the basic TESLA.

As a final analysis, we examine the relative impact on TESLA of the three compositionality methods, in terms of pairings of MT outputs where the ordering is reversed based on the revised TESLA scores. Table 3 details, for each language pairing, the number of pairwise judgements that were ranked correctly originally, but incorrectly when the compositionality score was incorporated ("P→N"); and also the number of pairwise judgements that were ranked incorrectly originally, and corrected with the incorporation of the compositionality judgements ("N→P").

Overall, the two compositionality methods perform better than the exact match method, and utilising compositionality has a more positive effect than negative. However, the difference between the numbers is, once again, very small, except for the ru-en language pair. The exact match method ("0/1") has a bigger impact, both positively and negatively, as a result of the polarisation of n-gram overlap scores for MWEs. We also noticed that the N→P sentences for SS+DS are a subset of the N→P sentences for DS. Moerover, the N→P sentences for DS are a subset of the N→P sentences for $0/1$; the same is true for the P→N sentences.

6 Discussion

As shown in the previous section, the incorporation of compositionality scores can improve the quality of MT evaluation based on TESLA. However, the improvements are very small and not statistically significant. Part of the reason is that we focus exclusively on noun compounds, which are contiguous and relatively easy to translate for MT systems (Koehn and Knight, 2003). Having said that, preliminary error analysis would suggest that most MT systems have difficulty translating non-compositional noun compounds, although then again, most noun compounds in the WMT 2013 shared task are highly compositional, limiting the impact of compositionality scores. We speculate that, for the method to have greater impact, we would need to target a larger set of MWEs, including non-contiguous MWEs such as split verb particle constructions (Kim and Baldwin, 2010).

Further error analysis suggests that incorrect identification of noun compounds in a reference sentence can have a negative impact on MT evaluation. For example, *year student* is mistakenly identified as an MWE in ... *a 21-year-old final year student at Temple ....*

Furthermore, when an MWE occurs in a reference translation, but not an MT system's output, incorporating the compositionality score can sometimes result in an error. For instance, in the first example in Table 4, the reference translation contains the compound noun *cash flow*. According to the dataset, the output of MT system 1 is better than that of MT sys-

Reference	This means they are much better for our cash flow.
MT system 1	That is why they are for our money flow of a much better.
MT system 2	Therefore, for our cash flow much better.
Reference	'I felt like I was in a luxury store,' he recalls.
MT system 1	'I feel as though I am in a luxury trade,' recalls soldier.
MT system 2	'I felt like a luxury in the store,' he recalled the soldier.

Table 4: Two examples from the all-en dataset. Each example shows a reference translation, and the outputs of two machine translation systems. In each case, the output of MT system 1 is annotated as the better translation.

tem 2. However, since the former translation does not contain an exact match for *cash flow*, our method decreases the alignment score by multiplying it by the compositionality score for *cash flow*. As a result, the overall score for the first translation becomes less than that of the second, and our method incorrectly chooses the latter as a better translation.

Incorrect estimation of compositionality scores can also have a negative effect on MT evaluation. In the second example in Table 4, the similarity score between *luxury store* and *luxury trade* given by TESLA is 0.75. The compositionality score, however, is estimated as 0.22. The updated similarity between *luxury trade* and *luxury store* is therefore 0.16, which in this case results in our method incorrectly selecting the second sentence as the better translation.

7 Conclusion

This paper described the first attempt at integrating MWE compositionality scores into an automatic MT evaluation metric. Our results show a marginal improvement with the incorporation of compositionality scores of noun compounds.

Acknowledgements

We thank the anonymous reviewers for their insightful comments and valuable suggestions. NICTA is funded by the Australian government as represented by Department of Broadband, Communication and Digital Economy, and the Australian Research Council through the ICT Centre of Excellence programme.

References

Otavio Acosta, Aline Villavicencio, and Viviane Moreira. 2011. Identification and treatment of multiword expressions applied to information retrieval. In *Proceedings of the Workshop on Multiword Expressions: from Parsing and Generation to the Real World*, pages 101–109, Portland, USA.

Timothy Baldwin and Su Nam Kim. 2009. Multiword expressions. In Nitin Indurkhya and Fred J. Damerau, editors, *Handbook of Natural Language Processing*. CRC Press, Boca Raton, USA, 2nd edition.

Timothy Baldwin, Jonathan Pool, and Susan M. Colowick. 2010. PanLex and LEXTRACT: Translating all words of all languages of the world. In *Proceedings of the 23rd International Conference on Computational Linguistics: Demonstrations*, pages 37–40, Beijing, China.

Satanjeev Banerjee and Alon Lavie. 2005. METEOR: An automatic metric for MT evaluation with improved correlation with human judgments. In *Proceedings of the acl workshop on intrinsic and extrinsic evaluation measures for machine translation and/or summarization*, pages 65–72.

Colin James Bannard. 2006. *Acquiring Phrasal Lexicons from Corpora*. Ph.D. thesis, University of Edinburgh.

Ondřej Bojar, Christian Buck, Chris Callison-Burch, Christian Federmann, Barry Haddow, Philipp Koehn, Christof Monz, Matt Post, Radu Soricut, and Lucia Specia. 2013. Findings of the 2013 Workshop on Statistical Machine Translation. In *Proceedings of the Eighth Workshop on Statistical Machine Translation*, pages 1–44, Sofia, Bulgaria.

Marine Carpuat and Mona Diab. 2010. Task-based evaluation of multiword expressions: a pilot study in statistical machine translation. In *Human Language Technologies: The 2010 Annual Conference of the North American Chapter of the Association for Computational Linguistics*, pages 242–245, Los Angeles, USA.

Jesús Giménez and Lluís Màrquez. 2008. A smorgasbord of features for automatic MT evaluation. In *Proceedings of the Third Workshop on Statistical Machine Translation*, pages 195–198.

Yvette Graham and Timothy Baldwin. 2014. Testing for significance of increased correlation with human judgment. In *Proceedings of the 2014 Conference on*

Empirical Methods in Natural Language Processing (EMNLP 2014), pages 172–176, Doha, Qatar.

Yvette Graham, Timothy Baldwin, Alistair Moffat, and Justin Zobel. 2014. Is machine translation getting better over time? In *Proceedings of the 14th Conference of the EACL (EACL 2014)*, pages 443–451, Gothenburg, Sweden.

David Kamholz, Jonathan Pool, and Susan Colowick. 2014. PanLex: Building a resource for panlingual lexical translation. In *Proceedings of the Ninth International Conference on Language Resources and Evaluation (LREC'14)*, pages 3145–3150, Reykjavik, Iceland.

Su Nam Kim and Timothy Baldwin. 2010. How to pick out token instances of English verb-particle constructions. *Language Resources and Evaluation*, 44(1-2):97–113.

Dan Klein and Christopher D. Manning. 2003. Fast exact inference with a factored model for natural language parsing. In *Advances in Neural Information Processing Systems 15 (NIPS 2002)*, pages 3–10, Whistler, Canada.

Philipp Koehn and Kevin Knight. 2003. Feature-rich statistical translation of noun phrases. In *Proceedings of the 41st Annual Meeting of the Association for Computational Linguistics (ACL 2003)*, Sapporo, Japan.

Philipp Koehn, Hieu Hoang, Alexandra Birch, Chris Callison-Burch, Marcello Federico, Nicola Bertoldi, Brooke Cowan, Wade Shen, Christine Moran, Richard Zens, Chris Dyer, Ondrej Bojar, Alexandra Constantin, and Evan Herbst. 2007. Moses: Open source toolkit for statistical machine translation. In *Proceedings of the 45th Annual Meeting of the Association for Computational Linguistics Companion Volume Proceedings of the Demo and Poster Sessions*, pages 177–180, Prague, Czech Republic.

Chang Liu, Daniel Dahlmeier, and Hwee Tou Ng. 2010. Tesla: Translation evaluation of sentences with linear-programming-based analysis. In *Proceedings of the Joint Fifth Workshop on Statistical Machine Translation and Metrics (MATR)*, pages 354–359.

Sebastian Padó, Michel Galley, Dan Jurafsky, and Chris Manning. 2009. Robust machine translation evaluation with entailment features. In *Proceedings of the Joint Conference of the 47th Annual Meeting of the ACL and the 4th International Joint Conference on Natural Language Processing of the AFNLP: Volume 1-Volume 1*, pages 297–305.

Kishore Papineni, Salim Roukos, Todd Ward, and Wei-Jing Zhu. 2002. BLEU: a method for automatic evaluation of machine translation. In *Proceedings of the 40th Annual Meeting of the Association for Computational Linguistics (ACL 2002)*, pages 311–318.

Carlos Ramisch. 2012. A generic framework for multiword expressions treatment: from acquisition to applications. In *Proceedings of ACL 2012 Student Research Workshop*, pages 61–66, Jeju Island, Korea.

Siva Reddy, Diana McCarthy, and Suresh Manandhar. 2011. An empirical study on compositionality in compound nouns. In *Proceedings of IJCNLP*, pages 210–218, Chiang Mai, Thailand.

Ivan Sag, Timothy Baldwin, Francis Bond, Ann Copestake, and Dan Flickinger. 2002. Multiword expressions: A pain in the neck for NLP. In *Proceedings of the 3rd International Conference on Intelligent Text Processing Computational Linguistics (CICLing-2002)*, pages 189–206, Mexico City, Mexico.

Bahar Salehi and Paul Cook. 2013. Predicting the compositionality of multiword expressions using translations in multiple languages. In *Second Joint Conference on Lexical and Computational Semantics (*SEM), Volume 1: Proceedings of the Main Conference and the Shared Task: Semantic Textual Similarity*, pages 266–275, Atlanta, Georgia, USA, June.

Bahar Salehi, Paul Cook, and Timothy Baldwin. 2014. Using distributional similarity of multi-way translations to predict multiword expression compositionality. In *Proceedings of the 14th Conference of the European Chapter of the Association for Computational Linguistics*, pages 472–481, Gothenburg, Sweden, April.

Hinrich Schütze. 1997. *Ambiguity Resolution in Language Learning*. CSLI Publications, Stanford, USA.

Matthew Snover, Bonnie Dorr, Richard Schwartz, Linnea Micciulla, and John Makhoul. 2006. A study of translation edit rate with targeted human annotation. In *Proceedings of Association for Machine Translation in the Americas*, pages 223–231.

Sriram Venkatapathy and Aravind K Joshi. 2006. Using information about multi-word expressions for the word-alignment task. In *Proceedings of the Workshop on Multiword Expressions: Identifying and Exploiting Underlying Properties*, pages 20–27.

Marion Weller, Fabienne Cap, Stefan Müller, Sabine Schulte im Walde, and Alexander Fraser. 2014. Distinguishing degrees of compositionality in compound splitting for statistical machine translation. In *Proceedings of the First Workshop on Computational Approaches to Compound Analysis (ComAComA 2014)*, pages 81–90, Dublin, Ireland.

The Bare Necessities: Increasing Lexical Coverage for Multi-Word Domain Terms with Less Lexical Data

Branimir Boguraev, Esme Manandise, Benjamin Segal
IBM Thomas J. Watson Research Center
1101 Kitchawan Road, Yorktown Heights, NY 10598, USA.
{bran, esme, bpsegal}@us.ibm.com

Abstract

We argue that many multi-word domain terms are not (and should not be regarded as) strictly atomic, especially from a parser's point of view. We introduce the notion of Lexical Kernel Units (LKUs), and discuss some of their essential properties. LKUs are building blocks for lexicalizations of domain concepts, and as such, can be used for compositional derivation of an open-ended set of domain terms. Benefits from such an approach include reduction in size of the domain lexicon, improved coverage for domain terms, and improved accuracy for parsing.

1 Introduction

Knowledge about collocations and multi-word expressions (MWEs) can be beneficial for parsing, ultimately improving a parser's accuracy (Nivre and Nilsson, 2004; Korkontzelos and Manandhar, 2010; Wehrli, 2014). Typically such knowledge is made present by treating collocations and MWEs as single lexical and syntactic units (Baldwin and Kim, 2010; Escartín et al., 2013; Fotopoulou et al., 2014). This practice is also reflected in domain adaptation, where domain-specific lexicons hold collocations and MWEs with 'domain terms' status.

In the medical domain, terminological and lexical resources list collocations and MWEs as varied as *history of trauma to toes of both feet* and *morning after pill* as single "words with spaces" (Sag et al., 2002). As mandated by the lexicon-parser interface, such domain terms parse as single lexical units, which improves parser performance by reducing the lexical, structural, and distributional complexity of these noun phrases. This simplification is intuitively appealing. However, when closely-related, or similar, multi-word domain terms such as *day after pill* or *history of trauma to toes of left foot* are unlisted in the terminology lexica, the potential for parse error resurfaces. Relying on explicitly listed terms alone compromises parser accuracy.

We present here an approach to lexicon enrichment, which mitigates the inherent incompleteness of such lists, inevitably arising during processes of populating domain term banks. In our work on extracting domain-specific terms from a medical terminology resource,[1] we observe certain compositional properties of a large subset of such domain-specific terms.[2] In particular, this subset is open-ended: through generative patterns, even if some such domain terms are not in the lexicon, a mechanism can be construed which can license them as terms (virtual entries in the lexicon). These patterns operate on smaller expressions, which exhibit a much more atomic status than the terms proper, and enable—through compositionality—the dynamic generation and interpretation of the longer domain terms. Such smaller expressions we call *lex-*

[1] Proper domain multi-word terms are derived from the Unified Medical Language System (UMLS) (NIH, 2009) knowledge bases (KBs), which contain medical concepts, relations, and definitions, spread over millions of concepts and terms from over 160 source vocabularies. Not all entries in UMLS qualify for 'term' status; term extraction proper is, however, outside of the scope of this paper. The UMLS-derived terminology lexicon—close to 56 million tokens comprising over 8 million terms—is the source data of our analysis.

[2] We focus on noun phrases of varying structural complexity.

Proceedings of NAACL-HLT 2015, pages 60–64,
Denver, Colorado, May 31 – June 5, 2015.

ical kernel units (LKUs).

For example, in the set of medical domain terms *history of spastic paraplegia, spastic paraplegia with retinal degeneration*, and *family history of spastic paraplegia with Kallmann's syndrome*, we see repeated patterns of behavior of the same multi-word expression, *spastic paraplegia*: it can be governed by *history of*; it co-occurs with the preposition *with*; an instance of *history of* is pre-modified by the noun *family*.

Spastic paraplegia is a lexical kernel unit. Regarding it as a 'kernel' for an open-ended set of expressions like the ones above—and deploying appropriate generative patterns and devices—we argue that a newly-encountered word grouping like *family spastic paraplegia with neuropathy* can be licensed as a domain-specific term, available to a parser, even if the term is a virtual one, absent from the static domain-dependent terminology lexicon.

This paper discusses the nature and some practical consequences of LKUs. Given that ours is very much work in progress, the intent is to hint at an algorithmic procedure for the identification and extraction of LKUs from an externally provided terminology lexicon. Additionally, the paper aims to show the ability afforded by LKUs to transform a finite, static, lexicon of domain collocations and multi-word expressions to an open-ended, dynamic (or virtual) lexicon which can better support parsing. While not in a position to present a formal evaluation of the benefit of an LKU lexicon, we offer examples of how such a lexicon benefits a parser.

2 Mining LKUs from terminology lexica

The essence of what makes lexical kernel units atomic can be illustrated by an analysis of sample subsets[3] of domain terms from which LKU status for certain word sequences can be inferred.

Consider the subset of term entries containing (not necessarily consecutively) the words in the multi-word expression *spastic paraplegia*:

a. *spastic paraplegia syndrome,*
b. *spastic congenital paraplegia,*
c. *infantile spastic paraplegia,*
d. *familial spastic paraplegia with Kallmann's syndrome,*
e. *familial spastic paraplegia with neuropathy and poikiloderma,*
f. *familial spastic paraplegia, mental retardation, and precocious puberty,*
g. *slowly progressive spastic paraplegia,*
h. *hereditary x linked recessive spastic paraplegia,*
i. *onset in first year of life of spastic paraplegia.*

Spastic and *paraplegia* appear in domain terms of varying length and with different noun phrase structures; additionally, the two words may or may not be adjacent. In the entries d.–f., *spastic paraplegia* shares the adjective *familial* on its left; but it can also co-occur with other adjectives as pre-modifiers, *infantile, hereditary,* and *progressive* among them (b.–c. and g.–h.) Further, the phrases to the right of *spastic paraplegia* in entries d.–f. are of different phrase types. For instance, in entries d.–e., *spastic paraplegia,* is immediately adjacent to the preposition *with.*

Looking at the examples together, it is intuitively clear that variability around (an LKU) phrase exists across all the elements of the term subset; furthermore, this variability can be captured by a relatively small number of patterns.

To reinforce the confidence with which *spastic paraplegia* can be putatively assigned lexical kernel unit status, these patterns can be put to the test by a broader search, against the terminology lexicon. A pattern like `[LKU [with NP]]` (see Section 3) inspired by the domain entries d. and e., can be tested with the query string *spastic paraplegia with.*

Such search returns, among many, the domain terms *spastic paraplegia with amyotrophy of distal muscle wasting, spastic paraplegia with mental handicap, spastic paraplegia with mental retardation,* and *spastic paraplegia with amyotrophy of hands and feet* (although the terminology lexicon does not list either *spastic paraplegia with amyotrophy of hands* or *spastic paraplegia with amyotrophy of feet* as domain terms).

As another example, of an LKU with different profile and distributional properties, consider the *[noun]-of* collocation instantiated by *history of.* In the terminology lexicon, there are 7,087 domain terms with the anchor *history of.* A few are:

a. *current social history of patient,*
b. *current history of allergies,*

[3] We will not discuss here the process of deriving such subsets from the terminology lexicon.

c. *family history of alcohol abuse,*
d. *history of current illness,*
e. *history of domestic violence at home,*
f. *history of falling into a swimming pool,*
g. *history of freckles,*
h. *past medical history of drug abuse,*
i. *personal history of alcohol abuse,*
j. *past personal history of allergy to other anti-infective agents.*

A cursory analysis of the semantic and syntactic composition of the above domain terms reveals that they are unexceptional (even though statistically salient in the domain). Looking at all examples together, an important question to consider is whether the variability in the terms is expressed by the contexts around *history of* or around *history* alone. A search keyed off the word *history* and based on a pattern with prepositional placeholder `[history [prep]]` returns, among many, the domain terms *history in family of hypertension, medical history relating to child,* and *current history with assessment of changing moles.* Clearly, in addition to *of, history* sanctions prepositional collocations *in, relating to,* and *with.* This is supporting evidence that LKU status can be attributed to *history*; it is also indicative of the kind of lexical (collocational) knowledge that needs to be associated with the LKU entry for *history*.

3 Capturing the essence of domain terms

The examples above suggest that *spastic paraplegia* and *history* function as building blocks from which an open-ended set of larger domain terms can be compositionally built, and interpreted. The many multi-word domain terms found in the terminology lexicon that contain *spastic paraplegia* and *history* can be informally represented with the following patterns:

a. `[[adjective* and/or noun*]`
`spastic paraplegia [with [noun]]]`
b. `[[adjective* and/or noun*] history`
`[[in | of | with] [noun]]]`

These capture the essence of multi-word expressions and collocations that can have many domain term instantiations—including ones beyond the closed sets which prompted the patterns (Section 2). The free slots, `noun` and `adjective`, must be filled by collocations with the appropriate part of speech, some of which can be LKUs themselves.

The many variations—potentially an open-ended set—of domain terms are thus collapsed into a single pattern, anchored by a putative LKU, and augmented with linguistic and usage information (part-of-speech, semantic types, collocation preferences, etc...) extracted from the terminology lexicon.

It may be tempting to collapse the patterns, and seek generalizations covering sets of LKUs: replacing the kernel units *spastic paraplegia* and *history* with a place-holder would have pattern a. to be subsumed by pattern b. This would be counter-productive, however: it would allow for over-generation, as well as fail to distinguish between frame-specific lexical knowledge to be associated with the individual LKUs (e.g. we would not want *spastic paraplegia* to allow for the full set of prepositional complements compatible with *history*).

The lexical knowledge discovered during this LKU extraction and captured in the domain terms patterns eventually ends up in LKU entries. For instance, from the patterns above, the preposition collocations would induce appropriately specified lexical frames. These would allow for uniform treatment, by a parser, of similar noun phrases—even if some of them lack 'domain term' status: e.g. both *spastic paraplegia with retinal degeneration* (a term, and therefore a single syntactic unit) and *spastic paraplegia with no retinal degeneration* (not designated a term, but inferred as such), would keep the *with-* PP attached to *spastic paraplegia*.

4 Some characteristics of LKUs

Lexical kernel units can be single- or multi-word sequences, as exemplified by the earlier analyses of *spastic paraplegia* and *history*. The degree to which LKUs by themselves are representative of a domain varies. However, what is more important is that through composition, they combine with other words or LKUs to construct larger, domain-specific, terms (consider, for example, *history of spastic paraplegia*). It is through analysis of such terms that an LKU lexicon is compiled.

Multi-word LKUs tend to be invariable and function as domain-specific, atomic, language units. A large subset of such LKUs have some of the linguistic features of MWEs. Two characteristics are particularly descriptive.

First, LKUs can display various degrees of semantic and syntactic opaqueness (e.g. *popcorn lung* or *airway morbidity*), as well as transparency (*small intestine* or *airway passage*).

Second, substitutability of a word within the LKU word sequence by another of the same or similar category may be barred. *Popcorn lung* and *popcorn disease symptom* cannot be substituted by **maize lung* or **edible corn disease symptom.*

As atomic units at the kernel of larger, compositionally built domain terms, it is much more revealing to look at what determines the exocentric pull (or valency) of LKUs, than analyzing their internal structure. LKUs determine the range and type of the larger phrases that can be construed around them.

While they serve as atoms for the creation of novel, longer domain expressions which can reflect a more general property of grammar as in *popcorn lung disease symptom* and *airway morbidity disorder*, the pool of words which LKUs can use to create longer domain units can be small and is highly domain-specific. Many collocations and novel creations are constrained by the semantics of the domain. In the medical and clinical domains, we do not see **popcorn lung morbidity, *popcorn lung rehabilitation,* or **popcorn lung remission.*

Finally, they need not operate in text as standalone words. For instance, the LKU *Silver Russell* does not function in domain texts as an individual noun compound. *Silver Russell* only functions as an LKU in longer domain terms as in *Silver Russell dwarfism* or *Silver Russell syndrome.*

5 Parsing with LKUs

The LKU notion allows for the creation of a domain-specific lexicon with a minimal number of entries that describe the nature of a given domain. As we saw in Section 2, there are thousands of domain terms anchored by collocations of the LKU *history* with prepositions *of, in,* or *with,* with variations both to the left (*family history of ..., medical history of ...,* and so forth) and right (*history of panic disorder ..., history of falling into ..., history of drug and alcohol abuse ...,* and so forth) of the anchor. Even so, it is unrealistic to expect that *all* instances of similar terms can be discovered for capture in a terminology lexicon. We also saw, however, that very simple patterns can be very expressive. Leveraging the contextual information captured in, for instance, pattern (b.; Section 3), as part of the lexical representation of the LKU entry for *history*, makes such discovery unnecessary, even for terms as complex in structure as the examples above.

When a lexical kernel unit becomes a part of the domain-dependent lexicon, none of the terms which were analyzed to derive it needs to be listed in that lexicon. Thus the 7,087 domain terms anchored by *history+of* (Section 2) can be replaced by a single, one-token, LKU entry (*history*) in the domain lexicon. This same entry would also account for the extra domain terms anchored by *history+in* and *history+with.*

While not in any way a formal evaluation, a preliminary, small scale experiment to determine impact of LKUs on parser[4] performance shows improvements, in particular in the area of coordination (itself a long-standing challenge to parsing). We created two domain lexicons (DLs): DL1 included all well-formed terms from the terminology lexicon with the words *history* and *spastic paraplegia,*; DL2 listed *history* and *spastic paraplegia* as LKU entries, while it eliminated the 7,000+ domain terms from the lexicon. Randomly extracted segments from medical corpus were parsed, in alternative regimes,[5] with DL1, and then with DL2.

Consider the segment *Bupropion has two absolute clinical contraindications (i.e., current or past history of seizures).* DL1 contains an entry for *past history of seizures* (but not one for *current history of seizures*). The parse derived with DL1 is wrong: *current* gets a 'noun' analysis, coordinated with the noun phrase *past history of seizures.* The correct analysis—a coordinated node joining *current* and *past*, and pre-modifying *history*—is achieved, however, with DL2, whose atomic *history* LKU allows a granular structured interpretation of what DL1 declares to be a single multi-word unit.

Another example illustrates the benefits of capturing the word-specific collocations within the repre-

[4]We use the English Slot Grammar (ESG) parser (McCord, 1990; McCord et al., 2012).

[5]We skip over how the parser interprets LKU entries, dynamically creating virtual domain terms anchored by the LKUs.

sentation of an LKU. In the DL1 parse of segment *Familial hereditary spastic paraplegias (paralyses) are a group of single-gene disorders*, the adjective *familial* pre-modifies both the noun *hereditary spastic paraplegia* (listed as a term in DL1) and the material in parentheses.[6] With the LKU-enabled DL2, ESG is instructed by the lexical information associated with the LKU *spastic paraplegia* (pattern (a.); Section 3) to treat both *familial* and *hereditary* as sister pre-modifiers to *spastic paraplegia* in particular.

6 Conclusion

Lexical kernel units give an embodiment to an intuition concerning the compositional aspects of domain terms in a conventional terminology lexicon. To the best of our knowledge, no attempts have been made to question the 'term entries are atomic' assumption.

We propose a view where lexical kernel units provide a more uniform partitioning of a terminology lexicon, teasing out its prominent lexical collocations. Once captured into an LKU lexicon, lexical kernel units allow for a granular view into that domain; this, in itself, is beneficial to a parser. Also, by virtue of being relevant to domain concepts, they allow for a degree of open-endedness of such a lexicon: in effect, they underpin a compositional mechanism to domain term identification and interpretation. Thanks to a pattern-driven generative device, instead of parsing with a fixed size terminology lexicon, we leverage a process aiming to license domain terms 'on demand'.

Pilot experiments to date show that LKUs have a positive impact on parsing. Future work will articulate an algorithm and heuristics for identifying and extracting LKUs from terminological lexica and other resources. In particular, we will address the questions of generating the sets of terms indicative of LKUs, abstracting the pattern specifications for LKU-to-term derivations, and deriving fully instantiated (canonical) LKU lexicon entries. We will also conduct an extensive contrastive evaluation of LKU-based parsing of medical corpora.

[6]ESG analyzes most parenthetical, appositive, constructions as coordinations around the opening parenthesis.

Acknowledgments

We thank three anonymous reviewers for in-depth, and helpful, comments.

References

Timothy Baldwin and Su Nam Kim. 2010. Multiword expressions. *Handbook of Natural Language Processing, Second Edition. Morgan and Claypool.*

Carla Escartín, Gyri Losnegaard, Gunn Samdal, and Pedro García. 2013. Representing multiword expressions in lexical and terminological resources: an analysis for natural language processing purposes. In *Electronic lexicography in the 21st century: thinking outside the paper: Proceedings of the eLex 2013 Conference, Tallinn, Estonia*, pages 338–357.

Aggeliki Fotopoulou, Stella Markantonatou, and Voula Giouli. 2014. Encoding MWEs in a conceptual lexicon. *EACL 2014*, page 43.

Ioannis Korkontzelos and Suresh Manandhar. 2010. Can recognising multiword expressions improve shallow parsing? In *Human Language Technologies: The 2010 Annual Conference of the North American Chapter of the ACL*, pages 636–644. Association for Computational Linguistics.

Michael C. McCord, J. William Murdock, and Branimir Boguraev. 2012. Deep parsing in Watson. *IBM Journal of Research and Development*, 56(3):3.

Michael C. McCord. 1990. Slot grammar: A system for simpler construction of practical natural language grammars. In R. Studer, editor, *Natural Language and Logic: Proc. of the International Scientific Symposium, Hamburg, FRG*, pages 118–145. Springer, Berlin, Heidelberg.

NIH. 2009. Unified Medical Language System (UMLS). `http://www.nlm.nih.gov/research/umls/`, July. US National Library of Medicine, National Institute of Health.

Joakim Nivre and Jens Nilsson. 2004. Multiword units in syntactic parsing. *Proceedings of Methodologies and Evaluation of Multiword Units in Real-World Applications (MEMURA).*

Ivan A Sag, Timothy Baldwin, Francis Bond, Ann Copestake, and Dan Flickinger. 2002. Multiword expressions: A pain in the neck for NLP. In *Computational Linguistics and Intelligent Text Processing*, pages 1–15. Springer.

Eric Wehrli. 2014. The relevance of collocations for parsing. *EACL 2014*, page 26.

Phrase translation using a bilingual dictionary and n-gram data: A case study from Vietnamese to English

Khang Nhut Lam, Feras Al Tarouti and Jugal Kalita
Computer Science Department
University of Colorado, Colorado Springs, USA
{klam2, faltarou, jkalita}@uccs.edu

Abstract

Past approaches to translate a phrase in a language L_1 to a language L_2 using a dictionary-based approach require grammar rules to restructure initial translations. This paper introduces a novel method without using any grammar rules to translate a given phrase in L_1, which does not exist in the dictionary, to L_2. We require at least one L_1–L_2 bilingual dictionary and n-gram data in L_2. The average manual evaluation score of our translations is 4.29/5.00, which implies very high quality.

1 Introduction

This paper tackles the problems of phrase translation from a source language L_1 to a target language L_2. The common approach translates words in the given phrase to L_2 using an L_1–L_2 dictionary, then restructures translations using grammar rules which have been created by experts or are extracted from corpora. We propose a new method for phrase translation using an L_1–L_2 dictionary and n-gram data in L_2, instead of grammar rules, with a case study in translating phrases from Vietnamese to English. We note that the given Vietnamese phrases for translation do not exist in the dictionary. For example, we translate Vietnamese phrases "bộ môn khoa học máy tính", "thuế thu nhập cá nhân" and "đợi một chút" to English: "computer science department", "individual income tax", and "wait a little", respectively. In particular, given a Vietnamese phrase, our algorithms return a list of ranked translations in English.

One purpose of the phrase translations in our work is to support language learners. Assume that, using a Vietnamese-English dictionary, a learner has looked up translations of "bộ môn", "khoa học" and "máy tính" as "department/faculty", "science" and "calculator/computer", respectively. Now, he wants to obtain the translation of "bộ môn khoa học máy tính", a phrase which does not exist in the dictionary. We present a method to generate phrase translations based on information in the dictionary.

2 Overall Vietnamese morphology

Vietnamese is an Austroasiatic language (Lewis et al., 2014) and does not have morphology (Thompson, 1963) and (Aronoff and Fudeman, 2011). In Vietnamese, whitespaces are not used to separate words. The smallest meaningful part of Vietnamese orthography is a syllable (Ngo, 2001). Some examples of Vietnamese words are shown as following:

- Single words: "nhà"- house, "lụa"- silk, "nhặt"- pick up, "mua"- buy and "bán"- sell.
- Compound words: "mua bán"- buy and sell, "bàn ghế"- table and chair, "đồng ruộng"- rice field, "mè đen"- black sesame, "cây cối"- trees, "đường xá"- street, "mẫu giáo"- kindergarden, "hành chánh"- administration, "thổ cẩm"- brocade, "vàng vàng"- yellowish, "ngại ngại"- hesitate, "gật gà gật gù"- nod repeatedly out of satisfaction, "lải nhải"- annoyingly insistent.

Thus, what we call a *word* in Vietnamese may consist of several syllables separted by whitespaces.

3 Related work

The two methods, commonly used for phrase translation, are dictionary-based and corpus-based. A

Proceedings of NAACL-HLT 2015, pages 65–69,
Denver, Colorado, May 31 – June 5, 2015.

dictionary-based approach, e.g., (Abiola et al., 2014) generate translation candidates by translating the given phrase to the target language using a bilingual dictionary. The candidates are restructured using grammar rules which are developed manually or learned from a corpus. In corpus-based approaches, a statistical method is used to identify bilingual phrases from a comparable or parallel corpus (Pecina, 2008), (Koehn and Knight, 2003), and (Bouamor et al., 2012). Researchers may also extract phrases from a given monolingual corpus in the source language and translate them to the target language using a bilingual dictionary (Cao and Li, 2002), and (Tanaka and Baldwin, 2003). Finally, a variety of methods are used to rank translation candidates. These include counting the frequency of candidates in a monolingual corpus in the target language, standard statistical calculations (Pecina, 2008), or even using Naïve Bayes Classifiers and TF-IDF vectors with the EM algorithm (Cao and Li, 2002). (Mariño et al., 2006) extract translations from a bilingual corpus using an n-gram model augmented by additional information, target-language model, a word-bonus model and two lexicon models.

More pertinent to our work is (Hai at al., 1997), who introduced a phrase transfer model for Vietnamese-English machine translation focusing on one-to-zero mapping, which means that a word in Vietnamese may not have appropriate single-word translation(s) and may need to be translated into a phrase in English. They translate Vietnamese words to English using a bilingual dictionary, then use conversion rules to modify the structures of the English translation candidates. The modifying process builds phrases level-by-level from simple to complex, restructures phrases using a syntactic parser and additional rules, and applies measures to solve phrase conflict.

4 Proposed approach

This section introduces a new simple and effective approach to translate from Vietnamese to English using a bilingual dictionary and n-gram data. An entry in n-gram data is a 2-tuple $< w_E, frq >$, where w_E is a sequence of n words in English and frq is the frequency of w_E. An entry in a bilingual dictionary is also a 2-tuple $< w_s, w_t >$, where w_s and w_t are a word or a phrase in the source language and its translation in the target language, respectively. If the word w_s has many translations in the target language, there are several entries such as $< w_s, w_{t1} >$, $< w_s, w_{t2} >$ and $< w_s, w_{t3} >$. We note that an existing bilingual dictionary may contain phrases and their translations. Our work finds translations for phrases which do not exist in the dictionary. The general idea of our approach is that we translate each word in the given phrase to English using a Vietnamese-English dictionary, then use n-gram data to restructure translations. Our work is divided into 4 steps: segmenting Vietnamese words, filtering segmentations, generating ad hoc translations, selecting the best ad hoc translation, and finding and ranking English translation candidates.

4.1 Segmenting Vietnamese words

A Vietnamese phrase *P*, consisting of a sequence of n syllables $< s_1\ s_2\ ...\ s_n >$, can be segmented in different ways, each of which will produce a segmentation *S*. A segmentation *S* is defined as an ordered sequence of words w_i separated by semicolons ";" such as $S =< w_1; w_2; w_3; ...; w_i; ...; w_m >$, where m is the number of words in S, $m \leq n$ and $1 \leq i \leq m$. We note that a word may contain one or more syllables s. Generally, we have 2^{n-1} possible segmentations for a Vietnamese phrase *P*. For example, the phrase "khoa khoa học" - science department/faculty, has 4 possible segmentations:
S_1 = <khoa; khoa; học>, S_2 = <khoa; khoa học>, S_3 = <khoa khoa; học>, and S_4 = <khoa khoa học>.

4.2 Filtering segmentations

Each word in each segment may have $k \geq 0$ translations in English. The total number of English translation candidates for a Vietnamese phrase, with m words, is $O(2^{n-1} * m^k)$. To reduce the number of candidates, we check whether or not every Vietnamese word in each segmentation has an English translation in a Vietnamese-English dictionary. If at least one word does not have a translation in the dictionary, we delete that segmentation. For example, we delete S_3 and S_4 because they contain the words "khoa khoa" and "khoa khoa học" which do not have translations in the dictionary. As a result, the phrase "khoa khoa học" has 2 remaining segmentations: S_1=<khoa; khoa; học> and S_2=<khoa; khoa học>.

4.3 Generating ad hoc translations

To generate an ad hoc translation *T*, we translate each word in a segmentation *S* to English using the Vietnamese-English dictionary. The ad hoc translations of a given phrase are the translations of segmentations. For instance, the translations of the segmentation S_1 for "khoa khoa học" are <faculty; faculty; study>, <department; department; study>, <subject of study; subject of study; study>; and the translations for S_2 are <faculty; science>, <department; science>, <subject of study; science>. Therefore, the six ad hoc translations of "khoa khoa học" are T_1="faculty faculty study", T_2="department department study", T_3="subject of study subject of study study", T_4="faculty science", T_5="department science", and T_6= "subject of study science".

4.4 Selecting the best ad hoc translation

We have generated several ad hoc translations by simply translating each word in the segmentations to English. Most are not grammatically correct. We use a method, presented in Algorithm 1, to reduce the number of ad hoc translations. We consider words in each entry in the English n-gram data as a bag of words NB (lines 1-3), i.e., the words in each entry is simply considered a set of words instead of a sequence. For example, the 3-gram "computer science department" is considered as the set {computer, science, department}. Each ad hoc translation T, created in Section 4.3, is also considered a bag of words TB (lines 4-6). For every bag of words TB, we find each bag of words NB', belonging to the set of all NBs, such that NB' contains all words in TB (lines 7-9), i.e., $TB \subseteq NB'$. Each bag of words TB is given a score $score_{TB}$ which is the sum of frequency of all bags of words NB' (line 10). The bag of words TB with the greatest score is considered the best ad hoc translation (lines 12-18).

After this step, only one ad hoc translation T will remain. For example, we eliminate 5 ad hoc translations (viz., T_1, T_2, T_3, T_4 and T_6) of the Vietnamese phrase "khoa khoa học", and select "department science" (T_5) as the best ad hoc translation of it. We note that the best ad hoc translation may still be grammatically incorrect in English.

Algorithm 1 Selecting the best ad hoc translation

Input: all ad hoc translations Ts
Output: the best ad hoc translation $bestAdhocTran$

```
1: for all entries N ∈ n-gram data do
2:     generate bags of words NB
3: end for
4: for all ad hoc translations T do
5:     generate bags of words TB
6: end for
7: for all TB do
8:     score_TB = 0
9:     Find all NB' ∈ set of all NBs that contain
       all words in TB
10:    score_TB = ∑ Frequency(NB')
11: end for
12: bestAdhocTran=TB_0
13: for all TB do
14:     if score_TB > score_bestAdhocTran then
15:         bestAdhocTran=TB
16:     end if
17: end for
18: return bestAdhocTran
```

4.5 Finding and ranking translation candidates

To restructure translations, we use n-gram data instead of grammar rules. We take advantage that the n-gram information implicitly "encodes" the grammar of a language. Having the best ad hoc translation TB and several corresponding bags NB' from the previous step, we find and rank the translation candidates. For every NB', we retrace its corresponding entry in the n-gram data, and mark the words in the entry as a translation candidate $cand$. Then, we rank the selected translation candidates.

- If there exists one or many $cands$ such that the sizes of each $cand$ and TB are equal, these $cands$ are more likely to be correct translations than other candidates. We simply rank $cands$ based on their n-gram frequencies. The candidate $cand$ with the greatest frequency is considered the best translation. For example, the best ad hoc translation of "khoa khoa học" is "department science". In the n-gram data, we find an entry <"science department", 112> which contains exactly the same words in the best ad hoc translation found. We accept "science department" as a correct translation of "khoa khoa học" and its rank is 112, which is the n-gram frequency of "science department'.

- The rest of the candidates are ranked using the following formula:

$$rank(cand) = \frac{Frequency(cand)}{|size(cand) - size(TB)| * 100}.$$

Our motivation for the rank formula is the following. If a candidate has a greater frequency, it has a greater likelihood to be a correct translation. However, if the size of the candidate and the size of TB are very different, that candidate may be inappropriate. Hence, we divide the frequency of $cand$ by the difference in the number of words between $cand$ and TB. To normalize, we divide results by 100.

5 Experiments

We work with the Vietnamese-English dictionary obtained from EVbcorpus[1]. The dictionary contains about 130,000 entries. We also use the free lists of English n-gram data available at the ngrams.info[2] Website. The free lists have the one million most frequent entries for each of 2, 3, 4 and 5-grams. The n-gram data has been obtained from the corpus of contemporary American English[3].

Currently, we limit our experiments to translation candidates with equal or smaller than 5 syllables. We obtain 200 common Vietnamese phrases, which do not exist in the dictionary, from 4 volunteers who are fluent in both Vietnamese and English. Later, these volunteers are asked to evaluate our translations using a 5-point scale, 5: excellent, 4: good, 3: average, 2: fair, and 1: bad.

The average score of translations created using the baseline approach, which is simply translating words in segments to English, is 2.20/5.00. The average score of translations created using our proposed approach is 4.29/5.00, which is quite high. The rating reliability is 0.72 obtained by calculating the Intraclass Correlation Coefficient (Koch, 1982). Our approach returns translations for 101 phrases out of the 200 input phrases. This means the precision and recall of our translations are 85.8% and 50.5%, respectively.

[1]https://code.google.com/p/evbcorpus/
[2]http://www.ngrams.info/
[3]http://corpus.byu.edu/coca/

We also compute the matching percentage between our translations and translations performed by the Google Translator. The matching percentage of our translations for phrases is 42%. The translations marked as "unmatched" do not mean our translations are incorrect. A few such examples are presented in Table 1.

Vietnamese phrase	Meaning of the Vietnamese phrase	Our translation	Google translation
ca sĩ nổi tiếng	a famous singer	famous singer	diva
giá cả thị trường	the price at which buyers and sellers trade the item in an open marketplace	prices on the world market	market prices
con chim non	young bird not yet fledged	a birdie	not with chim
đồng minh phương tây	alliance in the West	alliance with the West	Western allies
thuê phòng	rent a room	rent a room	rent
người trẻ tuổi	a young person	young man	young people
khả năng tư duy	the ability to think	thinking ability	thinking
tắt lửa	put out, as of fires, flames, or lights	put out the fire	quench
leo cây	to climb a tree	climb a tree	climbing tree

Table 1: Some translations we create are correct but do not match with translations from the Google Translator.

The average score of our translations is high; however, the recall is low. If our algorithms can return a translation for an input phrase, that translation is usually specific, and is evaluated as excellent or good in most cases. Our approach relies on an existing bilingual dictionary and n-gram data in English. If we have a dictionary covering the most common words in Vietnamese, and the n-gram data in English is extensive with different lengths, we believe that our approach will produce even better translations.

6 Conclusion and future work

We have introduced a new method to translate a given phrase in Vietnamese to English using a bilingual dictionary and English n-gram data. Our approach can be applied to other language pairs that have a bilingual dictionary and n-gram data in one of the two languages. We plan to compute Vietnamese n-gram data from a Wikipedia dump and try to translate phrases from English to Vietnamese next.

References

O.B. Abiola, Adetunmbi A. O., Fasiku A. I., and Olatunji K. 2014. A web-based English to Yoruba noun-phrases machine transaltion system. *International Journal of English and Literature*. Pages 71–78.

Mark Aronoff, and Kirsten Fudeman. 2011. What is morphology, vol. 8. *John Wiley & Sons*.

Dhouha Bouamor, Nasredine Semmar, and Pierre Zweigenbaum. 2012. Identifying bilingual Multi-Word Expressions for Statistical Machine Translation. In *Proceedings of LREC*. Istanbul, Turkey, May. Pages 674–679.

Yunbo Cao, and Hang Li. 2002. Base noun phrase translation using web data and the EM algorithm. In *Proceedings of the 19th international conference on Computational linguistics*. Pages 1–7.

Le Manh Hai, Asanee Kawtrakul, and Yuen Poovorawan. 1997. Phrasal transfer model for Vietnamese-English machine translation. In *NLPRS*.

Gary G. Koch. 1982. Intraclass correlation coefficient. *Encyclopedia of statistical sciences*.

Philipp Koehn, and Kevin Knight. 2003. Feature-rich statistical translation of noun phrases. In *Proceedings of the 41st Annual Meeting on Association for Computational Linguistics*. Sapporo, Japan, July. Volume 1, pages 311-318. Association for Computational Linguistics.

Paul M. Lewis, Gary F. Simons, and Charles D. Fennig (eds.). 2014. *Ethnologue: Languages of the World*, 17th edition. Dallas, Texas: SIL International.

José B. Mariño, Rafael E. Banchs, Josep M. Crego, Adrià de Gispert, Patrik Lambert, José A.R. Fonollosa, and Marta R. Costa-Jussà. 2006. *N-gram-based machine translation*. Computational Linguistics 32, no. 4 (2006): 527–549.

Binh N. Ngo. 2001. *The Vietnamese language learning framework* . Journal of Southeast Asian Language Teaching 10. Pages 1–24.

Pavel Pecina. 2008. A machine learning approach to multiword expression extraction. In *Proceedings of the LREC Workshop Towards a Shared Task for Multiword Expressions*. Marrakech, Morocco, June. Pages 54–61.

Takaaki Tanaka, and Timothy Baldwin. 2003. Translation selection for Japanese-English noun-noun compounds. In *Proceedings of Machine Translation Summit IX*. Marrakech, Morocco, June. Pages 378–385.

Laurence C. Thompson. 1963. The problem of the word in Vietnamese. *Word journal of the International Linguistic Association*, 19(1):39–52.

Annotation and Extraction of Multiword Expressions in Turkish Treebanks

Gülşen Eryiğit, Kübra Adalı, Dilara Torunoğlu-Selamet, Umut Sulubacak, Tuğba Pamay
Department of Computer Engineering,
Istanbul Technical University,
Istanbul, 34469, Turkey
{gulsen.cebiroglu|kubraadali|torunoglud|sulubacak|pamay}
@itu.edu.tr

Abstract

Multiword expressions (MWEs) present particular and distinctive semantic properties, hence their automatic extraction receives special attention from the natural language processing (NLP) and corpus linguistics community, and is still an active research area. Unfortunately, the creation of necessary resources for this task is quite rigorous and many languages suffer from the lack of these; as in the case for Turkish.

This study presents our MWE annotations on recently introduced Turkish Treebanks, which focuses on annotating various types of linguistic units and expressions, including named entities, numerical expressions, idiomatic phrases, verb phrases with auxiliaries and duplications. The paper aims to provide a benchmark and pave the way towards further MWE extraction research for Turkish. To this end, the paper also introduces our experimental results with seven baseline approaches, a dependency parser and a previously introduced rule-based extractor on these annotated corpora. Our highest performances achieved over these resources are about 60% F-scores.

1 Introduction

Automatic extraction of multiword expressions (MWEs) is an important and challenging task in natural language processing (NLP). They are introduced to be a key problem for the development of large-scale NLP technology (Sag et al., 2002). Multiword expressions are lexical items that can be decomposed into single words where these single words represent most of the time a totally different meaning compared to word sets within which they occur. Thus, MWEs pose significant problem for NLP and machine translation (MT) applications. The effect and the importance of MWE extraction techniques are being investigated by the NLP and CL communities. A recent ICT-Cost Action (IC1207-PARSEME "PARSing and Multi-word Expressions") focuses only on MWEs in a multidisciplinary level from different perspectives.

In the literature some studies are focused on deriving automatic MWE extraction techniques without using annotated data. Attia (2006) investigates the automatic acquisition of Arabic MWEs and proposes three complementary approaches to extract related MWEs automatically. Piao et al. (2006) propose similar approaches automatically identifying Chinese MWEs and achieve precision ranging from 61.16% to 93.96% for different types. Schone and Jurafsky (2001) seek a knowledge-free method for inducing MWEs from text corpora and provide two major evaluations of nine existing collocation-finders. Metin and Karaoğlan (2010) tries to explore Turkish collocations by using standard statistical methods (e.g Chi-square hypothesis test and mutual information). Tsvetkov and Wintner (2012) extract MWEs by using monolingual and parallel corpora (Hebrew-English), and then use the outcome to train a machine translation system. As mentioned in most of the aforementioned studies, although it might be feasible to automatically identify MWEs using these approaches, yet they need to be improved further. The need for and the importance of manually annotated large-scale data for MWE extraction purpose is not negligible. There exist many recent works on creating language resources for MWEs e.g. MWE databases, corpora and treebanks. The French corpora (Laporte et al., 2008a; Laporte et al., 2008b)

Proceedings of NAACL-HLT 2015, pages 70–76,
Denver, Colorado, May 31 – June 5, 2015.

and the Prague Dependency Treebank (Bejček and Straňák, 2010) may be given as examples of these studies among many others.

Dependency parsers are capable of providing quite acceptable performances for MWE extraction. Nivre and Nilsson (2004), Eryiğit et al. (2011), Vincze et al. (2013) and Candito and Constant (2014) investigate the impact of dependency parsers on Swedish, Turkish and Hungarian MWE extraction. Vincze et al. (2013) show that their results outperformed those achieved by state-of-the-art techniques for Hungarian LVC detection. Eryiğit et al. (2011) show that in the training stage, the unification of MWEs of a certain type, namely compound verb and noun formations, has a negative effect on parsing accuracy by increasing the lexical sparsity. In spite of their syntactic relations, MWEs still need special treatments in terms of semantic relations.

Inspired by these recent studies, to shed light and provide a direction for future studies on adequate MWE extraction techniques for Turkish, in this paper we present our annotation for MWEs on recently introduced Turkish Treebanks. We focus on annotating various types of linguistic units and expressions, including named entities, numerical expressions, idiomatic phrases, verb phrases with auxiliaries and duplications. The paper experiments with different lexical approaches together with automatic named entity recognition (NER). The results are compared with those of an available collocation extraction tool (Oflazer et al., 2004) and a dependency parser (Eryiğit et al., 2008). Although, the newly introduced methods improved the previous results by almost 20 percentage points (yielding ~60% F-score), we treat these results as the state-of-the-art baselines for Turkish.

The paper is structured as follows: Section 2 introduces the used language resources, Section 3 discusses MWEs in Turkish, Section 4 presents models for MWE extraction, Section 5 gives the experimental results and discussions, Section 6 presents the conclusion.

2 Language Resources

We use four different treebanks in our experiments, three of which have been annotated within this study. The first treebank, METU-Sabancı Treebank, (MST) (Oflazer et al., 2003) is from Eryiğit et al. (2011) where the authors state that most of the MWEs in the original treebank are not annotated. They use a semi-automatic way for annotating these MWEs. To this end, they first extracted a MWE list consisting the 30150 MWEs available in the Turkish Dictionary (TDK, 2011) and then automatically listed the entire treebank sentences where the lemmas of the co-occurring words could match the lemmas of the MWE constituents in the list. They then manually marked the sentences where the co-occurring words may be actually accepted as a MWE (but somehow missed during the construction of the original treebank). This semi-automatic annotation approach is incapable of detecting non-adjacent MWE constituents. IMST, IVS and IWT are recently introduced Turkish treebanks annotated with a new dependency scheme (Sulubacak and Eryiğit, 2014).

IMST contains exactly the same sentences thus the same MWEs as MST. But differing from the previous work, the annotation of MWEs are done fully manually without using a semi-automatic selection as explained above. The MWEs are annotated by the use of a specific dependency label (MWE) regardless of their category. In this study, we present our MWE annotations on these three treebanks: IVS with 300 sentences, IMST with 5,635 sentences collected from formally-written data and IWT with 5,009 sentences collected from Web 2.0.

Table 1 presents the resulting MWE statistics on each of these datasets. Since a MWE may consist of two or more words, the table provides both the exact number of MWEs (in the second line) and the total number of MWE relations between MWE constituents (in the first line). As may be noticed from this table, IMST contains almost 50% more MWE annotation than MST of Eryiğit et al. (2011) due to the full manual annotation. Finally the last line of the table gives the number of MWEs with different lengths.

3 MWEs in Turkish

Due to its morphological typology, MWE annotation and extraction methodologies developed for most prominent languages are not suitable for Turkish. Whereas the most well-researched European lan-

	MST			IMST			IVS			IWT		
# of MWE relations	2432			3544			295			2780		
exact # of MWEs	2038			3069			269			2597		
exact # of MWEs	L=2	L=3	L>3	L=2	L=3	L>3	L=2	L=3	L>3	L=2	L=3	L>3
with Word Lengths	1792	159	87	2757	205	107	247	18	4	2444	127	26

Table 1: MWEs in Turkish Treebanks

guages are typically fusional or analytic, Turkish is an agglutinative language, meaning that it is possible to derive and inflect words indefinitely through cascading suffixes. In fact, the derivation is so common that most sentences contain several derived words incorporating one or more suffixes, even in the colloquial language. The constituents of MWEs also commonly undergo inflection (Oflazer et al., 2004; Savary, 2008), giving way to numerous forms of the same expression each appropriate for a different syntactic function. Furthermore, many idiomatic MWEs may also be interpreted literally—that is, there are permissible expressions used in their literal meaning that are morphosyntactically identical to a MWE. Another point is that the constituents of a MWE may occur at nonadjacent positions in the sentence. Figure 1 gives an example for the MWE "ekmeğini yemek" (*to gain one's livelihood from (someone)*). In the given sentence, the words composing the MWE are both inflected (the first word "ekmek" (*bread*) with 1st person possessive agreement suffix in accusative form and the second word "yemek" (*to eat*) in past tense with 2nd singular person agreement) and written separately from each other.

For these reasons, ordered surface word form matches do not suffice in properly assessing the semantic quality of expressions. Therefore, the disambiguation of MWEs is a more complicated problem than could be resolved by use of look-up tables.

In the rest of this section, we describe the extent of MWEs we specified in our framework. We specify six major categories for MWEs, considering common idiosyncratic formations in Turkish in addition to well-recognized global conventions. We consider any word falling under these categories to be a MWE, as we later build our extraction models around them. The categories are given below:

Named Entities: Proper names and titles of unique persons such as "Genel Sekreter Ban Kimoon" (*Secretary-General Ban Ki-moon*), organizations such as "Avrupa İnsan Hakları Mahkemesi" (*European Court of Human Rights*) and locations such as "Papua Yeni Gine" (*Papua New Guinea*) occur very frequently in both edited and unedited texts. Commonly recognized as named entities, these expressions often span multiple words, thereby forming a category of MWEs.

Numerical Expressions: We mark any group of contiguous tokens denoting a numerical expression as MWEs, including spelled out numbers, quantities such as currency values and percentages, and temporal expressions such as date and time phrases. Such expressions are often considered to be a subgroup of named entities, but since they are among the most frequently encountered MWEs, we handle them under a separate category to emphasize their importance.

Idiomatic Phrases: Many common idiomatic phrases in Turkish are also occasionally used in their literal meanings, such as "yola düşmek" (*hit the road, or lit. fall on the road*). Since both meanings of the phrase would appear morphosyntactically similar, such cases lead to ambiguities in meaning that must be resolved using contextual information. For this reason, we consider idiomatic phrases to be a most challenging category of MWEs.

Light verb constructions: Turkish has a way of forming verb phrases using auxiliary verbs such as "olmak" (*to be*), "etmek" (*to do*), "yapmak" (*to make*) and "kılmak" (*to render*). Among the examples, especially the first two are extremely productive and often used in very common expressions like "teşekkür etmek" (*to thank, or lit. to do thank*). Although the figurative meanings of such phrases are usually predictable, they still comprise idiomatic phrases. We handle these outside the previous category due to their prevalence, much like numerical

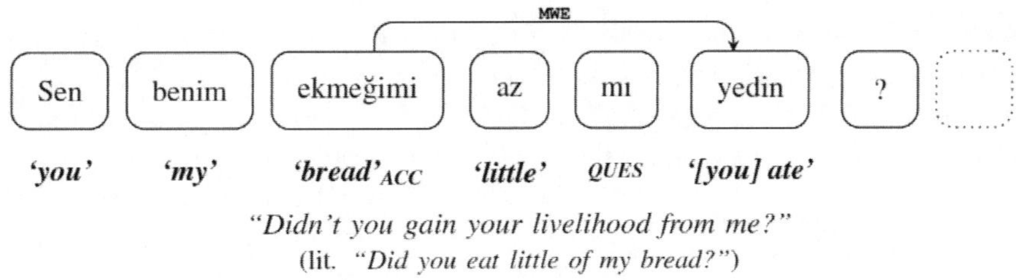

Figure 1: A sample Turkish MWE

expressions.

Compound Function Words: We include any compound particles, multi-word interjections and other function word compounds under MWEs. This category excludes function words modified by intensifiers such as "de" and "ise", which also regularly modify content words, as in "ya da" (*or*). Ultimately, there are few permissible function word compounds in Turkish, but they are often commonly used phrases, and warrant a category of MWEs.

Duplications: It is common to use word duplication as a grammatical mechanism in both formal and informal Turkish. Duplicating an adjective allows the word to be used as an adverb much like affixation, such as in "yavaş yavaş" (*slowly, or lit. slow slow*). Onomatopoeic or gibberish (and usually rhyming) pairs of words such as "allak bullak" (*topsy-turvy*) are also used fairly often to the same effect. Furthermore, there is the 'm'-duplication, which is a common mechanism in colloquial Turkish, where a word is repeated and an 'm' is prefixed to the duplicate (replacing the initial consonant) in order to add the '*and so on*' meaning, like in "form morm" (*forms and so*). We evaluate all such duplications as MWEs.

4 Models for MWE Extraction

For our MWE extraction experiments, we test with a Turkish dependency parser from Eryiğit et al. (2008), an existing collocation extraction tool (Oflazer et al., 2004) (which we call MorphoColl from this point on), and seven lexical models. The lexical models are based on the previous work by Eryiğit et al. (2011), three of which are identical to the models described in the study and the rest integrate different lexical approaches and a NER module into these models. The rest of this section gives the details about our extraction models and their methodologies.

4.1 Dependency Parser

This model comprises a generic dependency parser which includes **MWE** as one of the dependency relations. We extract MWEs by traversing these relations represented in the output dependency graphs.

4.2 MorphoColl

This model attempts to automatically extract collocations making use of lexical information and morphosyntactic rules. It is composed of three sequential layers, where each layer has its own set of rules and produces the input to the next layer as its output.

4.3 Lexical Models

We first filtered MWEs from a Turkish dictionary (TDK, 2011) into a list and used this list as a look-up table. We used the list in three elementary models with different validation criteria, as introduced previously in Eryiğit et al. (2011).

Model #0: The first MWE extraction model selects the sequences of words whose surface forms match those of the constituents of a MWE in the referenced list. Thus, this model extracts lexicalized collocations which are considered fixed MWEs (Oflazer et al., 2004). An example for this case is given below:

- "**Arka arkaya** iki operasyon geçirdi."
  lit. (Back to back) (two) (operations) (he/she had).
  (*He/she had two operations* ***consecutively***.)

Model #1: The second model selects the sequences of words whose surface forms except the last word (which may go under inflection) are the same as the constituents of a MWE in the referenced list. For the last constituent, the stem of the word is required to match. This model extracts collocations belonging to the semi-lexicalized category as stated in (Oflazer et al., 2004). Below is an example for this case:

- "Geleceğini **haber vermedi**."
  lit. *(*that he/she was coming) (he/she didn't give) (news).
  (*He/she didn't* ***inform***)

Model #2: The third model checks only the stems of the words and select the sequences of words matching the stems of a MWE in the referenced list. Non-lexicalized collocations (Oflazer et al., 2004) each of whose constituents can undergo inflection are extracted by this model. The following example demonstrates this case:

- "Asla **umudunu kesmeyeceksin**."
  lit. *(*Never) (your hope) (you will cut)
  (*You will never* ***despair***)

As a summary, Model 0 doesn't allow any inflections or derivations in the MWE candidate whereas Model 1 allows for only the last word, and Model 2 allows for all of its words. Since the used dictionary does not include proper names, the models introduced above are incapable of detecting named entities. Thus, our following two models which we name "**Model #1 + NER**" and "**Model #2 + NER**" use a Turkish named entity recognizer (Şeker and Eryiğit, 2012) on top of the mentioned models. Since the NER module may also return single word entities, only the extracted entities with multiple words are accepted as MWEs in these models. Below are some examples of the MWEs which are extracted by the NER in both models:

- "**Milli Savunma Bakanlığı'nın** toplantısı bugün yapılacak."
  lit. *(*National) (Defense) (of the Ministry) (the meeting) (today) (is to be held)
  (*The* ***Ministry of National Defense*** *meeting is to be held today.*)

- "**Bayındır Sokak'taki** evimden çıktım."
  lit. *(*Bayındır) (located in Street) (from my house) (I left)
  (*I left my house located in* ***Bayındır Street.***)

The used NER tool which is trained on a data set following the MUC guidelines (Chinchor and Robinson, 1997) for named entity annotation does not extract the titles of the proper names as part of the entity such as in "Başkan Barack Obama" (*President Barack Obama*) where the word 'president' is not extracted as part of the MWE. On the other hand, in our annotations on Turkish Treebanks, these words are also annotated as part of the MWEs. The **Model #1 + Enlarged_NER** implicates the previous and/or the next word of the proper name to the extracted MWE if their first characters are in uppercase letter with the aim to detect the missing title words. The following example shows a MWE consisting of titles and proper names as would be extracted by this model:

- "**Kaymakam Arif Beyi** davet ettik."
  lit. *(*Mister) (Arif) (Governor) (invite) (we have made)
  (*We have invited* ***Mister Governor Arif.***)

It is impractical to expect from a dictionary list to contain duplications (especially for m-duplications) because there is a theoretically infinite number of duplications (Section 3). Our last model **Model #1 + Enlarged_NER + Dup** contains an additional module which detects these repetitions on top of the previous model. Below is an example showing a MWE formed by word repetition handled by this model:

- "Onu **yavaş yavaş** sakinleştirdi."
  lit. *(*him/her) (slow slow) (he/she calmed down).
  (*He/she* ***slowly*** *calmed him/her down*)

5 Experimental Results and Discussions

Table 2 gives the precision, recall and F-scores (based on the number of MWEs) for the evaluation of the presented models on the introduced datasets. As stated previously, IMST, which contains higher number of annotated MWEs (Section2) yields lower recall scores compared to MST for all of the models. This is because of the newly annotated MWEs with non-adjacent constituents (Section3). On the other hand, all of the models give higher precision scores on IMST where the missing MWE annotations of MST are eliminated due to careful manually annotations on IMST.

Although, Model #1 is a very straightforward lexical matching approach, it outperforms MorphoColl and the dependency parser on newly annotated

	MST			IMST			IVS			IWT		
	P	R	F	P	R	F	P	R	F	P	R	F
Dependency Parser	38.77	44.7	41.52	42.04	32.16	36.44	37.41	19.33	25.49	43.05	39.74	41.33
MorphoColl	80.77	22.67	35.40	77.5	15.71	26.12	82.93	12.64	21.94	86.24	15.44	26.19
Model #0	20.89	9.47	13.32	39.92	12.38	18.1	52.06	14.13	22.22	43.72	13.94	21.14
Model #1	32.65	42.89	37.07	46.73	40.27	43.26	63.13	42.01	50.45	51.5	39.7	44.84
Model #2	27.62	45.93	34.49	39.23	43.99	41.48	45.59	44.24	44.91	43.95	44.17	44.06
Model #1+NER	42.85	56.28	48.65	57.69	49.72	53.41	70.95	47.21	56.7	59.49	45.86	51.79
Model #2+NER	35.67	59.32	44.56	47.66	53.44	50.38	50.96	49.44	50.19	50.08	50.33	50.2
Model #1+Enlarged_NER	51.92	68.2	58.96	66.59	57.38	61.64	71.51	47.58	57.14	67.38	51.95	58.67
Model #1+Enlarged_NER+Dup	52.74	70.46	60.32	67.25	59.14	62.93	72.43	47.58	57.44	68.13	53.75	60.1

Table 2: Baseline System Results

datasets. The reason is because, the literal interpretation of MWEs with adjacent constituents is less probable compared to idiomatic usage. Such as the MWE "ayvayı yemek" which is close in meaning to *to be in hot water* (*slang to be in trouble*) may also be used literally in the case of *eating a quince* which is a much less probable usage.

The impact of adding a NER layer improves the results almost 10 percentage points. Our Enlarged_NER adds almost 10 percentage points on top of this, and the impact ($\sim$2 percentage points) of duplication detection is also promising although not as high as the previous two. Our best performed model **Model #1 + Enlarged_NER + Dup** achieves 60.32%, 62.93%, 57.44% and 60.1% F-scores in MST, IMST, IVS and IWT respectively.

The extractors that we presented in this paper are limited to an individual dependency parser, a rule-based model and dictionary-based models with rule-based additions. Since these models do not go beyond considering the lexical forms and syntactic structures of constituents, they have an equally limited performance in determining MWEs, which are essentially semantic entities. As such, our models should only be considered baseline models. We expect the models to be a benchmark for future work on more sophisticated MWE extraction systems for Turkish and facilitate comparison with studies on other languages analogous to Turkish in their morphosyntactic structure, such as other agglutinative languages like Finnish and Hungarian, as well as various morphologically rich languages like French and Arabic.

Our premise is that, in order to properly pick out MWEs from within texts, a model needs to integrate morpho-lexical, syntactic and semantic modules all in one, in order to respectively extract critical constituents, appoint the grammatical relations between them, and determine the nature of the extracted phrases. One of our future plans is to design and implement such a model following this study, making use of machine learning and incorporating sequential modules, each working out a separate aspect of the candidate expressions. Additionally, we aim to expand our survey and test our new model on other languages besides Turkish for a more thorough performance evaluation.

6 Conclusion

In this study, we described the various challenges in annotating and extracting MWEs in Turkish, due to the typology and certain idiosyncratic features of the language. We outlined the framework we established on what constitutes a MWE, along with the exceptional cases that have been considered. Afterwards, we discussed our elementary approach to extracting MWEs in Turkish, then presented the basic extraction models we developed and tested on four Turkish treebanks. Our best model which uses a lexical look-up approach allowing the inflection of the final MWE constituent, an enhanced named entity recognition module and a duplication extraction module obtains about 60% F-measure in these treebanks.

Acknowledgment

We would like to acknowledge that this work is part of a research project entitled "Parsing Web 2.0 Sentences" subsidized by the TUBITAK (Turkish Scientific and Technological Research Council) 1001 program (grant number 112E276) and part of the

ICT COST Action IC1207 PARSEME (PARSing and Multi-word Expressions).

References

Mohammed A. Attia. 2006. Accommodating multiword expressions in an arabic lfg grammar. In *Proceedings of the 5th International Conference on Advances in Natural Language Processing*, FinTAL'06, pages 87–98, Berlin, Heidelberg. Springer-Verlag.

Eduard Bejček and Pavel Straňák. 2010. Annotation of multiword expressions in the Prague dependency treebank. *Language Resources and Evaluation*, 44(1-2):7–21.

Marie Candito and Matthieu Constant. 2014. Strategies for contiguous multiword expression analysis and dependency parsing. In *ACL 14-The 52nd Annual Meeting of the Association for Computational Linguistics*. ACL.

Nancy Chinchor and Patricia Robinson. 1997. Muc-7 named entity task definition. In *Proceedings of the 7th Conference on Message Understanding*, page 29.

Gülşen Eryiğit, Tugay İlbay, and Ozan Arkan Can. 2011. Multiword expressions in statistical dependency parsing. In *Proceedings of the Second Workshop on Statistical Parsing of Morphologically Rich Languages (IWPT)*, pages 45–55, Dublin, Ireland, October.

Gülşen Eryiğit, Joakim Nivre, and Kemal Oflazer. 2008. Dependency parsing of Turkish. *Computational Linguistics*, 34(3):357–389.

Eric Laporte, Takuya Nakamura, and Stavroula Voyatzi. 2008a. A French corpus annotated for multiword expressions with adverbial function. In *Language Resources and Evaluation Conference (LREC). Linguistic Annotation Workshop*, pages 48–51.

Eric Laporte, Takuya Nakamura, and Stavroula Voyatzi. 2008b. A French corpus annotated for multiword nouns. In *Language Resources and Evaluation Conference. Workshop Towards a Shared Task on Multiword Expressions*, pages 27–30.

Senem Kumova Metin and Bahar Karaoğlan. 2010. Collocation extraction in Turkish texts using statistical methods. In *Advances in Natural Language Processing*, pages 238–249. Springer.

Joakim Nivre and Jens Nilsson. 2004. Multiword units in syntactic parsing. *Proceedings of Methodologies and Evaluation of Multiword Units in Real-World Applications (MEMURA)*.

Kemal Oflazer, Bilge Say, Dilek Zeynep Hakkani-Tür, and Gökhan Tür. 2003. Building a Turkish treebank. In *Treebanks*, pages 261–277. Springer.

Kemal Oflazer, Özlem Çetinoğlu, and Bilge Say. 2004. Integrating morphology with multi-word expression processing in Turkish. In *Proceedings of the Workshop on Multiword Expressions: Integrating Processing*, pages 64–71. Association for Computational Linguistics.

S Piao, Guangfan Sun, Paul Rayson, and Qi Yuan. 2006. Automatic extraction of Chinese multiword expressions with a statistical tool. In *Workshop on Multiword-expressions in a Multilingual Context (EACL 2006)*.

Ivan A Sag, Timothy Baldwin, Francis Bond, Ann Copestake, and Dan Flickinger. 2002. Multiword expressions: A pain in the neck for NLP. In *Computational Linguistics and Intelligent Text Processing*, pages 1–15. Springer.

Agata Savary. 2008. Computational inflection of multiword units. *A contrastive study of lexical approaches*, 1(2).

Patrick Schone and Daniel Jurafsky. 2001. Is knowledge-free induction of multiword unit dictionary headwords a solved problem. In *Proceedings of the 2001 Conference on Empirical Methods in Natural Language Processing*, pages 100–108.

Gökhan Akın Şeker and Gülşen Eryiğit. 2012. Initial explorations on using CRFs for Turkish named entity recognition. In *Proceedings of COLING 2012*, Mumbai, India, 8-15 December.

Umut Sulubacak and Gülşen Eryiğit. 2014. A redefined Turkish dependency grammar and its implementations: A new Turkish web treebank & the revised Turkish treebank. under review.

TDK. 2011. *Turkish Language Association Turkish dictionary*. http://www.tdk.gov.tr.

Yulia Tsvetkov and Shuly Wintner. 2012. Extraction of multi-word expressions from small parallel corpora. *Natural Language Engineering*, 18(04):549–573.

Veronika Vincze, János Zsibrita, and TI Nagy. 2013. Dependency parsing for identifying Hungarian light verb constructions. In *Proc. of the Sixth International Joint Conference on Natural Language Processing*, pages 207–215.

Event Categorization beyond Verb Senses

Aron Marvel
University at Buffalo
609 Baldy Hall
Buffalo, NY 14260, USA
aronmarv@buffalo.edu

Jean-Pierre Koenig
University at Buffalo
609 Baldy Hall
Buffalo, NY 14260, USA
jpkoenig@buffalo.edu

Abstract

Verb senses are often assumed to distinguish among different conceptual event categories. However, senses misrepresent the number of event categories expressed both within and across languages and event categories may be "named" by more than a word, i.e. a multi-word expression. Determining the nature and number of event categories in an event description requires an understanding of the parameters relevant for categorization. We propose a set of parameters for use in creating a Gold Standard of event categories and apply them to a corpus sample of 2000 sentences across 10 verbs. In doing so, we find an asymmetry between subjects and direct objects in their contributions to distinguishing event categories. We then explore methods of automating event categorization to approximate our Gold Standard through the use of hierarchical clustering and Latent Semantic Analysis (Deerwester et al., 1990).

1 Introduction

A word form is associated with one or more senses, each of which may denote a distinct conceptual category. This association is many-to-many; one word may have many senses, while different words may also share the same sense. Additionally, just as two different words may denote the same concept, so may a sequence of words. Consider the sentences in (1).

(1) a. The officer entered the building.
b. The officer went into the building.

How many concepts do these sentences contain? Probably *officer* and *building* each count as one and so does *enter*. But it is difficult to justify labeling *enter* as a single concept while treating *go* and *into* as separate. *Enter* and *go into* seem to denote the same concept, the first by means of a single word and the second through a multi-word expression (MWE). The mapping between concept and lexicalization becomes a real problem for AI reasoning systems. These systems often translate natural language input into a lingua franca, such as the HPSG representation used by SNePS (Shapiro & Rappaport, 1992), and there is no clear way for them to know when they have encountered a MWE that represents a single concept.

While the sentences in (1) indicate that a single conceptual category may span syntactic boundaries and involve different verbs, it is also possible for distinct conceptual categories to be denoted using a single verb sense as in (2).

(2) a. The senator raised a glass in celebration.
b. The crane raised the car out of the water.

Both (2a) and (2b) employ the same sense of *raised*[1] but denote very different categories of events. In prototypical contexts, (2a) describes a toast, while (2b) describes the extraction of a large object. The events described in (2) differ in a number of ways, among them duration, complexity,

[1] To determine whether two uses of a word instantiate the same sense, we use the American Heritage Dictionary (AHD), which features several notable linguists among its contributors and consultants.

Proceedings of NAACL-HLT 2015, pages 77–86,
Denver, Colorado, May 31 – June 5, 2015.

available inferences, and the types of agents involved. Further, several inferences one can draw from (2a) arise non-compositionally, i.e. cannot be inferred from just the meaning of the parts and the sentence's syntactic structure.

What is crucial for our purposes in (2) is that the two distinct event categories described by the sentences are differentiated by information outside of the verb sense. Recognition of this fact prompts the question of what kinds of information beyond verb sense are relevant for differentiating event categories, as well as how to distinguish between MWEs that denote distinct event categories and those that do not. In this paper, we explore these problems and develop a new method of automatically categorizing event descriptions.

The paper is structured as follows. Section 2 briefly discusses the limitations of lexical approaches to event categorization and outlines an alternative approach that takes into account clausal constituents beyond the verb. In Section 3, we propose a set of six general parameters by which categories of events may be distinguished beyond the verb sense. Those parameters are applied to a categorization task in Section 4 using a sample of corpus sentences for 10 different verbs. In Section 5, we describe an attempt to automate the sorting task using relatedness measures from Latent Semantic Analysis in combination with hierarchical clustering.

2 Event categories as MWEs

Lexical approaches to event categorization, i.e. those that only rely upon the verb, encounter significant problems stemming from the arbitrariness of lexicalization both within and across languages. Within a language, the same conceptual event category may be expressed by a verb or a verb plus non-verbal expressions as in (1). Confining event categorization to the verb may additionally miss important differences between event categories as in (2). Additionally, languages differ both in the sizes of their verbal lexicons and in the number of senses assigned to each verb. The average adult English speaker knows approximately 4,000 verbs (Koenig et al. 2003), each of which has on average three (COBUILD, pc, 2006) or four (WordNet Statistics, 2015) senses. Under the assumption that verb senses approximate event categories, this results in a total of 12,000 - 16,000 distinct event categories. Speakers of a language such as Wagiman, a northern Australian language, have an inventory of only about 500 verbal expressions, 90% of which have only a single recorded sense (Wilson, 1999). The upshot of only using verb senses to distinguish event categories would be the claim that speakers of Wagiman are capable of (linguistically) distinguishing only 4% of the event categories distinguished by speakers of English – an implausible statistic.

Wagiman speakers achieve parity with speakers of other languages by combining verbal expressions to create what Wilson calls 'complex predicates': the English word *watch* translates to a combination of two words in Wagiman: the word *nanda*, meaning 'to see', from a closed class of basic verbs, and the word *letta*, meaning 'to look', from an open class of verbal expressions called coverbs. Wagiman verb-coverb combinations provide an example of a multi-word expression in one language serving the purpose of a single-word expression in another. This phenomenon has received due attention within the MWE literature (see, e.g., Sag et al., 2001; Villavicencio, 2007), though most often as it relates to idiom translation. It has also received attention in the typological literature, e.g. in discussion of 'verb-framed' vs. 'satellite-framed' languages, the former of which express motion path as part of verb meaning and the latter of which express it verb-externally through 'satellite' phrases (Talmy, 1985a).

In addition to the above motivations, the problems we investigate are related to a large body of research devoted to selectional preferences, including efforts from both psycholinguistics (e.g. McRae et al. 1998, 2005) and computational modeling (e.g. Erk & Padó 2008, Lenci 2011). These efforts are primarily concerned with measuring the sensitivity of people and NLP systems to distributional properties of verbs, though some, such as FrameNet (Baker et al. 1998) and Corpus Pattern Analysis (Hanks 2004), do flesh out the boundaries within these distributions more fully. Our aim here is to explore the parameters that underpin divisions within these distributions. Many of the parameters involve non-compositional meaning components and thus benefit from an understanding of event descriptions as MWEs. We propose here that all events, not just idiomatic and institutionalized phrases, may be categorized at the level of multiword expressions.

Consider again the two uses of *raised* in (2). In comparing the two different categories of raising events, we may look beyond the verb and investigate the contribution of other parts of the clause: How is the kind of raising involved in raising a glass distinct from the kind involved in raising a car? How is the kind of raising a senator does predictably different from the kind of raising a crane does? We propose partial answers to these questions and motivate them with examples in the next section.

3 Parameters for event categorization

What follows is an attempt to extract from both previous research and common sense a set of general parameters by which event categories may be distinguished beyond the level of the verb sense. We should be clear at the outset that the following parameters are not to be taken as complete, but rather as a subset of dimensions of experience that are available for event categorization. Examples are drawn from our corpus sample and, importantly, share the same verb sense as per the AHD.

3.1 Complexity

Event complexity often refers to the number of sub-events represented in the semantics of a verb (see e.g. Dowty 1979). However, such accounts ignore the contribution of event participants in influencing event categorization. Consider the two uses of *sell* in (3).

(3) a. He refused to sell any of his antiques.
b. The support staff sells their expertise to the community beyond the school.

Though the sense of *sell* remains constant between (3a) and (3b), selling done by a support staff to a community is likely to include a larger total number of sub-events than selling done by or to an individual. This sub-event information, though, is only available to language users when they combine verb information with information they glean from disparate parts of the clause.

In addition to the number of sub-events, complexity includes the relations among sub-events and the participants within them. Sensitivity to this kind of complexity has been found as a general trait in infants and adults. Infants have a harder time processing complex relations like containment than they do processing simpler relations such as interposition (Baillargeon & Wang, 2002). Additionally, recent research suggests that adult speakers are sensitive to event complexity in their willingness to violate iconicity expectations during narrative discourse (Dery & Koenig, in press). We therefore consider both the quantitative and qualitative aspects of complexity to be relevant for event categorization.

3.2 Time scale

The parameter of time scale includes binary distinctions such as events that are permanent rather than temporary or bounded rather than unbounded, but also includes differences in duration along a continuum, e.g. events that occur in the space of one second in comparison to events that happen over the course of several months, years or millennia. An example of a difference along a continuum is found in (4).

(4) a. Royal Bank of Scotland bought Bank Worcester at the end of 1990.
b. I stopped at a bar just long enough to buy two cheese rolls.

While buying a couple of cheese rolls as in (4b) takes only a moment, the consolidation of two banks as in (4a) generally does not.

The linguistics literature on event structure is rife with binary time scale distinctions. Events are often discussed in terms of whether or not they are telic, bounded (Verkuyl, 1972), culminating (Moens & Steedman, 1988), or delimited (Tenny, 1987). In addition to the latter theoretical support, experimental evidence for sensitivity to binary time scale distinctions may be found within both the acquisition literature — e.g. children's marking those distinctions even when their languages do not (Clark, 2001 & 2003) — and studies of adult narrative discourse, where situations with inherent endpoints bias narrators towards different types of continuations (Dery & Koenig, in press). In establishing Gold Standard categories for our data, we consider both the binary and continuous dimensions of temporal distinctions described above.

3.3 Agent type

We use the term 'agent' here in a broad sense; while characteristics such as animacy and volition are prototypical, they are not required. Agents are distinguishable from one another according to such properties as whether they are individuals or groups, animate or inanimate, physical or abstract, etc., and the type of agent exerts an influence on event interpretation and categorization. Example (5) presents two sentences that involve distinct types of agents.

(5) a. A Genoese fleet rescued the city.
b. Archaeologists rescue information about the past before it is destroyed.

From differences in agent type it is possible to predict that the rescuing events described are different categories of rescuing. (5a) describes a large concerted operation involving many individuals, machinery, national resources, extensive planning and so on, while (5b) involves none of these things.

Evidence for the parameter of agent type also comes from reading time experiments and experiments using event-related potentials (ERPs) in which participants show sensitivity to the combination of agent and verb when processing event patients (Bicknell et al. 2010).

3.4 Sociocultural salience

A factor that, to our knowledge, has been entirely missed or ignored in the literature on event categorization – perhaps because it is so difficult to quantify – is social or cultural salience. Yet it is uncontestable that some objects, characteristics, or events are set apart from others because of their importance within the practices of a community. (6a) differs from (6b) because the event category described, book-borrowing, has become institutionalized to the extent that we have public buildings devoted solely to facilitating that practice.

(6) a. The room is for pupils to borrow books.
b. Can you borrow an iron for me?

To our knowledge, the borrowing of irons has yet to achieve such lofty status on the public agenda. The salience of any particular category of event will vary across populations of language users, as well as across languages, to the extent that language and cultural practices co-vary.

3.5 Inferences

As additional information combines with that of the verb, more inferences become available, and many of these inferences may be relevant to event categorization. Consider the examples in (7).

(7) a. She adjusted the scarf to cover the bruises forming on her neck.
b. The children covered their eyes and turned away as the needle went in.

In (7a), the agent presumably desires to hide a bruise from the sight of others, while in (7b), the inference is not that the children are trying to prevent others from seeing their eyes; rather, they are trying to keep themselves from witnessing something unpleasant. Such inferences are often unavailable compositionally. World knowledge associated with the description conveyed by the verb *and* its arguments must be added to the compositional meaning before such inferences can be drawn.

3.6 Specific motion sequence

Certain events are characterized by a sequence of motions that set them apart from events that can be performed in any number of ways. These events may often be described as actions performed according to a recognizable motor program put into action by the event participant(s). Though distinctions along this dimension are admittedly rarer than those made via many of the other parameters, they do exist, as the examples in (8) show.

(8) a. Charlery pulled the ball behind Halsall.
b. The General shouted at his men to pull the barricade down.

The category of event described in (8a) requires a specific motion in which the leg is moved forward over the ball, the toe is brought down into contact with the top of the ball, and the leg and ball are pulled back together; pulling down a barricade as in (8b), however, may be accomplished through a variety of unspecified means.

4 Experiment 1: Manual categorization

While the above parameters for distinguishing event categories may sound plausible, there is no guarantee that their application will result in a division of event descriptions that is equally plausible. In order to make such a determination, each of the authors categorized the same large set of event descriptions by hand. The results of this process were then used as a Gold Standard for subsequent automation of the categorization task. For the purposes of this exploratory study, we elected to limit our investigation to variation within the head noun included in subjects and direct objects for a given verb, while recognizing that information from other portions of the clause may play a role in event categorization. The methods we employ are easily extendible to include other constituents such as prepositional phrases.

4.1 Materials and procedure

Through the use of the software package Tgrep2 (Rohde, 2005), a full list of sentences containing the following 10 verbs was obtained from the British National Corpus (BNC): *bake*, *borrow*, *buy*, *cover*, *deliver*, *frighten*, *immerse*, *pull*, *rescue*, and *sell*. The total sample comprised approximately 43,000 sentences. The sentences in the sample were then randomized and a list of the first 100 sentences with unique subjects was compiled for each verb. Items with pronominal subjects were excluded because without access to an anaphoric or deictic referent, pronouns contribute relatively little information beyond that contributed by the verb. Items with subjects that were proper names, which similarly contribute little or no information useful for categorization, were also excluded. Lastly, sentences with ambiguous or incorrect parses were removed from the sample by hand. Sentences in the sample were then randomized once more and another list for each verb was compiled containing the first 100 sentences with unique direct objects. The product of this process was 20 lists — two for each of ten verbs — totaling 1602 sentences.[2]

Because pronouns constitute a much larger proportion of subjects than direct objects, our decision to exclude pronouns may artificially inflate the contribution of subjects (vs. direct objects) to the diversity of event categories, though this is primarily an issue only with small sample sizes. In total, pronouns constituted 49.64% of subjects and 19.51% of direct objects for the verbs included in our sample and proper names constituted 12.23% of subjects and 3.18% of direct objects.

Each of the authors independently categorized each list of sample sentences. The event categories discovered were discussed until consensus was reached.[3] The resulting event categories were then compared against verb senses obtained from the American Heritage Dictionary (AHD) in order to determine the efficacy of verb senses in capturing the event category distinctions we found. Dictionary senses that were not found in any of our sample sentences were ignored.

4.2 Results

The AHD provides an average of 3.8 senses per verb in our list.[4] Categorization by application of our parameters provided an average of 16.5 event categories per verb. Of these categories, 62% came from the direct object sentence lists, suggesting that there is an asymmetry between subjects and direct objects in distinguishing among event categories (p = .009, n = 165 categories). A comparison of AHD senses to event categories is shown in Table 1.[5]

4.3 Discussion

Several regularities arose during the categorization process. The direct object lists almost always contributed larger numbers of categories than the subject lists. In some respects, this finding is not unexpected. Agents generally play a minor role in characterizing events. Intuitively, "A man raised a finger" could be paraphrased as a finger-raising event, but not as a man-raising event (as opposed to a woman-raising event). We also found that

[2] Not all lists were 100 items in length, simply because some verbs had fewer than 100 valid BNC results after filtering; while we do not explicitly address these cases here, the proper n value for each list was used in all analyses.

[3] Because stable categories were not yet available (the task being to create them), inter-rater agreement was not measured. It is worth noting, however, that our categorizations overlapped to a surprisingly high degree.

[4] The total average number of senses per verb, including those senses not found in our sample sentences, was 5.7 for our 10 verbs.

[5] Event category counts are summed for each verb from subject and direct object lists.

Verb	AHD senses	Categories
bake	2	10
borrow	2	18
buy	3	18
cover	8	30
deliver	7	17
frighten	2	14
immerse	3	8
pull	6	24
rescue	1	13
sell	4	13
Average	**3.8**	**16.5**

Table 1. Comparison of AHD senses to event categories discovered by application of the parameters discussed in Section 3.

some of our proposed parameters were more frequently applicable than others. Unsurprisingly, agent type played a major role in distinguishing event categories within the subject sentence list. It most often followed from differences in plurality (*an uncle borrowed* vs. *the crew borrowed*), animacy (*an uncle borrowed* vs. *an atom borrowed*) and abstractness (*the crew borrowed* vs. *the agenda borrowed*). Complexity, sociocultural salience and inferences also played a large part, while time scale and specific motion sequence tended to take a back seat in both subject and direct object lists.

One further finding not directly evident from the reported results concerns the verb *frighten*. This verb belongs to a relatively small class of psych verbs known as 'object-experiencer' verbs, where one sees a reversal of what otherwise occurs in subject and direct object positions – e.g., a verb like *watch* may occur in *Anne watched the storm*, but *frighten* may only occur in the reverse pattern *the storm frightened Anne*. This reversal was found in our corpus data. The general asymmetry in the number of pronominal subjects and direct objects we observed did not apply to *frighten*, and proper names were found in direct object position more than twice as often for *frighten* as they were for other verbs. If it is world knowledge about what the verb and its arguments describe that is informing event categorization, one would expect that, when the kinds of items typically found in direct object position are instead found in subject position and vice versa, the asymmetry in the relative importance of subjects and objects in distinguishing event categories is also reversed. This is exactly what we found: 64% of the *frighten* categories were distinguished by the combination of verb and subject. The results for *frighten* suggest that the asymmetry between subjects and objects is not due to grammatical function, lending support to our claim that the parameters outlined in Section 3 are independent of a language's morphosyntax.

One final finding of our first experiment is worth noting and bears directly on the design of Experiment 2. In general, the more semantically similar to one another any pair of a verb's subjects or direct objects were, the more likely the events described by the combination of those items with the verb were to be put in the same event category. For example, the events described by *covered their hands* and *covered their feet* are more likely to be in the same category than either is to be in a category with *covered their city*, simply because *hands* and *feet* are more semantically similar to one another than either is to *city*. We adopt this finding as an assumption for automating event categorization in Experiment 2.

5 Experiment 2: LSA categorization

Categorizing even a relatively short list for only ten verbs turned out to be quite difficult and time-consuming. It is therefore desirable to find a dynamic and automatic way to categorize any event description as it is encountered. Below we describe a first try at such automation, using Latent Semantic Analysis (LSA) and hierarchical clustering to approximate our Gold Standard categories.

LSA is a method for evaluating semantic similarity from corpora containing collections of independent documents. It requires the creation of large, sparse matrices which track each word's frequency of co-occurrence with each other word within each document. The matrix is reduced to a target number of only the most salient dimensions, usually between 50 and 400, and within the resulting semantic space it is possible to locate each word as a vector (see Deerwester et al., 1990 for a detailed description). The upshot of this process is that those words which occur together in the same documents most often (and whose frequent companions also occur together most often) are considered highly related and will usually occur near each other in the semantic space. LSA predictions matched scores of non-native college applicants in

TOEFL tests of word similarity (Landauer et al., 1998).

5.1 Materials and Procedure

Through the application of latent semantic analysis to a 400-dimensional semantic space created from the British National Corpus, pair-wise relatedness value were calculated for each subject list and each direct object list. The result was approximately $\sum_{i=1}^{100} i = 5050$ relatedness values for each list. The `hclust` command in R (R Core Team, 2015) was then used to construct an average-linkage dendrogram from the half matrix containing each list of relatedness values. Though the full 100-item dendrograms cannot fit a page in a readable form, a slice from the *borrow* direct object list is included here as Figure 1 for illustrative purposes.

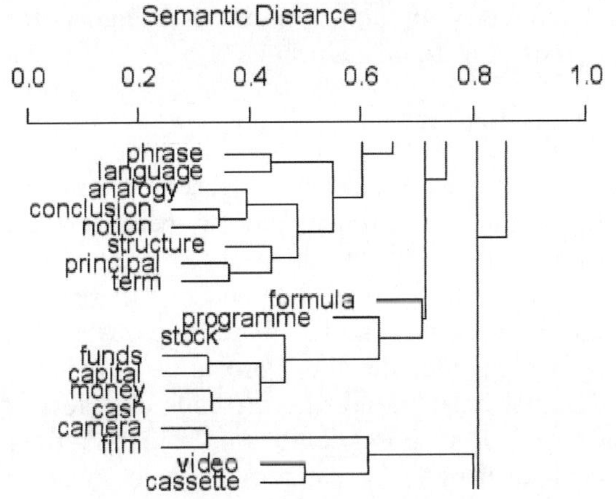

Figure 1. A section of the dendrogram created by using LSA semantic distance values to group direct objects of the verb *borrow*.

At a glance, three distinct categories are visible in Figure 1: a category of language-related items, a category of currency-related items, and a category containing videography-related items. Dendrograms are built from the bottom up (from left to right in Figure 1) by combining the most closely related branches at each step, eventually fusing the final two clusters into one unified tree. Using R's `cutree` command, this process can be reversed by counting splits from the top down until the number of categories identified in the Gold Standard categorization is reached – for the *borrow* direct objects list, that number was 13. Each list's full dendrogram was deconstructed in this way.

Precision and recall were obtained as they are for V-measures (Rosenberg and Hirschberg, 2007). For each subject or direct object in its respective list, we found the set **H** of all other words that had been assigned to the same category by LSA. The cardinality of this set represents the total number of *hypothesized* items in that word's category. We then found the set **A** of all words that had been assigned to the same category in the Gold Standard. The cardinality of this set represents the total number of *actual* items in that word's category. Thirdly, we found the intersection of the latter two sets $\mathbf{H} \cap \mathbf{A}$. The cardinality of this set represents the total number of items correctly categorized by the automated categorization.

Precision ($p = |\mathbf{H} \cap \mathbf{A}|/|\mathbf{H}|$) and recall ($r = |\mathbf{H} \cap \mathbf{A}|/|\mathbf{A}|$) values were then calculated for each item and combined for an *F*-score that is their harmonic mean ($F = 2pr/(p + r)$). Finally, 100 random categorizations were performed for each list as a measure of comparison.

5.2 Results

The average LSA and randomized *F*-scores for each list type are reported in Table 2.[6]

List	p LSA	r LSA	F LSA	F rand	Ratio
Subj	40%	80%	.53	.39	1.38
DO	35%	66%	.46	.32	1.46
Overall	**38%**	**73%**	**.50**	**.35**	**1.42**

Table 2. *F*-scores for LSA categories, compared to *F*-scores for randomized categories. Ratios represent how much better than chance LSA categorization performed.

The LSA automated categorization resulted in an average of 42% more accurate categorization than that obtained by random categorization.

[6] Average *F*-scores are weighted by list length, i.e. those lists significantly shorter than 100 items – specifically lists for *bake* and *immerse* in our sample – were given proportionally less weight in calculating overall averages.

5.3 Discussion

The combination of high recall and low precision suggests that the automated categorization tends to lump a large portion of each list into only a few categories, populating the remaining categories with only a small number of outliers. Our categorization when creating the Gold Standard, in contrast, tended to distribute items more evenly over event categories. The imbalance turns out to be a consequence of the particular clustering method used in creating the LSA categories – in this case, the average linkage method. Some methods (e.g. the Ward method) instead favor increased precision over recall. In our tests, recall-biased methods invariably resulted in better F-measures.[7]

Looking at the differences in category members within Gold Standard and LSA results may provide insight into both where LSA fails and where alternative parameters may have escaped our notice. The *bake* object list yields several such exemplars. In creating our Gold Standard, we categorized baking events according to such criteria as whether or not the baked item requires preparation (e.g. making and rolling dough, etc.), which adds to the complexity of the baking event, and whether the item undergoes a transformation in the baking process (e.g., dough becomes bread, but a potato remains a potato). The LSA categorization, in contrast, appeared to reflect ethnic/cultural cuisine categories rather than processes undergone by the materials involved: the cluster containing *soufflé*, *aubergine*, *fillet* and *flan* was separated from that containing *potato*, *pie* and *cake*. This makes sense when one considers that the relatedness measures used by the LSA are obtained from co-occurrence of words within documents – and recipes, from which many of the baking event clauses were extracted, are often found in documents that focus on a specific kind of cuisine. It is worth stressing that this difference in categorization is not simply an indication of the limitations of LSA. Rather, it brings to light an important dimension of categorization that was not considered in our Gold Standard; baking events may quite plausibly be divided into French baking, American baking, etc. It is possible that in this instance we simply missed differences in sociocultural salience (the fourth parameter in Section 3) that stem from the role that baking plays in cultural nutrition.

We also found reflexes of the asymmetry between subjects and objects within LSA relatedness measures. Average relatedness among direct objects for a given verb was significantly higher than relatedness among subjects for seven of the eight verbs listed in the results. The one verb for which this did not hold was *frighten*, where we expected and saw a reversal in number of categories discovered when sorting by hand. When *frighten* is excluded, inter-object relatedness is on average 35% higher than inter-subject relatedness. In other words, the direct objects for a verb tend to be more closely related to one another than the subjects of that verb are. The exact nature of the relationship between this asymmetry in relatedness scores and the asymmetry in contribution to category formation remains to be determined.

6 Conclusion

Preliminary categorizations suggest that language users are capable of much finer-grained event categorization than that provided at the level of verb senses (at a ratio of over 4:1) and that these event categories are associated with multi-word expressions which include the verb plus direct object/subject head. Using the methods described in this paper, it is possible to automate this finer-grained level of event categorization to some degree. With respect to both of these findings, there is an asymmetry between English subjects and direct objects in their contribution to categorization – the combination of direct objects and verbs accounts for a greater share of category distinctions than the combination of subjects with verbs. This asymmetry is purely conceptual, independent of any theoretical assumptions regarding order of syntactic composition, and is reflected in LSA relatedness measures.

We are at the time of writing conducting experiments with naïve speakers to norm our Gold Standard categorization and assess the independent contribution of different parameters in event categorization. The contribution of information other than the subject and direct object also deserves to be explored in more detail and the analysis should be expanded both to languages beyond English.

[7] Methods tested in order of improvement over random categorization were average linkage (42%), single linkage (41%), McQuitty (33%), complete linkage (18%) and Ward (7%). Note that single linkage prefers 'lumping' to a greater degree than average linkage, but results in slightly less improvement.

Additionally, LSA is only one source of relatedness measures among many; it competes with various WordNet algorithms, mutual information measures, and newer predictive measures (see e.g. Baroni et al. 2014). Though one might expect a high correlation among these measures, it turns out that very often the correlation is surprisingly low, and thus one could conceivably obtain very different categories depending on the method used to measure semantic similarity (Maki et al., 2004). It may be that some methods result in relatedness scores that better approximate human categorization than others, and these alternatives deserve exploration.

References

Baillargeon, R. & Wang, S. (2002). Event categorization in infancy. *Trends in Cognitive Sciences, 6,* 85-93.

Baker, C., Fillmore, C. & Lowe, J. (1998). The Berkeley FrameNet project. In *Proceedings of COLING-ACL 1998*, pp. 86-90.

Baroni, M., Dinu, G. & Kruszewski, G. (2014). Don't count, predict! A systematic comparison of context-counting vs. context-predicting semantic vectors. In *Proceedings of the 52nd Annual Meeting of the Association for Computational Linguistics*, pp. 238-247.

Bicknell et al. (2010). Effects of event knowledge in processing verbal arguments. *Journal of Memory and Language, 63,* 489-505.

Clark, E. V. (2001). Emergent categories in first language acquisition. In M. Bowerman & S.C. Levinson (Eds.), *Language acquisition and conceptual development* (pp. 379-405). Cambridge: Cambridge University Press.

Clark, E.V. (2003). *First language acquisition.* New York: Cambridge University Press.

Deerwester, S., Dumais, S., Furnas, G., Landauer, T., & Harshman, R. (1990). Indexing by latent semantic analysis. *Journal of the American Society for Information Science*, 41(6): 391-407.

Dery, J. & Koenig, J.P. (in press). A Narrative-Expectation-Based Approach to Temporal Update in Discourse Comprehension. *Discourse Processes*, 00: 1-26.

Dowty, D. (1979). *Word Meaning and Montague Grammar*. Dordrecht: Reidel.

Erk, K. & Padó, S. (2008). A structured vector space model forword meaning in context. In *Proceedings of the 2008 Conference on Empirical Methods in Natural Language Processing*, pp. 897-906.

Evans, G. (1980). Pronouns. *Linguistic Inquiry,* 11: 337-362.

Hanks, P. (2004). Corpus Pattern Analysis. In *Proceedings of the 2004 Conference of the European Association for Lexicography (EURALEX)*, pp. 87-97.

Landauer, T. K., Foltz, P. W., & Laham, D. (1998). Introduction to Latent Semantic Analysis. *Discourse Processes, 25*(2&3).

Lenci, A. (2011). Composing and updating verb argument expectations: A distributional semantic model. In *Proceedings of the 2nd ACL Workshop on Cognitive Modeling and Computational Linguistics*, pp. 58-66.

Maki, W., McKinley, L., Thompson, A. (2004). Semantic distance norms computed from an electronic dictionary (WordNet). *Behavior Research Methods, Instruments, & Computers, 36* (3): 421-431.

McRae, K., Spivey-Knowlton, M. & Tanenhaus, M. (1998). Modeling the influence of thematic fit (and other constraints) in on-line sentence comprehension. *Journal of Memory and Language, 38*: 283–312.

McRae, K., Hare, M., Elman, J. & Ferretti, T. (2005). A basis for generating expectancies for verbs from nouns. *Memory & Cognition, 33*(7): 1174–1184.

R Core Team (2015). R: A language and environment for statistical computing. R Foundation for Statistical Computing, Vienna, Austria. Available from http://www.R-project.org/

Rohde, Douglas (2005). Tgrep2 [Computer software]. Department of Brain and Cognitive Science, Massachusetts Institute of Technology. Retrieved March 19, 2014. Available from http://tedlab.mit.edu/~dr/Tgrep2/

Rosenberg, A. & Hirschberg, J. (2007). Vmeasure: A conditional entropy-based external cluster evaluation measure. In *Proceedings of the 2007 Joint Conference on Empirical Methods in Natural Language Processing and Computational Natural Language Learning* (EMNLP-CoNLL), pp. 410–420.

Sag, I., Baldwin, T., Bond, F., Copestake, A. & Flickinger, D. (2001). Multiword expressions: A pain in the neck for NLP. In *Proceedings from 3rd International Conference on Intelligent Text Processing and Computational Linguistics*: CICLing.

Shapiro, S. C., & Rapaport, W. J. 1992. The sneps family. *Computers & Mathematics with Applications*, 23, 243-275.

Talmy, L. (1985a). Force Dynamics in language and thought. In *Papers from the Regional Meetings, Chicago Linguistic Society*, 21, 293–337.

Talmy, L. (1985b). Lexicalization patterns: Semantic structure in lexical form. In T. Shopen (Ed.). *Language typology and syntactic description: Vol. 3. Grammatical categories and the lexicon,* pp. 57–149. Cambridge: Cambridge University Press.

Tenny, C. (1987). *Grammaticalizing aspect and affectedness*. Doctoral dissertation, MIT.

Verkuyl, H.J. (1972). *On the compositional nature of the aspects*. Dordrecht: Reidel.

Villavicencio, A., Kordoni, V., Zhang, Y., Idiart, M., and Ramisch, C. (2007). Validation and evaluation of automatically acquired multiword expressions for grammar engineering. In *Proceedings of the 2007 Joint Conference on Empirical Methods in Natural Language Processing and Computational Natural Language Learning* (EMNLP-CoNLL), pp. 1034–1043.

Wilson, S., and Center for the Study of Language and Information (U.S.). (1999). *Coverbs and Complex Predicates in Wagiman*. Stanford, Calif: CSLI Publications.

WordNet Statistics. Princeton University. 2015. < https://wordnet.princeton.edu/wordnet/man/wnstats.7WN.html>

Muddying The Multiword Expression Waters: How Cognitive Demand Affects Multiword Expression Production

Adam Goodkind
CUNY Graduate Center
agoodkind@gradcenter.cuny.edu

Andrew Rosenberg
CUNY Queens College
andrew@cs.qc.cuny.edu

Abstract

Multiword expressions (MWEs) are vexing for linguists, psycholinguists and computational linguists, as they are hard to define, detect and parse. However, previous studies have not taken into account the cognitive constraints under which MWEs are produced or comprehended. We present a new modality for studying MWEs, keystroke dynamics. We ask subjects to respond to a variety of questions, varying in the level of cognitive demand required to generate an answer. In each response, a subject's pause time preceding each word – within and outside an MWE – can illuminate distinct differences in required effort across tasks. By taking advantage of high-precision keystroke loggers, we show that MWEs produced under greater cognitive demands are produced more slowly, at a rate more similar to free expressions. We hypothesize that increasingly burdensome cognitive demands diminish the capacity of lexical retrieval, and cause MWE production to slow.

1 Introduction

Multi-word expressions (MWEs) are vexing for both theoretical linguists and those working in Natural Language Processing. For theoretical linguists, MWEs occupy a liminal space between the lexicon and syntax (Langacker, 2008). For NLP practitioners, MWEs are notoriously difficult to detect and parse (Sag et al., 2002).

This paper presents a new modality for studying MWE production, keystroke dynamics, which allows for large-scale, low-cost, high-precision metrics (cf. (Cohen Priva et al., 2010)). Keystroke dynamics looks at the speed at which a user's hands move across a keyboard (Bergadano et al., 2002). It has the distinct advantage of using written text, with clear word and sentence boundaries, while combining it with dynamic production features, allowing for greater insight into the language creation process.

This study explores the notion that many of the principles that guide intonation and speech prosody are also present during the typing production process. Principles related to prosody need not be limited to spoken language production. The *Implicit Prosody Hypothesis*, for example, posits that a "silent prosodic contour" is projected onto a stimulus, and may help a reader resolve syntactic ambiguity (Fodor, 2002). Previous studies applied this hypothesis to silent reading (Fodor, 2002). The present study, in turn, applies this same principle to (silent) typing: Language users take advantage of prosodic contours to help organize and make sense of language stimulus, whether in the form of words they are perceiving or words they are producing.

Moreover, in previous studies, the *type* of question a subject is asked, in order to elicit a response, has not been taken into consideration. We take advantage of the low cost and high precision of keystroke dynamics to uncover trends in MWE production, by eliciting responses from subjects using a variety of questions with very different cognitive demands. Our findings show that the cognitive demands of an elicitation task have a noticeable effect on how MWEs are produced during a response. These findings have important ramifications for linguists performing MWE-related experiments, and cognitive scientists studying how lexical items are stored and retrieved.

In order to run our analysis, we collected free response typing data from a large set of subjects. The subjects responded to a wide array of cognitively demanding prompts, from simple recall to more complex, creative analysis. From this data, we then perform two experiments. In a preliminary experiment, we analyze how linguistic attributes such as word length and predictability shape keystroke produc-

Proceedings of NAACL-HLT 2015, pages 87–95,
Denver, Colorado, May 31 – June 5, 2015.

tion. In our main experiment, we then use these findings to analyze how multiword expression production is affected by the cognitive demands imposed upon the subjects.

We hypothesize that the cognitive demands of a task will impede MWE production, as the overall demands will interfere with lexical retrieval, creating a cognitive bottleneck. Our study aims to shed light on three sets of questions:

- Are MWEs produced differently depending upon the type of task they are produced within? If so, how?
- Can patterns in MWE production provide insights regarding constraints on lexical retrieval?
- What are the benefits of keystroke dynamics for psycholingistics studies?

The rest of the paper is organized as follows: Section 2 situates our study in context, illustrating how prosody is affected by MWEs, and keystroke dynamics relates to cognition. Section 3 outlines our experiments, with results reported in Section 4. Our results are discussed in Section 5, with a conclusion and look towards future work in Section 6.

2 Related Work

Our study brings together MWEs, cognition and keystroke dynamics in a novel manner. In order to situate our investigation in context, we explore relevant previous studies below, and explain how their findings contribute to the present work.

2.1 MWEs in speech production

Many studies have concluded that multiword expressions are stored and retrieved as single lexical units (Wray, 2005; Dahlmann and Adolphs, 2007, and references therein). As such, MWEs exhibit unique phonological and prosodic characteristics. For example, MWEs have been found to exhibit greater phonological consistency than free expressions (Hickey, 1993). Specifically, pauses have been found to be less acceptable in lexicalized phrases (Pawley, 1985). In addition, and most relevant to our study, Dahlmann and Adolph study how pausality differs in and around MWEs (Dahlmann and Adolphs, 2007). They conclude that "...where pauses occur they give valuable indications of possible [MWE] boundaries". (Dahlmann and Adolphs, 2007, p. 55)

In many ways, the present study can, and should, be viewed as an extension of Dahlmann and Adolphs' study. If we view keystroke dynamics as a reflection of many speech production principles in the typing process, then this is a reasonable extension. We augment the previous findings, though, by investigating how varying cognitive demands affect MWE production.

In studies of speech, Erman (2007) notes that a pause can be caused by the cognitive demands of lexical retrieval, and Pawley (1985) notes that pauses are much less acceptable within a lexicalized phrase than within a free expression. This led Dahlmann and Adolphs (2007) to study pausing within spoken MWEs. A central finding of Dahlmann & Adolphs is that MWEs are often surrounded by pauses, and that pausality is unique within and around MWEs.

In addition, Dahlmann & Adolphs note the difficulty of accurately measuring pauses in speech; keystroke dynamics does not face that obstacle.

2.2 Typing Behavior and Cognition

Typing is an interesting blend of cognitive and physical activity. On the cognitive side, a typist must undertake the cognitively demanding task of text production. Although literate people produce text on a nearly daily basis, researchers have gone so far as to call the writing process "one of the most complex and demanding activities that humans engage in" (Alves et al., 2008, p. 2). The act of typing involves juggling both the high-level text creation process, and low-level motor execution.

Beginning in the 1980s (Rumelhart and Norman, 1982), investigators used typing data to construct cognitive and motor models of language production. As expounded by Salthouse (1986), a typist must simultaneously employ multiple cognitive and motor schemata, often with a formidable amount of noise between signals. Translating from lexical retrieval into physical action is a non-trivial task, which involves multiple pipelines that can be occluded, and also result in mixed up signals.

The typing task is especially daunting for novice typists. Gentner, et al. (1988) investigated the linguistic characteristics of skilled versus unskilled typists, finding marked differences in the behavior (and thus cognitive model) of each population. A novice typist is so burdened by the physical execution cycle of typing that the quality of his or her writing is noticeably diminished.

However, Alves et al. (2008), in studying narrative construction in typing conclude that while differences do exist between the populations, this might not be as significant a differentiation as originally thought. They conclude, "Although motor execution is more demanding for slow typists, this higher demand neither prevented them from activating high-level processes concurrently with typing, nor changed the distribution of occurrences of the writing processes." (Alves et al., 2008, p. 10)

The importance of pauses during the typing process is borne out in a number of studies. Schilperoord (2002) concludes that writers pause for a number of reasons, such as cognitive overload, writing apprehension or fatigue. Alves et al. (2008) similarly concluded that pauses are usually a sign of cognitive competition. Many of the reasons given for pausing during typing are similar to the reasons given for pausing during speech production, thus providing further motivation to use the typing process to test phenomena observed during speech.

3 Methodology

3.1 Procedure

Our typing data was collected from 189 Louisiana Tech students (hereinafter referred to as "subjects"). The subjects reported themselves to be 41.3% female, 56.4% male and 88.3% right-handed and 9.1% left-handed. (Note that these do not sum to 100%; on each question some percentage of subjects chose not to respond to one or more of the demographic questions.)

We limited our study to only native English speakers. This was to avoid the additional confound of language familiarity, though this is certainly an important area for study. Specifically, Riggenbach (1991) found that in speech, placement and length of pausing around MWEs is seen as a sign of fluency.

Further, we limited our study to only "touch typists", or those subjects who only look at the screen when typing. This is in comparison to "visual typists" who look at their fingers when typing. As proposed by Johanssen et al. (2010), touch-typists and visual typists employ distinct cognitive models, as visual typists also need to dedicate cognitive effort to figuring out where the next key is. For touch typists, this is a less conscious process.

Subjects were seated at a desktop computer with a QWERTY keyboard, and freely responded to prompts of varying complexity. A keylogger with 15.625 millisecond clock resolution was used to record text and keystroke event timestamps. There was no time limit, although subjects had to type at least 300 characters before proceeding to the next prompt. Each subject responded to $10 - 12$ prompts, with the average response comprising 448 characters and 87 words.

Prompts were designed to test all aspects of Bloom's Taxonomy of learning (Krathwohl, 2002), from simple to more complex tasks. Bloom's Taxonomy includes six different types of tasks: *remember, understand, apply, analyze, evaluate* and *create*. The Bloom Taxonomy is ordered by complexity, in that mastery of one learning objective is necessary in order to progress to the next. It is a useful way for educators to structure a curriculum, in order to ensure that learners possess the necessary cognitive abilities before progressing to more complex tasks. The taxonomy has been refined and expanded in recent years; as such, we treat each type of task as a discrete type of task, rather than having a continuous relationship.

The order that the prompts were presented in was randomized, with an equal distribution from each type of task. Examples of prompts include (1) and (2):

(1) *List the recent movies you've seen or books you've read. When did you see or read them? What were they about?* [Remember]

(2) *How would you design a class if you were the teacher? What subject would you teach? How would you structure your course?* [Create]

The full data set is part of a long-term longitudinal study relating to subject biometrics. Although the current data is not publicly available, we hope to release future data sets.

3.2 Materials

All texts were tokenized using OpenNLP (Baldridge, 2005). We then automatically extracted all multiword expressions using jMWE (Finlayson and Kulkarni, 2011). For the present studies we only looked at contiguous MWEs. jMWE has reported an F_1 measure of 83.4 in detecting continuous, unbroken MWEs in the Semcor (Mihalcea, 1998) Brown Concordance (Finlayson and Kulkarni, 2011).

Contiguous MWEs should show more signs of being a cohesive lexical unit, although non-contiguous MWEs should still exhibit some degree of the same. As a result of this exclusion, MWEs such as *ran up* in (3) would be included in our study, while the same non-contiguous MWE in (4) would not.

(3) *Jack ran up the bill.*

(4) *Jill ran the bill up.*

While keystroke dynamics is concerned with a number of timing metrics, such as key holds (*h* in Figure 1) and pauses between every keystroke (*p* in Figure 1), the current study looked only at the pause preceding a word (the second *p* in Figure 1). This interval consists of the time between the spacebar being released and the first key of the word being pressed.

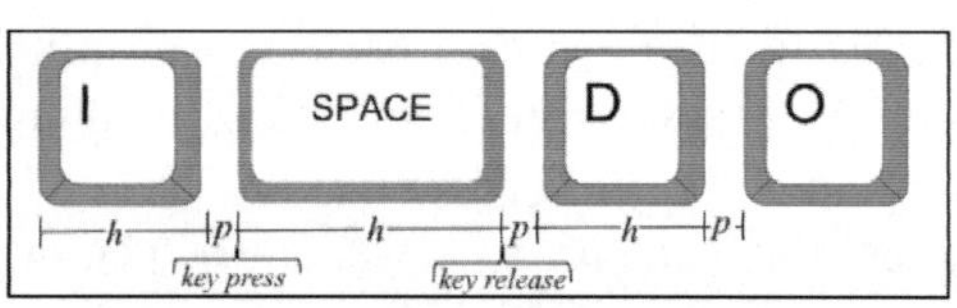

Figure 1: Timing Intervals in Keystroke Dynamics
p = pause *h* = hold

We also did not remove any outliers, although this is common in keystroke dynamics (Epp et al., 2011; Zhong et al., 2012). We feel it is difficult-to-impossible to discriminate between a "true" pause that is indicative of a subject's increased cognitive effort and any other type of pause, such as those caused by distraction or physical fatigue. As such we include any idiosyncrasies, such as long pauses, in our analyses rather than dismiss them as noise.

4 Experiments

4.1 Experiment 1: Creating A Baseline

In the main experiment, we measure the pause preceding each word. However, we wanted to remove as many confounds as possible that were not related to whether the word was part of an MWE.

Our first line of investigation aimed to understand the distribution of pauses overall. As seen in Figure 2, pauses are not distributed normally around a mean (non-Gaussian). Rather, there is a strong log-linear relationship between length of pause and frequency. As such, results reported below use the logarithm of the pause time. We felt that reporting the raw pause time would obfuscate important patterns within pausality.

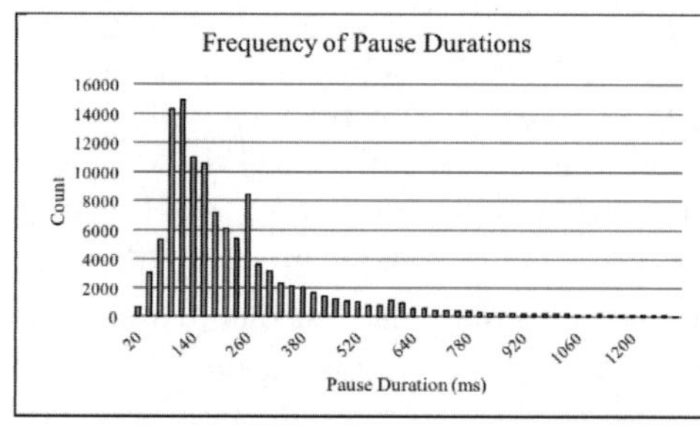

Figure 2: Distribution of All Pauses

As noted by Nottbusch & Weingarten (2007), the length of a written word affects pre-word pausing. We quantified this by mapping each pre-word pause to the length of the word, and found a strong logarithmic relationship, where pause length increased as a function of the log of the word length (see Figure 3). Since we expect cognitive demand to affect typing, we measured this affect on each task, and created different α and β parameters for our "Expected Pause" algorithm, as described in (5).

(5) $Pause_{expected}(w) = \alpha \cdot \ln(length(w)) + \beta$

The regression model illustrated in (5) provided a very reliable fit for all tasks. Between tasks α ranged from $0.107-0.112$ while β ranged from $2.20-2.24$. In the various versions of the Expected Pause algorithm, R^2 ranged from $0.93 - 0.98$ yet the differences were never significant, with $0.22 < p < 0.58$.

In our main experiment, all pauses were quantified as a deviation from the expected pause, based on word length and cognitive demand.

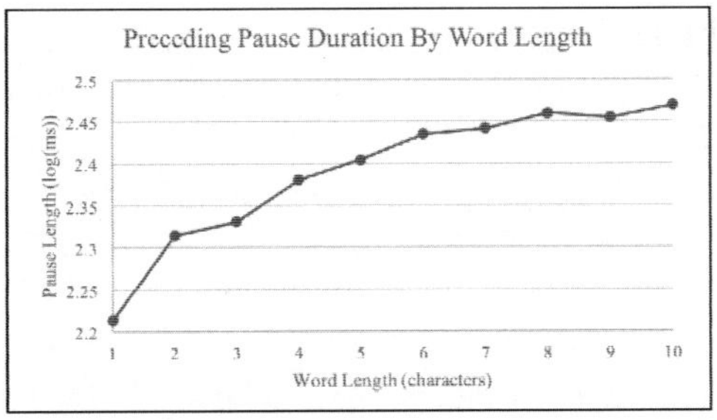

Figure 3: Duration of Pre-Word Pause By Word Length

A final confound to be investigated was sequence likelihood. The effects of predictability are well documented, in that more likely sequences are produced and comprehended at a faster rate (Goldman-Eisler, 1958; Hale, 2006; Nottbusch et al., 2007; Levy, 2008; Smith and Levy, 2013, and references therein). Since MWEs are frequently made up of collocations, i.e. words that are often seen together, they are inherently highly predictable.

For the present study, we wanted to ensure that we were not simply detecting faster rates of highly predictable sequences, but rather that we were detecting a signal idiosyncratic to MWEs. To test this, we grouped all word tokens according to the bigram predictability of the sequence they occurred within. Bigram predictability was calculated using a development set of users to create a language model. Smoothing was done using the Laplace technique with the inverse vocabulary size, as described in (6), where V is the total number of possible bigrams, i.e., the vocabulary size for a bigram model, and C is the total count of occurrences.

(6) $$P(w_n|w_{n-1}) = \frac{C(w_{n\text{-}1}w_n)+1}{C(w_{n\text{-}1})+V}$$

The grouping was done by rounding the log probability of the bigram sequence. We looked at the most highly predictable groups, to see if MWEs were still produced differently from free expressions, when compared to sequences of similar likelihood.

Our results are illustrated in Figure 4. Using a two-tailed t-test, and assuming equal variance, the differences for the two most highly predictable groups (where rounded log probability was -1 and 0) is significant at the 0.00001 level, while it is not significant for left-most grouping (rounded log probability of -2). The overall difference for all levels of predictability is significant at the 0.000001 level.

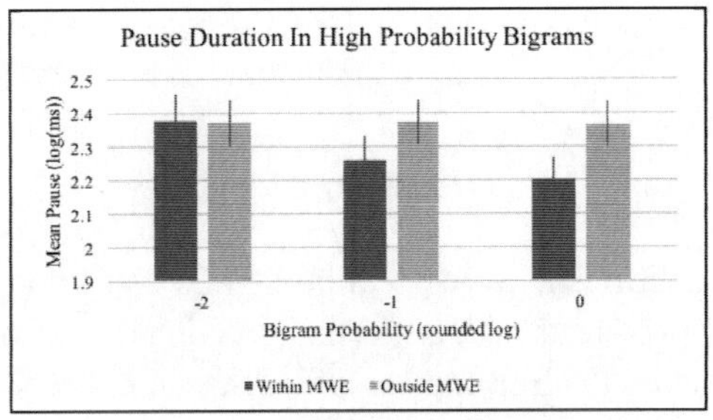

Figure 4: MWE Production in High Predictability Sequences.

4.2 Experiment 2: MWEs in Varying Cognitive Tasks

MWEs were produced at a fairly consistently rate across all tasks, comprising approximately $12-13\%$ of all word tokens, as reported in Table 1. It should be noted that this figure is markedly lower than often cited figures such as Erman & Warren (2000), who point out that half of spoken and written language comes from multiword constructions. In the present case, however, we are dealing with a small subset of MWEs, namely those that were produced contiguously (cf. examples (3) and (4) above). A total of $1,982$ different MWEs were produced, across the entire spectrum of "MWE types," from verb-particle constructions to idioms.

Task	Within-MWE Tokens	Outside MWE Tokens	Total Tokens	MWE Rate (%)
Remember	3,285	23,631	26,916	12.2%
Understand	3,986	25,008	28,994	13.7%
Apply	1,807	12,674	14,481	12.5%
Analyze	3,375	21,300	24,675	13.7%
Evaluate	4,957	35,290	40,247	12.3%
Create	3,629	24,042	27,671	13.1%
Total	**21,039**	**141,945**	**162,984**	**12.9%**

Table 1: MWE Production Rates and Counts By Task

Pauses that took place before the first word and directly after the last word of an MWE were not considered to be 'within' the MWE. An example of the pauses we *did* measure is seen in Figure 5. In this figure, the underscores represent measured pauses, while a whitespace gap represents a pause that was not taken into consideration for the present study. Pauses that occur on the edges of MWEs may represent distinct "barrier" pauses (Dahlmann and Adolphs, 2007), and therefore merit a further, but distinct study.

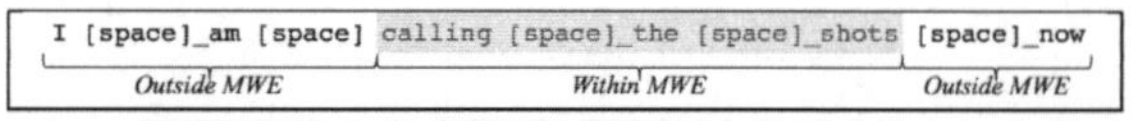

Figure 5: An example sentence. Measured pauses are represented with an underscore.

In each task, words within MWEs were consistently produced with a shorter preceding pause than were words in free expressions. As seen in Figure 6, pauses are shorter within MWEs across all tasks.

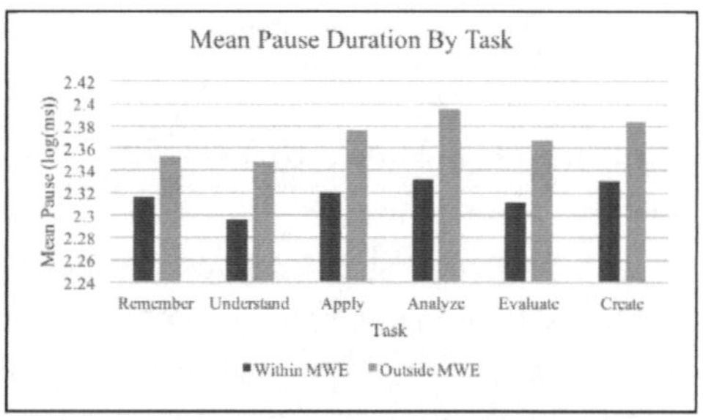

Figure 6: Pause Duration By Task, Within and Outside MWEs

However, the distributions of the means as reported in Figure 7 is not uniform[1].

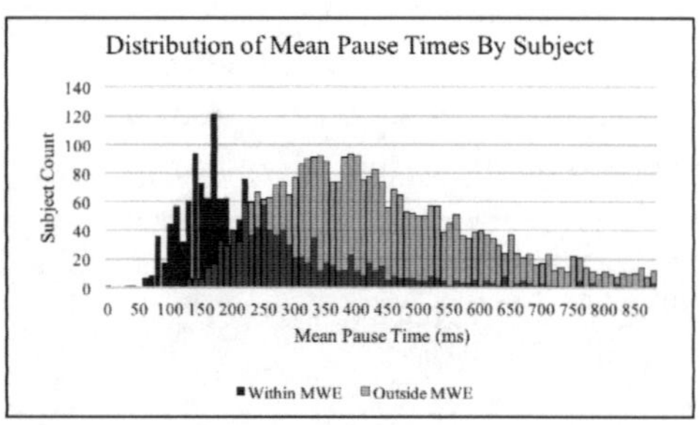

Figure 7: Distribution of Mean Pauses Within and Outside MWEs

Within-MWE pauses are not only shorter in duration, but we see evidence that the distribution is somewhat more concentrated around the mean. Although the standard deviations of each distribution are similar ($s_{within-mwe} = 197.5$, $s_{outside-mwe} = 209.8$), the interquartile ranges were more distinct ($IQR_{within-mwe} = 160$, $IQR_{outside-mwe} = 240$).

However, our investigation aimed to look at how pausing within MWEs varies between cognitive loads, rather than an overall distribution. These results are illustrated in Figure 8. A one-way between category ANOVA was conducted on the pause times, to compare the effects of cognitive demands on pausality. There was a significant effect of cognitive demand at the $p < 0.001$ level, $[F(5, 11796) = 4.19, p = 0.000815]$.

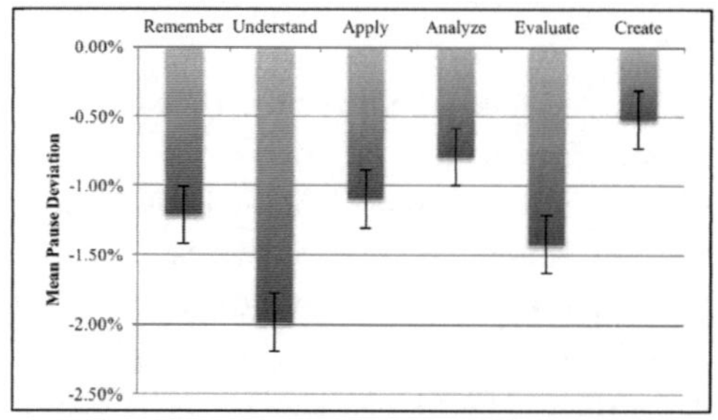

Figure 8: Within-MWE Pause Duration Deviation By Cognitive Task (Tasks are arranged from (generally) simplest to most complex)

5 Discussion

As demonstrated above, the overall cognitive demands of a task have a significant effect on pauses within an MWE. While the trend is generally upward, in that MWEs produced under greater cognitive demand behave more similar to free expressions, i.e. they exhibit longer pauses, we note that this is not perfectly consistent. This is to be expected, as there are many dimensions to each of Bloom's tasks, and each dimension could have greater or lesser effects on pauses within typing. This could also be an artifact of the difficulty of assigning labels using Bloom's Taxonomy, as has been demonstrated even among a group of subject-matter experts (van Hoeij et al., 2004)

These results seem to demonstrate competing cognitive demands, operating in parallel. The canonical theory of MWE production holds that MWEs are retrieved as a single unit. Our results, however, imply that a more nuanced view may be

[1] Figure 7 took the mean pause per subject, rather than mean pause per word token, which is why it uses a linear scale, rather than a logarithmic scale.

justified. If an MWE is retrieved as a single unit, then somewhere between retrieval and execution the overall cognitive demands can interfere. Specifically, we theorize that the overall cognitive demands serve to narrow the bandwidth of lexical retrieval, occluding large units from being holistically moved into the executive buffer, as illustrated in Figure 9. To clarify this idea, though, subsequent investigations will investigate pauses at the boundaries of MWEs.

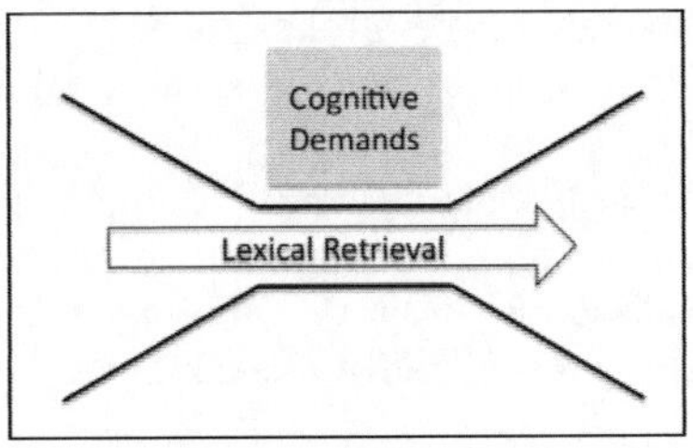

Figure 9: Model of Cognitive Bottleneck

The notion of various schemata interacting is supported by Kellogg (1996), who proposes that "resources from the central executive of Baddeleys model of the working-memory, e.g., Baddeley (1974), are needed to perform both lower-level writing processes such as spelling, grammar and motor movements and higher-level writing processes such as planning and revising." (qtd. in Johansson, 2010).

By comparing the production rates of different types of lexical unit retrieved from working memory – MWES versus free expressions – along with varying the overarching cognitive task, we believe our experiment lends quantifiable support to this notion.

Our findings also bear relevance to investigators performing psycholinguistic experiments. Although most experiments are prepared with careful attention to the linguistic structure of stimulus, such as an elicitation prompt, there exists little attention to the overall cognitive demands a stimulus response requires. Our results, however, demonstrate that overarching cognitive demands can have a significant effect on results.

Finally, we hope our results serve as an illustration of the utility of keystroke dynamics within the linguistic and cognitive science domains. Many studies cite the difficulty of accurately transcribing speech data, delineating word boundaries and quantifying pause duration. Keystroke dynamics is not impeded by any of these factors. Additionally, although the data of this study was collected in a laboratory study, similar studies could be conducted using much less overhead, e.g. Amazon Mechanical Turk (Cohen Priva et al., 2010), where subjects can participate remotely without compromising experiment quality (Snow et al., 2008). This allows for low-cost, high-precision experimentation, with a wider selection of experiment participants.

6 Conclusion and Further Work

In this paper, we found that pauses within an MWE can vary significantly, depending upon the cognitive demands of the task within which they were produced. We first controlled for linguistic factors that affect typing rate, such as word length and predictability, and formed an Expected Pause metric. This metric measures the length of time we expected a subject to pause before a word, based on linguistic attributes. We then measured the divergence of pauses within MWEs, and found they varied significantly depending on the overarching cognitive task.

We believe our study represents a significant finding within MWE and lexical retrieval research. We have been able to directly quantify the effects of overall cognitive demand as it interacts with lexical retrieval. These results should be kept in mind when performing MWE research, as they clearly demonstrate that MWE production can be significantly affected by the cognitive complexity of a task, even if the method of elicitation is kept consistent.

A potentially important factor in MWE production is "MWE type," such as verb-particle construction or idiom. Vincze et al. (2011) found useful differences between types, as they relate to MWE identification. Similarly, Schneider et al. (2014) classified MWEs using "strong" and "weak" dimensions, depending on "the strength of association between words...ranging from fully transparent collocations to completely opaque idioms (Hermann et al., 2012)" (Schneider et al., 2014, p. 456). Future studies will investigate the effects of these dimensions on the dynamics of MWE production.

Subsequent studies will also look into other elements of MWE production, such as errors (typos) produced within and outside of MWEs. In the cognitive science tradition, errors are a telltale window into the mind's inner workings.

Finally, we will expand our investigation to all intervals surrounding and within an MWE. Similar to Dahlmann & Adolphs (2007), we will investigate pauses at the beginning and end of a multiword expression. In addition, we will investigate non-contiguous MWEs, to determine how their production differs from contiguous MWEs.

Acknowledgements

Thank you to Janet Fodor, Uriel Cohen Priva and David Guy Brizan for many discussions, feedback and edits. Thank you also to three anonymous reviewers for your feedback and suggestions. This work was supported in part by DARPA Active Authentication Phase I grant FA8750-12-2-0201 and FA8750-13-2-0274.

References

Rui Alexandre Alves, Sao Luis Castro, and Thierry Olive. 2008. Execution and pauses in writing narratives: Processing time, cognitive effort and typing skill. *International journal of psychology*, 43(6):969–979.

Alan D Baddeley and Graham Hitch. 1974. Working memory. *Psychology of learning and motivation*, 8:47–89.

J. Baldridge. 2005. The opennlp project. `www.opennlp.sourceforge.net`.

F. Bergadano, D. Gunetti, and C. Picardi. 2002. User authentication through keystroke dynamics. *ACM Transactions on Information and System Security (TISSEC)*, 5(4):367–397.

U Cohen Priva, S Ohlsson, and R Catrambone. 2010. Constructing typing-time corpora: A new way to answer old questions. In *Proceedings of the 32nd annual conference of the cognitive science society*, pages 43–48.

Irina Dahlmann and Svenja Adolphs. 2007. Pauses as an indicator of psycholinguistically valid multi-word expressions (mwes)? In *Proceedings of the Workshop on a Broader Perspective on Multiword Expressions*, pages 49–56. Association for Computational Linguistics.

Clayton Epp, Michael Lippold, and Regan L Mandryk. 2011. Identifying emotional states using keystroke dynamics. In *Proceedings of the SIGCHI Conference on Human Factors in Computing Systems*, pages 715–724. ACM.

Britt Erman and Beatrice Warren. 2000. The idiom principle and the open choice principle. *Text*, 20(1):29–62.

Britt Erman. 2007. Cognitive processes as evidence of the idiom principle. *International Journal of Corpus Linguistics*, 12(1):25–53.

Mark Alan Finlayson and Nidhi Kulkarni. 2011. Detecting multi-word expressions improves word sense disambiguation. In *Proceedings of the Workshop on Multiword Expressions: from Parsing and Generation to the Real World*, pages 20–24. Association for Computational Linguistics.

Janet Dean Fodor. 2002. Prosodic disambiguation in silent reading. In *PROCEEDINGS-NELS*, volume 1, pages 113–132.

Donald R Gentner, Serge Larochelle, and Jonathan Grudin. 1988. Lexical, sublexical, and peripheral effects in skilled typewriting. *Cognitive Psychology*, 20(4):524–548.

Frieda Goldman-Eisler. 1958. Speech production and the predictability of words in context. *Quarterly Journal of Experimental Psychology*, 10(2):96–106.

John Hale. 2006. Uncertainty about the rest of the sentence. *Cognitive Science*, 30(4):643–672.

Karl Moritz Hermann, Phil Blunsom, and Stephen Pulman. 2012. An unsupervised ranking model for noun-noun compositionality. In *Proceedings of the First Joint Conference on Lexical and Computational Semantics-Volume 1: Proceedings of the main conference and the shared task, and Volume 2: Proceedings of the Sixth International Workshop on Semantic Evaluation*, pages 132–141. Association for Computational Linguistics.

Tina Hickey. 1993. Identifying formulas in first language acquisition. *Journal of Child Language*, 20(01):27–41.

Roger Johansson, Åsa Wengelin, Victoria Johansson, and Kenneth Holmqvist. 2010. Looking at the keyboard or the monitor: relationship with text production processes. *Reading and writing*, 23(7):835–851.

Ronald T Kellogg. 1996. A model of working memory in writing. In C. Michael Levy and Sarah Ransdell, editors, *The science of writing: Theories, methods, individual differences, and applications*, pages 57–71. Lawrence Erlbaum Associates, Inc.

D. Krathwohl. 2002. A revision of bloom's taxonomy: An overview. *Theory Into Practice*, 41(4):212–218.

Ronald W Langacker. 2008. *Cognitive grammar: A basic introduction*. Oxford University Press.

Roger Levy. 2008. Expectation-based syntactic comprehension. *Cognition*, 106(3):1126–1177.

Rada Mihalcea. 1998. Semcor semantically tagged corpus. *Unpublished manuscript*.

Guido Nottbusch, Rüdiger Weingarten, and Said Sahel. 2007. From written word to written sentence production. *STUDIES IN WRITING*, 20:31.

A. Pawley. 1985. *Lexicalization*. the interdependence of theory, data, and application. Georgetown University Round Table on Languages and Linguistics, 98-120, Languages and Linguistics.

Heidi Riggenbach. 1991. Toward an understanding of fluency: A microanalysis of nonnative speaker conversations. *Discourse processes*, 14(4):423–441.

David E Rumelhart and Donald A Norman. 1982. Simulating a skilled typist: A study of skilled cognitive-motor performance. *Cognitive Science*, 6(1):1–36.

Ivan A Sag, Timothy Baldwin, Francis Bond, Ann Copestake, and Dan Flickinger. 2002. Multiword expressions: A pain in the neck for nlp. In *Computational Linguistics and Intelligent Text Processing*, pages 1–15. Springer.

T. A. Salthouse. 1986. Perceptual, cognitive, and motoric aspects of transcription typing. *Psychological bulletin*, 99(3):303.

Joost Schilperoord. 2002. On the cognitive status of pauses in discourse production. In *Contemporary tools and techniques for studying writing*, pages 61–87. Springer.

Nathan Schneider, Spencer Onuffer, Nora Kazour, Emily Danchik, Michael T Mordowanec, Henrietta Conrad, and Noah A Smith. 2014. Comprehensive annotation of multiword expressions in a social web corpus. *Proc. of LREC. Reykjavík, Iceland*.

Nathaniel J Smith and Roger Levy. 2013. The effect of word predictability on reading time is logarithmic. *Cognition*, 128(3):302–319.

Rion Snow, Brendan O'Connor, Daniel Jurafsky, and Andrew Y Ng. 2008. Cheap and fast—but is it good?: evaluating non-expert annotations for natural language tasks. In *Proceedings of the conference on empirical methods in natural language processing*, pages 254–263. Association for Computational Linguistics.

Maggy JW van Hoeij, JCM Haarhuls, Ronny FA Wierstra, and Peter van Beukelen. 2004. Developing a classification tool based on bloom's taxonomy to assess the cognitive level of short essay questions. *Journal of veterinary medical education*, 31:261–267.

Veronika Vincze, István Nagy, and Gábor Berend. 2011. Multiword expressions and named entities in the wiki50 corpus.

Alison Wray. 2005. *Formulaic language and the lexicon*. Cambridge University Press.

Yu Zhong, Yunbin Deng, and Anil K Jain. 2012. Keystroke dynamics for user authentication. In *Computer Vision and Pattern Recognition Workshops (CVPRW), 2012 IEEE Computer Society Conference on*, pages 117–123. IEEE.

Building a Lexicon of Formulaic Language for Language Learners

Julian Brooke[*†] **Adam Hammond**[‡] **David Jacob**[†]
Vivian Tsang[†] **Graeme Hirst**[*] **Fraser Shein**[*†]

[*]Department of Computer Science
University of Toronto
jbrooke@cs.toronto.edu
gh@cs.toronto.edu

[†]Quillsoft Ltd.
djacob@quillsoft.ca
vtsang@quillsoft.ca
fshein@quillsoft.ca

[‡]School of English and Theatre Studies
University of Guelph
adam.hammond@uguelph.ca

Abstract

Though the multiword lexicon has long been of interest in computational linguistics, most relevant work is targeted at only a small portion of it. Our work is motivated by the needs of learners for more comprehensive resources reflecting formulaic language that goes beyond what is likely to be codified in a dictionary. Working from an initial sequential segmentation approach, we present two enhancements: the use of a new measure to promote the identification of lexicalized sequences, and an expansion to include sequences with gaps. We evaluate using a novel method that allows us to calculate an estimate of recall without a reference lexicon, showing that good performance in the second enhancement depends crucially on the first, and that our lexicon conforms much more with human judgment of formulaic language than alternatives.

1 Introduction

A significant portion of a speaker's lexical knowledge consists not of atomic lexical entries, i.e. words, but rather sequences built from their combination; in fact, the working multiword lexicon of the average native speaker is almost certainly much larger than the single-word lexicon (Church, 2011). Language learners, due to lack of exposure to the new language and interference from their native language, often fail to use these larger sequences proficiently, a fact which has been demonstrated via corpus analysis using high frequency *n*-grams (Chen and Baker, 2010; Granger and Bestgen, 2014). Although high frequency *n*-grams, known in corpus linguistics as lexical bundles, are useful for certain kinds of analysis, they are inappropriate for a fully-featured multiword learning system, which would ideally involve an electronic lexicon corresponding roughly to the internal lexicon of native speakers. In this work, we adopt the creation of such a lexicon as our goal.

Though much work has been done and many resources created which focus on specific aspects of the multiword vocabulary, most notably in fields such as multiword expressions (MWEs) (Baldwin and Kim, 2010) and keyphrase/term extraction (Newman et al., 2012), our pedagogical perspective leads us towards a somewhat broader theoretical foundation, the *formulaic sequence* theory of Wray (2002; 2008). We are interested in any multiword sequence that could plausibly be lexicalized, not simply those that are noncompositional (idiomatic) or that are otherwise useful for information retrieval applications. With our goal of helping advanced learners produce more fluent language, we are more interested in sequences that underpin the structure of sentences and not just terms that reflect its topic. As much as possible, we do not want to limit the syntactic composition, size, or frequency of our lexical items, and we want methods that allow us to build distinct, high-coverage lexicons for varying genres.

Working on top of an existing pipeline for unsupervised multiword unit segmentation (Brooke et al., 2014), the current work presents two key improvements on that initial model that allow us to build high-coverage lexicons of formulaic language. With respect to improving the quality of the sequences, we present a new measure for distinguishing true (lexicalized) affinity from background syntactic effects, the *lexical predictability ratio*, and integrate it into the model to improve the quality of the out-

Proceedings of NAACL-HLT 2015, pages 96–104,
Denver, Colorado, May 31 – June 5, 2015. ©2015 Association for Computational Linguistics

put lexicon. The second major advance expands the coverage of the lexicon beyond directly contiguous sequences, allowing for sequences with gaps. Note that these are not independent, since the class imbalance between possible and actual gap phrases means that the second depends on the first.

Our main evaluation is novel for this space: rather than comparing with (necessarily) incomplete reference lexicons, we view our task as a n-gram (or gapped n-gram) filtering task, sampling n-grams to annotate from our full (frequency-filtered) set, which allows us to calculate a reliable precision, recall, and F-score. We also test the relevance of our lexicon to contextual recognition of multiword expressions, using a recently released dataset. In both cases, our method outperforms a variety of alternatives, including the original segmentation approach that was our starting point; like that original approach, our lexicon creation method is highly scalable and deterministic, and has only one key parameter (minimum frequency in the corpus).

2 Related Work

There is a long-standing area of research in computational linguistics focusing on lexical association measures, often, though not exclusively, for the creation of multiword lexicons (Church and Hanks, 1990; Schone and Jurafsky, 2001; Evert, 2004; Pecina, 2010): for two-word sequences there are, in fact, far too many to list in this context, though most of the research has centered upon popular options such as the t-test, log-likelihood, and pointwise mutual information (PMI). When these methods are used to build a lexicon, particular syntactic patterns and thresholds for the metrics are typically chosen. Critics note that many of the statistical metrics do not generalize at all beyond two words, but PMI (Church and Hanks, 1990), the log ratio of the joint probability to the product of the marginal probabilities, is a prominent exception. Other measures specifically designed to address sequences of larger than two words include the c-value (Frantzi et al., 2000), a metric designed for term extraction which weights term frequency by the log length of the n-gram while penalizing n-grams that appear in frequent larger ones, and mutual expectation (Dias et al., 1999), which produces a normalized statistic that reflects how much a candidate phrase resists the omission of any particular word.

Overlapping with this area is the research on multiword expressions (Baldwin and Kim, 2010), which is generally (though not exclusively) understood to refer to idiomatic, non-compositional multiword units; even so restricted, there is a huge variety of distinct types, and research in the area has tended to be rather focused, looking at, for instance, just verb/noun combinations (Fazly et al., 2009). The recent work of Schneider et al. (2014a) is a rare example of a comprehensive MWE identification model which distinguishes a full range of MWE sequences, including those involving gaps, using a supervised sequence tagging model; like other models in this space, Schneider et al. make use of existing manual lexical resources and they note that an (unsupervised) automatic lexical resource could be useful addition to the model. Otherwise, gaps in MWEs have generally addressed by using full syntactic representations (Seretan, 2011).

Beyond association metrics, other unsupervised approaches to the multiword problem include that of Newman et al. (2012), who used a generative Dirichlet Process model which jointly creates a linear segmentation of the corpus and a multiword vocabulary. Gimpel and Smith (2011) focus specifically on deriving word sequences with gaps using a generative model, with the intent of improving machine translation. The drawback to these generative methods, relative to association metrics, is scalability and a certain degree of randomness, since these methods generally involve Gibbs sampling with many iterations through the corpus to reach an acceptable model. The approach presented here is based on that of Brooke et al. (2014), which was developed explicitly to work well for larger corpora, in the order of a billion words or more; we will leave further discussion of that work for Section 4.

3 Theory and Rationale

Though the approach to identification of phrases presented in this paper should not be viewed as entirely distinct from work on multiword expressions, collocations, lexical bundles, or phraseology, we nonetheless will make use of a somewhat less familiar term to refer to our objects of interest: *for-*

mulaic sequences. A formulaic sequence is defined by Wray (2002; 2008) as "a sequence, continuous or discontinuous, of words or other elements, which is, or appears to be, prefabricated: that is, stored and retrieved whole from memory at the time of use, rather than being subject to generation or analysis by the language grammar." In other words, a formulaic sequence shows signs of being lexicalized. Other than the psycholinguistic fact of being a lexical item for native speakers of a language, there is no other single necessary condition for some collection of words to be a formulaic sequence, but there are many indicators: Wray (2008) lists 11 diagnostic criteria, including exact repetition, a lack of semantic transparency, genre associations, pragmatic effects, nonstandard syntax, and phonological properties; she reports that native speaker intuition is usually sufficient to make a reliable judgment of whether or not a sequence is formulaic.

Wray's conception of formulaic language is explicitly not that of mere exception to the combinatorial creativity of syntax and semantics; she argues that most language can be viewed to some degree as formulaic, and that the use of formulaic sequences is the default mode for most genres, both written and oral. Moreover, her view is that the processing of language in general should be viewed not so much as a bottom-up construction of larger phrases from individual lexical units, but rather as a top-down process where larger chunks are split apart and analyzed as discrete parts only when there is clear evidence for flexibility, a strategy that has a direct analogy in the decomposition approach used here. Another important aspect of the theory is a focus on the linear sequence rather than some other kind of syntactic abstraction (e.g. a dependency relationship) as being primary to the internal representation of multiword phenomena, a perspective which allows for much cleaner analysis of longer and more varied expressions: when cases of sequence-internal flexibility occur, they are handled by the inclusion of a slot or gap which is also part of the sequence. Note that, since humans are fairly skilled at interpreting noisy input of various kinds, the notion of sequence as the default glue of the internal multiword lexicon does not rule out the possibility of greater creativity (e.g. reversing word order), but this should be understood as the speaker abandoning one of the benefits of formulaic sequences (easy processing) for other communicative purposes (e.g. humor).

Second language acquisition is one of the major areas of application for work on formulaic sequences (Ellis et al., 2008). Wray (2008) posits that the difficulty many adult second language learners have reaching fluency reflects, at least in part, an inattention to the role of formulaic sequences, coupled with an expectation that a language should allow for free combination of words governed only by the basic rules of syntax. Modern communicative approaches to teaching tend to encourage learners to express themselves freely so long as they are able to make themselves understood, i.e. to satisfy the short-term communicative goal. However, if full fluency and social integration into the culture of native speakers is a long-term goal, as it is for many immigrant learners for instance, these learners also need to correctly process and eventually produce a wide range of formulaic sequences. Creating high-coverage vocabularies based on real, modern language usage is a first step in helping learners with these challenging but ubiquitous units of language.

4 Method

4.1 Preliminaries

Although there are several key additions that bring the resulting vocabulary much closer to being a comprehensive collection of formulaic sequences, the overarching structure of our method is adapted from Brooke et al. (2014): first, basic statistics are collected from the corpus, and, based on these an initial segmentation of the corpus is carried out. Once a preliminary lexicon is built from these segments, the lexicon is refined based on both the initial statistics as well as the initial segmentation. Brooke et al. applied this refinement process in the corpus to create a final segmentation, but, since the lexicon is our main interest, we will not address that step here. We will first present the use of lexical predictability in the context of the basic (no-gap) model, and then introduce the changes required to accommodate gaps.

First, a few details that would distract from the main discussion of the method below. Following Brooke et al, we set our frequency threshold to be at least one instance in 10 million tokens; all of the work here (including alternatives to our method) are based on that restriction. Our corpus is a filtered version of the tier 1 blogs in the ICWSM 2009 Spinn3r dataset (Burton et al., 2009), including about 2.4 million blogs or about 890 million tokens of text; for this and other work, we have made a significant effort to exclude texts with spurious repetition (e.g. spam, multiple postings). The part of speech (PoS) information is provided by the TreeTagger (Schmid, 1995), which relative to our needs is quite fast and available for many languages. We collected our statistics using the lemmatized, lower-case forms of words, and accordingly dropped the inflectional information from the PoS tag. We will not discuss the specifics of the algorithms and representations used to collect the statistics except to say that a great deal of attention was paid to keeping the process both fast and memory efficient.

4.2 N-gram decomposition using the lexical predictability ratio

The central mechanism in the n-gram decomposition approach is a measure for choosing among a set of possible segmentations of a text span. Brooke et al. (2014) select a segmentation based on maximizing the conditional probability of each word when the conditioning context is limited to words within the same segment. Our measure also uses conditional probabilities, but we need to distinguish between two types: let $p(w_i|w_{j,k})$ refer to the conditional probability of some particular word/tag pair given a surrounding sequence of word/tag pairs $w_{j,k}$, and $p(w_i|t_{j,k})$ refer to the probability of a particular word/tag pair given only the PoS tags ($j \leq i < k$). For some w_i within some segment whose endpoints are m and n, the *lexical predictability ratio* (LPR) of w_i within span (m, n) is:

$$LPR(w_i, w_{m,n}) = \max_{m \leq j < k \leq n} \frac{p(w_i|w_{j,k})}{p(w_i|t_{j,k})}$$

The LPR for the entire span is defined as:

$$LPR(w_{m,n}) = \prod_{i=m}^{n-1} LPR(w_i, w_{m,n})$$

We use the word *lexical* to refer to this measure because it represents an increase in probability that is apparently due to a lexical rather than syntactic affinity. Other than eliminating syntactic noise, one obvious advantage of using a ratio here is that it naturally emphasizes open-class lexical items, which will tend to have low probability independent of any lexical context, and minimizes the influence of closed-class words; the opposite is true for a measure based on difference, where the influence of a relatively small change to a word with a relatively high initial probability might dwarf a huge relative increase in a low probability word. Given our lexical interests, it is important that our measure be especially sensitive to words in the general vocabulary.

Other than this key change and those relevant to the inclusion of gaps to be discussed in the next section, we preserve intact the initial segmentation algorithm of Brooke et al. (2014). Briefly, the key steps of this process are as follows: First, for each sentence in the corpus, we identify maximal length n-grams, i.e. n-grams above our frequency threshold where any $n+1$-grams that contain them are below the threshold. Where these maximal n-grams overlap, one or more segment boundaries must be inserted in order to create a proper segmentation, with all segments corresponding to an n-gram in our statistics; in this case, the best segmentation is chosen based on maximizing the lexical prediction ratio of the relevant segments, and the segments are counted and taken as the initial vocabulary of the vocabulary decomposition step.

Vocabulary decomposition proceeds by considering each sequence in the initial vocabulary, starting with the longest, and deciding whether or not to break it into two smaller pieces: the counts are added to the smaller pieces which are considered later on in the process. The original algorithm treated the two substrings equally, but here we do not: in practice, in most decompositions there is one, rarer piece that contains the core lexical information, which we call the nucleus (u), while the other is the satellite (s) and is most often a function word or other relatively common word or phrase; the vocabulary decomposition process should be viewed as a process of shaving off satellites until we are left with a lexical nucleus (possibly a single word) that resists further splitting. For each sequence length n, we proceed from the n-gram with the lowest count to the highest. An entry w is broken when either its count $c(w)$ in the lexicon is below the frequency threshold, or when inequality (1) is false for at least one break index b, $0 < b < n$; here $y(t)$ refers to the number of word types for a given tag, and $c(*)$ refers to the count of all tokens in the corpus:

$$\frac{LPR(w_{0,n})}{LPR(w_{0,b})LPR(w_{b,n})} > \frac{\frac{c(u)}{c(t_u)/y(t_u)}}{\frac{c(w)}{c(t_w)/y(t_w)}} \log \frac{c(*)}{c(s)} \quad (1)$$

The left-hand side of the inequality represents the amount of lexical predictability that is lost (over all words in w) when a break is inserted at b. The higher this number, the more the sequence resists decomposition. The first term on the right side represents a ratio of the counts of the lexical nucleus to the full entry: the higher the count of the lexical nucleus relative to the count of the full entry, the more likely we are to break. However, we do not compare these counts directly: mirroring what we have done with the conditional probability in the calculation of LPR, we consider these marginal probabilities relative to the expected marginal probability (count) of a term with that tag sequence, which is simply the total count for the tag divided by the number of types. All these counts are derived from the statistics of the initial vocabulary. In the second term on the right, more common satellites decrease the chance of a break, which counters the property, mentioned earlier, that the LPR can be rather low even for entirely predictable satellites if the marginal probability is already high. Since $c(*)$ is necessarily larger than $c(s)$, this term also serves an initial threshold that must be overcome by increased LPR and/or a higher than expected count. Finally, when there are multiple breakpoints which render the inequality false, or when a break is forced due to low counts, the break which is actually carried out is that which maximizes the difference between the right-hand side and the left-hand side. When all entries have been examined in this fashion, the entries which have been preserved are the final vocabulary.

4.3 Including gaps in the decomposition model

Although it is essentially impossible to describe all formulaic sequences using a single syntactic representation, the slots or gaps within English formulaic sequences are relatively well behaved: in the MWE corpus of Schneider et al. (2014b), for instance, a manual analysis revealed that essentially every gap consisted of a noun phrase (e.g. *point * out*) or a noun modifier (*have * complaints about*). Although it is possible for a gap to have complex content, this is not typical, and anyway it is not necessary to cover all possible cases to do successful lexical induction; for English, we define our gaps as a sequence of 1 to 4 words whose tags satisfy this regular expression:

PP|[(PDT)(DT)JJ*[NN|NP]*(POS|PP$)JJ*NN*]

For us, a gap n-gram is just a regular n-gram with an additional index indicating the location of the gap: in essence, we can collect gap n-gram statistics by first searching for a tag sequence that matches our gap regex, and then counting n-grams around the sequence as if it were not there. This is efficient and defensible, since in many cases knowing the syntactic content of the gap would be redundant, since it entirely predictable from the surrounding context. We do not consider the possibility of multiple gaps: though such patterns exist, they are quite rare (Schneider et al., 2014a).

When we have collected the same statistics for our gap n-grams as we had previously collected for our regular n-grams, we can carry out an initial segmentation. When we are able to match a gap n-gram with a gap size of m, for the purposes of proposing initial segmentation alternatives we treat it as if it were a regular $n{+}m$-gram spanning the full extent of the gap n-gram. When a segment which corresponds to one or more possible gap n-grams is considered, we have to solve a new segmentation problem: inserting two special gap breaks which define the outer gap n-gram, plus (possibly) additional breaks within the gap if needed. For the purposes of calculating LPR, we treat the two outer pieces as a single span, and the contents of the gap as an entirely independent segment. Under those restrictions, we choose breaks to optimize LPR across the entire segment, and, eventually, the entire local context.

After segmentation, the resulting initial lexicon has a mixture of contiguous and gap n-grams. During the lexicon decomposition process, the two kinds are not differentiated with respect to the order in which they are examined. The main difference is that when decomposing regular contiguous n-grams we now have a new option: we can split to create a gap n-gram. For gap n-grams, we do not allow additional gaps; only a single break is possible, though a break at the gap creates two regular n-grams, while one in any other location preserves a gap n-gram. There are only minor changes to the inequality that decides whether a break should occur; if we are considering decomposing by adding a gap, then the denominator of the left-hand term of (1) is now $LPR(w_{b_1,b_2})LPR(w_{0,b_1+b_2,n})$, where $w_{0,b_1+b_2,n}$ is understood to be the string consisting of the concatenation of w_{0,b_1} and $w_{b_2,n}$; when calculating LPR, any conditional probabilities involving spans that cross the gap must use the appropriate gap statistics.

5 Evaluation

Evaluation of large-scale automatically-generated lexicons is notoriously problematic: comparing to a reference lexicon is usually not valid because the reference lexicon, if one exists, is not complete (if it were, why build an automatic lexicon at all?) and therefore it is impossible to accurately estimate precision. The output of a particular approach (i.e. the lexicon) can be judged directly, but this only measures precision, not recall, and it is a short-sighted approach with regards to evaluating future improvements. In this work, we take advantage of the fact that we are assuming an initial n-gram frequency threshold, which greatly reduces the space of all possible n-grams (both contiguous and gap) that we are actually considering as possible formulaic sequences. Although there are still many more bad n-grams than good, the imbalance is not so great as to make annotation impossible: we can sample from the set of possible n-grams, judge them as being good or bad formulaic sequences, and then compare with the output of lexicon creation processes to calculate precision, recall, and F-score.

Our annotation project involved 3 judges, a number chosen so we could use consensus for the creation of a gold standard. The judges, all college-educated native English speakers, were introduced to the basic theory of formulaic sequences and their diagnostics (Wray, 2008), and then instructed that their main task was to identify canonical formulaic sequences, where *canonical* was understood to mean a sequence that contains all the words that would most commonly be used as part of the formula, and no words whose presence seems incidental or the result of rule-driven processes: if an n-gram was larger, smaller, or otherwise distinct from a canonical sequence but the formulaic sequence was nonetheless identifiable, we offered another option (the n-gram "recalls" a formulaic sequence), which we don't use directly in our evaluation, but which we used to help the judges focus in on canonical formulaic sequences. To help them make their annotation, the judges were presented with 5 sample sentences from our corpus.

We annotated 1000 contiguous n-grams and 1000 gap n-grams in this fashion, with the n-grams randomly selected from sets of roughly 1.5 million n-grams in both cases. For contiguous n-grams, 16.9% of the n-grams were judged to be canonical formulaic sequences, but from gap n-grams this number was much lower, only 2.9%. Kappa is problematic with such a serious class imbalance (Di Eugenio and Glass, 2004), so instead we calculated an average F-score across the 3 annotations[1], which was found to be 0.62 for contiguous n-grams and 0.42 for gap n-grams, numbers which reflect a certain amount of subjectivity in the judgment task, but also considerable agreement. These F-scores also provide an estimate of a practical upper bound for our evaluation. To create a gold standard annotation, we used the majority judgment. We also had a single judge produce separate sets for development purposes.

Our second evaluation uses an existing resource, a section of the English Web TreeBank (Bies et al., 2012) that has been annotated for a full range of MWEs (Schneider et al., 2014b). As mentioned earlier, formulaic sequences are a broader category than MWEs (as traditionally understood), and indeed a manual analysis of a portion of the corpus revealed many formulaic sequences in this set which are not annotated. Nevertheless, since all MWEs are formulaic expressions, we can make use of the annotation as a secondary evaluation: for positive examples, we extracted all MWEs in the corpus (except for MWE-internal MWEs, which we ignored) above the frequency threshold (which was the vast majority of them, since the genres of the ICWSM and the Web TreeBank are similar), and as negative examples we extracted all n-grams (both contiguous and

[1]That is, treating one set of judgments as a gold standard and each of the others as an attempt to reproduce it. For all calculations of F-score in this paper, a "positive" classification is a judgment that the sequence is indeed formulaic.

Table 1: Comparison of various automatically generated lexicons with two annotated test sets. P = Precision, R = Recall, F = F-score, ME = mutual expectation, pred decomp = prediction decomposition method of Brooke et al. (2014). Bold is best in column.

	FS test set						**MWE test set**					
	Regular			**Gap**			**Regular**			**Gap**		
Method	**P**	**R**	**F**	**P**	**R**	**F**	**P**	**R**	**F**	**P**	**R**	**F**
Count	0.21	0.24	0.23	0.00	0.00	0.00	0.18	0.77	0.29	0.05	0.47	0.09
c-value	0.22	0.23	0.23	0.05	0.07	0.06	0.11	0.08	0.10	0.01	0.01	0.01
PMI	0.23	0.22	0.22	0.12	0.14	0.13	0.13	0.11	0.12	0.03	0.01	0.02
ME	0.23	0.23	0.23	0.00	0.00	0.00	0.18	0.59	0.28	0.05	0.27	0.09
Pred decomp	0.35	0.50	0.42	0.09	0.14	0.11	0.26	**0.83**	0.40	0.09	**0.59**	0.16
Simple LPR	0.40	**0.54**	0.46	0.10	**0.48**	0.17	0.38	0.74	0.50	0.17	**0.59**	0.27
LPR decomp	**0.51**	0.45	**0.48**	**0.22**	0.31	**0.26**	**0.47**	0.72	**0.57**	**0.33**	0.50	**0.40**

gap) above the frequency threshold where at least one word in the *n*-gram is contained within a MWE, and at least one word is not. This tests to see whether our lexicon would be potentially useful for this task while at the same staying agnostic about the status of other potential formulaic expressions beyond the scope of the MWEs. For regular *n*-grams, this process yields 1273 positive examples and 7272 negative examples: for gap *n*-grams, there are 263 positive examples, and 6764 negative examples, for both types the class imbalance corresponds roughly to the class imbalances in our formulaic sequence annotation. Note that, relative to our main evaluation, this test set is populated with common expressions; for comparison, only 5.2% of postitively identified formulaic sequences from our test set are in WordNet, whereas 31.5% of the MWEs from the Web TreeBank test set are. As with our main evaluation, we use precision, recall, and F-score.

We compare our model first with lexicons built using established measures which can be applied to general sequences beyond 2 words: pointwise mutual information (Church and Hanks, 1990), mutual expectation (Dias et al., 1999), *c*-value (Frantzi et al., 2000), and raw frequency: all can be calculated for both regular and gap *n*-grams using the statistics extracted for our LPR-based method, and then a threshold selected which builds a lexicon of the size we would expect to be ideal given the ratio of good to bad sequences found in our annotation (i.e. the best 16.9% of regular *n*-grams, the best 2.9% of gap *n*-grams). We also build a vocabulary using the original Brooke et al. (2014) prediction-based *n*-gram decomposition method (pred comp), using the same statistics; though it did not originally handle gaps, we updated it to allow gaps, in the same way as our approach. Finally, we consider a simplified version of the LPR approach which does not carry out an initial segmentation: Starting with all *n*-grams, we use inequality (1) to make a decision whether to keep the *n*-gram in the lexicon. In this version of (1), $c()$ is now the original count from the full corpus statistics, not the initial lexicon, except that we subtract from their counts the occurrences of u and s that are also occurrences of w.

6 Results and Analysis

The results for the various automatically generated lexicons for both test sets are in Table 1. First, we note that none of the simple measure-based lexicons offer competitive results, and the results for gap *n*-grams are consistently poor. There is also no clear standout, though ME seems to have the edge on average, a result which is consistent with previous work. Relative to these simpler methods, the original *n*-gram decomposition approach does fairly well in the regular test sets; its results for gap *n*-grams, however, are not impressive. The simpler LPR method is almost indistinguishable from our full method with respect to regular *n*-grams, but its performance with regards to gap *n*-grams indicates a benefit from using the full decomposition process, though it is not as large an effect as the use of LPR. Our LPR n-gram decomposition is consistently the best for both test sets and n-gram types and the F-scores in our test set indicate that, relative to the original n-gram decomposition technique, we have made real progress towards the practical upper bound suggested by the between-human F-score.

Our final formulaic sequence lexicon has 227,188 entries; 184,246 are contiguous, and 42,942 have gaps. For comparison, our single-word vocabulary with the same frequency cutoff is 72,117, supporting the long-standing claim that the multiword lexicon of a language is significantly larger than the single-word lexicon. For contiguous n-grams, 2-word entries compose 36.5%, 3-word entries 33.3%, 4-word entries 20.2%, and 5-word entries 7.7%; for non-contiguous entries, 3-word entries are the most common (44.0%), followed by 4-word entries (27.1%), 2-word entries (17.2%), and 5-word entries (9.9%). With respect to variety, although three 2-word part-of-speech combinations (NN NN, NP NP, and JJ NN) make up close to 21% of the contiguous lexicon, beyond those three there is significant variety, with no single PoS combination accounting for more than 2%, and the top 20 part-of-speech combinations covering only 37.6%. The situation for gaps is even more extreme: only verb/noun combinations (4.9%) stand out as being particularly common. Though a certain amount of this variety might be due to error, in general we believe it reflects the huge variety of potential syntactic realizations of formulaic sequences; essentially any words that regularly appear in sequence could be formulaic.

Looking at just the first 50 (randomly ordered) entries in our lexicon for each type we indeed see much variety, clearly formulaic contiguous phrases like *just the two of us, into the depths of, would not have been possible without, interestingly enough* and gap sequences like *watch * in action, about * or so, millions of * worldwide, implementation of * program, gave * a heart attack, scold * for not, beyond * capabilities* and *back to where * started.* There are some systematic errors, however: probably the biggest single problem is pronouns, which are often highly predictable in a particular context despite being theoretically flexible, e.g. *find myself wanting to.* Another clear problem is lexical predictability that is due to word classes (e.g. *in Long Beach*); information about these classes should be integrated into our background syntactic predictability. When there is enough variability in usage that smaller pieces of a larger phrase get segmented, LPR will often hold these incomplete pieces together, e.g. *your way through.* Looking at the gap lexicon, there are some syntactic patterns (*a * or a*), some semantic patterns (*parents of * kids*), and other cases where it is not clear why a gap was necessary since we would expect little or no variation (*as * weapon against*): often these last cases were close to the frequency threshold and there was just enough variation that the canonical sequence (in this case, *use * as a weapon against*) fell below the threshold. Future work should look at having a more flexible threshold.

7 Conclusion

We have presented here a very general approach to automatic acquisition of multiword lexicons, to our knowledge the broadest to date. By focusing on (apparently) lexical effects using the lexical predictability ratio, while at the same expanding the scope of the output to include gap phrases, we can make a genuine claim that our lexicon reflects a significant portion of the formulaic vocabulary of the language, especially given the size of our corpus that this method can accommodate and the choice to avoid filtering of particular syntactic types, which was justified by the diversity we found in our output lexicon. Our interest here is in educational applications, where having an explicit representation (rather than the implicit lexical information contained in, for instance, language models) can be used to help a learner expand their multiword vocabulary; this is particularly true for formulaic language which is fairly compositional, and therefore may not be obviously formulaic to a learner nor likely to appear in a standard dictionary. There is still work to be done in addressing the errors we see in our lexicon, but our results nonetheless represent significant progress towards the human upper bound suggested by our annotation project, and the evaluation method and resources introduced here should spur future work.[2]

[2]The test set, the automatically-generated lexicon, and the lexicon-creation software are available at http://www.cs.toronto.edu/~jbrooke

Acknowledgments

This work was supported by the Natural Sciences and Engineering Research Council of Canada and the Mitacs Elevate program.

References

Timothy Baldwin and Su Nam Kim. 2010. Multiword expressions. In Nitin Indurkhya and Fred J. Damerau, editors, *Handbook of Natural Language Processing, Second Edition*. CRC Press, Taylor and Francis Group, Boca Raton, FL.

Ann Bies, Justin Mott, Colin Warner, and Seth Kulick. 2012. English Web Treebank. LDC2012T13, Linguistic Data Consortium, Philadelphia.

Julian Brooke, Vivian Tsang, Graeme Hirst, and Fraser Shein. 2014. Unsupervised multiword segmentation of large corpora using prediction-driven decomposition of n-grams. In *Proceedings of The 25th International Conference on Computational Linguistics (COLING 2014)*.

Kevin Burton, Akshay Java, and Ian Soboroff. 2009. The ICWSM 2009 Spinn3r Dataset. In *Proceedings of the Third Annual Conference on Weblogs and Social Media (ICWSM '09)*, San Jose, CA.

Yu-Hua Chen and Paul Baker. 2010. Lexical bundles in L1 and L2 academic writing. *Language Learning & Technology*, 14(2):30–49.

Kenneth Ward Church and Patrick Hanks. 1990. Word association norms, mutual information, and lexicography. *Computational Linguistics*, 16(1):22–29.

Kenneth Church. 2011. How many multiword expressions do people know? In *Proceedings of the Workshop on Multiword Expressions*, pages 137–144.

Barbara Di Eugenio and Michael Glass. 2004. The kappa statistic: a second look. *Computational Linguistics*, 30(1):95–101, March.

Gaël Dias, Sylvie Guilloré, and José Gabriel Pereira Lopes. 1999. Language independent automatic acquisition of rigid multiword units from unrestricted text corpora. In *Proceedings of Conférence Traitement Automatique des Langues Naturelles (TALN) 1999*.

Nick C. Ellis, Rita Simpson-Vlach, and Carson Maynard. 2008. Formulaic language in native and second language speakers: psycholinguistics, corpus linguistics, and TESOL. *TESOL Quarterly*, 42:375–396.

Stefan Evert. 2004. *The statistics of word cooccurrences–word pairs and collocations*. Ph.D. thesis, University of Stuttgart.

Afsaneh Fazly, Paul Cook, and Suzanne Stevenson. 2009. Unsupervised type and token identification of idiomatic expressions. *Computational Linguistics*, 35(1):61–103.

Katerina Frantzi, Sophia Ananiadou, and Hideki Mima. 2000. Automatic recognition of multi-word terms: the c-value/nc-value method. *International Journal on Digital Libraries*, 3:115–130.

Kevin Gimpel and Noah A. Smith. 2011. Generative models of monolingual and bilingual gappy patterns. In *Proceedings of the Sixth Workshop on Statistical Machine Translation*.

Sylviane Granger and Yves Bestgen. 2014. The use of collocations by intermediate vs. advanced non-native writers: A bigram-based study. *International Review of Applied Linguistics in Language Teaching*, 52:229–252.

David Newman, Nagendra Koilada, Jey Han Lau, and Timothy Baldwin. 2012. Bayesian text segmentation for index term identification and keyphrase extraction. In *Proceedings of the 24th International Conference on Computational Linguistics (COLING '12)*.

Pavel Pecina. 2010. Lexical association measures and collocation extraction. *Language Resources and Evaluation*, 44:137–158.

Helmut Schmid. 1995. Improvements in part-of-speech tagging with an application to German. In *Proceedings of the ACL SIGDAT Workshop*, pages 47–50.

Nathan Schneider, Emily Danchik, Chris Dyer, and Noah A. Smith. 2014a. Discriminative lexical semantic segmentation with gaps: running the MWE gamut. *Transactions of the Association for Computational Linguistics*, 2:193–206, April.

Nathan Schneider, Spencer Onuffer, Nora Kazour, Emily Danchik, Michael T. Mordowanec, Henrietta Conrad, and Noah A. Smith. 2014b. Comprehensive annotation of multiword expressions in a social web corpus. In *Proceedings of the Ninth International Conference on Language Resources and Evaluation*, pages 455–461.

Patrick Schone and Dan Jurafsky. 2001. Is knowledge-free induction of multiword unit dictionary headwords a solved problem? In *Proceedings of Empirical Methods in Natural Language Processing (EMNLP '01)*.

Violeta Seretan. 2011. *Syntax-Based Collocation Extraction*. Springer.

Alison Wray. 2002. *Formulaic Language and the Lexicon*. Cambridge University Press, Cambridge.

Alison Wray. 2008. *Formulaic Language: Pushing the Boundaries*. Oxford University Press, Oxford.

Author Index

Association for Computational Linguistics
209 N. Eighth Street
Stroudsburg, Pennsylvania 18360

CURRAN ASSOCIATES INC
proceedings.com